AF661808

KASHRUT, CASTE AND KABBALAH

The Religious Life of the Jews of Cochin

Also by Nathan Katz and Ellen S. Goldberg

Ethnic Conflict in Buddhist Societies: Sri Lanka, Thailand and Burma (co-eds. & contrs., London and Boulder, 1988)

The Last Jews of Cochin: Jewish Identity in Hindu India (Columbia, 1993)

A Jewish King at Shingly: The Story of the Jews of Cochin (forthcoming)

Also by Nathan Katz

Buddhist and Western Philosophy (ed. & contr., New Delhi, 1981)

Buddhist Images of Human Perfection (Delhi, 1982, 2nd edn., 1989)

Buddhist and Western Psychology (ed. & contr., Boulder, 1983)

Tampa Bay's Asian-Origin Religious Communities (Tampa, 1991)

Studies of Indian Jewish Identity (ed., New Delhi, 1995)

Who Are the Jews of India? (Berkeley and London, 2000)

Kashrut, Caste and Kabbalah

The Religious Life of the Jews of Cochin

NATHAN KATZ
ELLEN S. GOLDBERG

MANOHAR
2005

First published 2005

© Nathan Katz and Ellen S. Goldberg, 2005

All rights reserved. No part of this publication may be reproduced or transmitted, in any form or by any means, without prior permission of authors and the publisher

ISBN 81-7304-638-7

Published by
Ajay Kumar Jain for
Manohar Publishers & Distributors
4753/23 Ansari Road, Daryaganj
New Delhi 110002

Typeset by
A J Software Publishing Co. Pvt. Ltd.
New Delhi 110005

Printed at
Lordson Publishers Pvt. Ltd.
Delhi 110007

Distributed by
FOUNDATION BOOKS
4381/4 Ansari Road, Daryaganj
New Delhi 110002
and its branches at Mumbai, Hyderabad,
Bangalore, Chennai, Kolkata

Contents

List of Illustrations 7

Introduction 11

1. Rituals and Identity 19

THE RELIGIOUS LIFE OF THE JEWS OF COCHIN

2. The Royalty of the Autumn Sacred Cycle 27

3. Spring Rites: An Ascetic Passover 50

4. A Shabbat Interlude 73

5. Life Cycle Rituals: 'Every Bridegroom is Joseph Rabban' 77

6. Jewish 'Apartheid' and a Jewish Gandhi 98

7. Some Speculations about Caste, Jewish Survival and Hindu Tolerance 134

8. Why Did They Leave India? 139

9. Rebirth in Israel 160

Bibliography 169

Index 179

Contents

Bibliography

Illustrations

Between pages 64-5

Plate 1: Sarah Cohen prepares 'Rosh Hashanah cakes' for the New Year, (Photo by Ellen S. Goldberg, 1986.)

Plate 2: A white curtain covers the Holy Ark in the Cochin Synagogue for Rosh Hashanah. (Photo by Ellen S. Goldberg, 1986.)

Plate 3: White silk covers the upstairs *bimah*, where the Torah will be read on Rosh Hashanah in the Cochin Synagogue. (Photo by Ellen S. Goldberg, 1986.)

Plate 4: Hereditary priest Jackie Cohen raises his glass to toast Simhat Cohen, a unique Indian Jewish observance. (Photo by Ellen S. Goldberg, 1986.)

Plate 5: A *lulav* (bundle of myrtle, willow and palm branches) and etrog (citron) on the downstairs bimah in the Cochin Synagogue. (Photo by Ellen S. Goldberg, 1986.)

Plate 6: Raymond Salem blesses the lulav and etrog in the Cochin Synagogue. (Photo by Ellen S. Goldberg, 1986.)

Plate 7: A 'tree of light' blazes before the Cochin Synagogue to proclaim the holiday of Simhat Torah. (Photo by Ellen S. Goldberg, 1986.)

Plate 8: The Cochin Synagogue decorated for Simhat Torah. (Photo by Ellen S. Goldberg, 1986.)

Plate 9: Afternoon Torah procession in the courtyard of the Cochin Synagogue. (Photo by Ellen S. Goldberg, 1986.)

Plate 10: Shalom Cohen and Raymond Salem kindle the Hanukkah lamp in the Cochin Synagogue. (Photo by Ellen S. Goldberg, 1986.)

Plate 11: Sattu Koder's Scroll of Esther. (Photo by Ellen S. Goldberg, 1987.)

Plate 12: Workmen clean out the well in the Salem home, also part of Passover preparations. (Photo by Ellen S. Goldberg, 1987.)

Plate 13: Shalom Cohen helps his sister, Sarah, make wine for Passover. (Photo by Ellen S. Goldberg, 1987.)

Plate 14: Sarah Cohen cools an earthen jug of water that will be used to make' *matzah* for Passover. (Photo by Ellen S. Goldberg, 1987.)

Plate 15: Abigail Elias prepares *matzah* for the Seder plate. (Photo by Ellen S. Goldberg, 1987.)

Plate 16: The Salem family's Seder. (Photo by Ellen S. Goldberg, 1987.)

Between pages 112-13

Plate 17: Sattu Koder sanctifies the wine at the family Seder. (Photo by Ellen S. Goldberg, 1987.)

Plate 18: Emulating their Hindu and Muslim neighbours, Cochin's Jews leave their shoes at the door of their house of worship. (Photo by Ellen S. Goldberg, 1987.)

Plate 19: Jacob Cohen reads from the Torah scroll on Shabbat. (Photo by Ellen S. Goldberg, 1987.)

Plate 20: Women pray upstairs, in the *ezrat nashim* (women's section). (Photo by Ellen S. Goldberg, 1987.)

Plate 21: Elias Hai Elias of Ernakulam holds a traditional bridegroom's vest. (Photo by Ellen S. Goldberg, 1987.)

Plate 22: Bride Glennis Simon in the Cochin Synagogue. (Photo courtesy of Esther 'Pearlie' Simon.)

Plate 23: Sarah Cohen lifts the Cochin veil from Glennis Simon as she drinks from the synagogue's gold wine cup, offered by bridegroom Leslie Salem. (Photo courtesy of Esther 'Pearlie' Simon.)

Plate 24: Cochin women safeguard their *ketubot* (wedding contracts) in silver holders, like this one displayed by Malkah 'Queenie' Hallegua. (Photo by Ellen S. Goldberg, 1987.)

Plate 25: A *milah* (circumcision) celebration in the Salem household. Baby Nathan Hertzman was in Toronto, but celebrations were held in Cochin nevertheless. (Photo by Ellen S. Goldberg, 1987.)

Plate 26: A funeral in the rural village of Chendamangalam. (Photo courtesy of P.A. Aron.)

Plate 27: Avraham Barak Salem. (Photo courtesy of Prem Doss S. Yehudi.)

Plate 28: Avraham Barak Salem (r.) meets with President Yitzhak Ben-Zvi in Jerusalem in 1953. Salem was sent to Israeli on a mission to facilitate the emigration of the Malabari Jews. (Photo courtesy of Raymond Salem.)

Plate 29: Avraham Barak Salem in the Cochin Synagogue in 1964 on Simhat Torah. Ephraim Roby is in the background. (Photo courtesy of Raymond Salem.)

Plate 30: The wedding that caused a minor revolution. Balfour Salem and Seema 'Baby' Koder were married in Bombay in 1950. (Photo courtesy of Raymond Salem.)

Plate 31: Torah scrolls from Cochin in the Ark at the Cochini style Synagogue near Beersheva in Israel. (Photo by Ellen S. Goldberg, 1987.)

Introduction

Upon learning that we had recently spent a year with the Cochin Jews in India, we were asked a question which is as inevitable as it is naive: 'Are they Jewish *or* are they Indian?' The question is naive only because it demonstrates a lack of familiarity with that corner of the diaspora known as India, *galut Hodu* in Hebrew, but also because it reflects a disturbing lack of self-awareness.

An American Jew would be pained by the question: 'Are you American *or* are you Jewish?' The question is offensive because the charge of dual loyalties has been levied against the Jews throughout the Western world. But more than that, it is offensive because it bifurcates one's very sense of self, alienating oneself from oneself, and resulting in the painful condition imposed upon the Jews which Jean-Paul Sartre perceptively described as 'a Jewish complex'.[1] In short, the question offends because it violates the human condition.

American Jews would be puzzled as well as offended by this question. For them, Americanness and Jewishness are not two separate domains, the one inhabited on weekdays and the other on Shabbat and Jewish festivals. Intertwined, Americanness and Jewishness form a whole, a 'natural' self which is violated by the very asking of the question. This bifurcation of identity is imposed from without, not generated from any inner, hidden contradictions.

Despite this condition, American Jews feel it 'natural' to ask of their coreligionists in India: 'Are they Indian *or* are they Jewish?'—as if that were somehow a choice. Similarly, Indian Hindus ask the same question about their Jewish compatriots, the very asking of which splits the world as well as the self. For far too long, we have all believed the imperial lie, that 'east is east and west is west'. A perspective rooted in Jewish experience would be that there never were two separable halves of our world, but the ghost of Kipling haunts by asking the 'natural' question.

For the Cochin Jews, Indianness and Jewishness are not neatly demarcated categories, but together form a seamless universe of meanings, customs, aesthetics and rituals. Their Indian-Jewish identity is experienced as a whole. In questioning this identity, the outsider, whether a foreign Jew or a non-Jewish Indian, betrays certain presuppositions about 'Jewishness' on the one hand, and about 'Indianness' on the other. And it is precisely these presuppositions which are vigorously challenged by the Cochin Jews. If American Jews can understand Indian-Jewish identity, then their sense of American-Jewish identity would be modified; the Western model would no longer be taken as normative. Similarly, Indian Hindus would come to view 'Indianness' in a way which includes Jews, as well as other minorities of foreign origin. As is the case with all true scholarly investigations, it is never simply the other which is the object of our study, but always and ultimately oneself. In learning about the Jews of Cochin, one's identity as an American Jew (or an Indian Hindu) is thereby revised.

Another basis for this inappropriate, yet 'natural', question is the way in which modern academic fields inelegantly divide our world. The Jews of Cochin have been studied largely by Western scholars of Judaism, and to a lesser extent by students of India, either Indian and foreign. When approached from either the perspective of Jewish studies or South Asian studies, the core of Cochin identity—which is to say the key explanatory factor for their historical legends, social structures and rituals—becomes lost. It falls between the cracks, lost in the interstices of academic conventions. Marginality upon marginality, the Cochin Jews occupy the remotest corner of the Jewish diaspora, while at the same time forming the most microscopic of India's myriad minorities. They are so tiny that they disappear from the usual cognitive maps. They become exotic commodities for the tourism industry, or human interest stores for journalists. The result is that they ceased to be treated as humans. The Cochin Jews often complained about their synagogue being reduced to a tourist curiosity. 'We are like animals in the zoo', Lily Koder bemoaned as a ferry load of tourists strolled past the houses of Synagogue Lane, peering through windows to see how Jews lived. 'The outsiders defile our synagogue and they mock our ways', she continued.[2]

This book aims to demonstrate the inappropriateness of the either/or question about their identity. Further, it shows precisely how this Indian-Jewish identity came to be established through historical legends, and how it is ritually enacted on a regular basis. Identity is never a mere given, but it is an achievement. It must be earned. In the case of Cochin, the Jews achieved a well integrated identity through four interrelated means.

1. Identity is achieved in part by narrating a historical legend which emphasizes long-standing residence in India and attestable origin in ancient Israel—a double *yichus* or lineage. Nearly 2,000 years of residence in Kerala, most of it spent idyllically in an independent principality at Cranganore, is their story. Some of them trace their

origin to the Roman destruction of the Second Temple of Jerusalem. Jerusalem and Cranganore are the two moorings of their identity, the *leitmotif* of their historical legends, as is explored in our companion volume, *A Jewish King at Shingly: The Story of the Jews of Cochin*.

2. Identity is also achieved by constructing a social order which is reflective of that of the larger society. In India, social order is sacralized in the *Dharmashastra*, and known pejoratively in the West as the caste system. The Jews of Cochin not only organized themselves as a caste vis-á-vis the larger Kerala society, but they also mimicked other castes in their proliferation into endogamous subcastes. Indeed, the one fact Western Jews are most likely to know about their Cochin coreligionists is their self-segregation into 'white' and 'black' groups. In dividing themselves into endogamous subcastes, they did precisely what other 'foreign' religious groups in India have always done, be they the Bene Israel Jews of Mumbai and environs, or Kerala's Christians and Muslims.
3. One of the two sources of prestige and power in traditional Indian society is land, and the landholding noble caste of Kerala is the Nayars. Like every caste in India, the Nayars have their own distinctive religious symbols and practices. In order to integrate into Kerala society, the Cochin Jews appropriated some Nayar symbols of nobility. They did this by matching them with indigenous, Jewish symbols of divine royalty (*malkhut*) when possible, and by direct borrowing of Nayar ritual behaviour at other times. According to the Cochin Jews, 'In order to understand Jew Town, you must see three things: Simchat Torah, a wedding, and Pesach.' They were even more correct than they realized, and our analysis will show how specifically Nayar symbols were Judaized and enacted at Simchat Torah and at weddings.
4. Similarly, at Pesach the symbols of the other Indian pole of power—the purity of the hereditary priests, in Kerala the Nambudiri Brahmins—became part and parcel of Passover preparations and celebrations. In Cochin, Pesach was observed in a mood quite unlike that found elsewhere in the Jewish world, and this 'mood' reflected the chaste, purity-conscious religion of the Nambudiris.

The three most distinctive—or as some would say 'exotic'—aspects of the Cochin *minhag* (local system of observance), Simchat Torah, weddings and Pesach, are distinctive precisely because they contain symbolic and ritualistic motifs which were adopted from the Hinduism of the Nayar nobility on the one hand, and the priestly Nambudiris on the other.

Religious studies is a rich field of investigation, and the unique position of the Cochin Jews, their attenuated marginality in particular, raises many issues for theoretical consideration. One is the process by which the symbols and behaviours of one religious tradition blend with those of another. It is obvious that the Cochin *minhag* borrowed heavily from Hinduism. But this was no blind historical process of accretion. The Cochin Jews were educated and knowledgeable about Jewish norms and standards. Hindu practices were not uncritically and unconsciously incorporated into their *minhag*, but were judiciously weighed against the standard of Jewish law (*Halakha*) before being accepted and Judaized. The one exception to this rule of judicious accommodation was the Jews' caste-like social structure in which they contravened, even defied, *halakhic* standards. The case of the Cochin Jews raises the question of how one religion 'borrows' symbol and ritual complexes from another. In Cochin, the process was not unconscious but fairly deliberate, a serious strategy for integrating into the larger, Hindu society without sacrificing their own distinctiveness.

Our understanding of asceticism, too, needs revision in the light of the data from Cochin. According to accepted theory, asceticism is the denial of physical pleasure, or even the infliction of pain, for the purpose of spiritual attainment. In viewing the interrelation between social position and ritual behaviour in Cochin, ascetical practices which came to be associated with Pesach served more than spiritual purposes: they were a key to high caste status as well. Asceticism bestows social status as well as spiritual experience. Therefore, asceticism needs to be understood both in terms of its other-worldly and very practical, down-to-earth outcomes.

This book addresses several groups of audiences, which is to say we assume several sets of responsibilities. First, it is meant for scholars of religious studies. There are several important theoretical issues facing them which constellate differently when viewed from the perspective of Jew Town. Such issues include asceticism and acculturation.

More generally, all these four identity-generating aspects of Cochin Jewish culture raise intriguing questions about the complex interactions between great cultures. In their historical legend, social structure, nobility symbolism enacted at Simchat Torah and at weddings, and asceticism and purity at Passover, the Cochin Jews behaved in typically Indian ways. These unique Jewish expressions reveal the complexity and richness of tradition—Jewish tradition in particular, but any great religious tradition bears similarly rich symbol complexes. To borrow a metaphor from Gestalt psychology, what is especially tantalizing is how certain aspects of a tradition become the foreground and how others recede into the background, depending on the cultural and historical context. In Hindu culture, Jewish symbol complexes of royalty and of purity rose to the fore, and others receded, mirroring the twin poles of power of Indian culture. From this point of view, it is interesting to reflect how in Protestant America, Judaism's prophetic strands are so emphasized that even many Jews believe prophetism to be constitutive of Judaism. It is no surprise that this belief is shared with most Protestants. How bizarre such a notion would seem to a Cochin Jew, in whose culture purity and nobility are much more central to one's religious identity. The interactions between the guest and host religions, especially in terms of ritual enactments, form the substance of this book.

For colleagues in South Asian studies, the case of the Cochin Jews offers a striking perspective on Hindu society. The question of what is Indian about India comes into a sharper focus when we ask what is Indian about the Cochin Jews. Precisely how foreign groups were assimilated into the Indian social order is understood here as a matter of ritual behaviour, social structure and historical legends. The much lauded Hindu 'tolerance' is also seen in a new light. Unlike the liberal tolerance of the modern West, Hindu tolerance is rooted in its hierarchical social structure. This is not the Western, liberal tolerance which 'wishes to destroy (the individual) . . . as a Jew and leave nothing in him but the man, the abstract and universal subject of the rights of man and the rights of the citizen'.[3] Hindu tolerance, on the contrary, embraces the person in particularity, as a member of a community, and not as a universalistic abstraction to which one is compelled to conform.

Scholars of Jewish studies will find many assumptions challenged by the case of the Cochin Jews. For one, a Jewish community which was never subjected to persecution or discrimination is striking. Common wisdom holds that Jewish identity is largely defensive in nature, shaped by the hostility of a host culture, whether Christian or Muslim. In Cochin, not only were the Jews never persecuted, but also they were always regarded with affection and respect by their neighbours. What is this Jewish identity with no defensive parameters? What is the psyche of a Jewish community which has never tasted hatred? And why did they become such passionate Zionists if their homeland was so hospitable? How can we understand the irony that this Jewish community, perhaps the most comfortable and well integrated in all of diaspora history, was one of the first to extinguish itself through mass emigration to Israel? If the Cochin Jewish identity was not defensive in nature, so also Cochin Zionism lacked the impetus of pogroms. Yet Zionism was so successful in Cochin, today there a mere two dozen Jews left. As Jacob Cohen ruefully commented, 'The birth of Israel marked the doom of this community.'[4]

This book is targeted at non-academic Jews as well as Indians, and we have attempted to retain the undeniable charm of the tale in recounting it. We make no apology for our enthusiasm because the story of the Cochin Jews is a matter of pride for Jews and Hindus alike. The Jews in Cochin were entirely free to pursue their religion according to their own lights, something not found elsewhere in the world. All Jews ought to celebrate the fact that some of their coreligionists lived as all of them should have lived: as free people. Justly, the story of the Cochin Jews is a source of pride for Indians, whose hospitality and affection make India unique among nations of the diaspora. Indeed, India's record of welcoming religious refugees is one of its most noteworthy cultural achievements. First Jews, then Nestorian Christians, followed by Zoroastrians, and more recently Tibetan Buddhists—all were forced to flee their homelands because of religious persecution, and all found a secure haven in India.

Even among scholars, very few would be sufficiently knowledgeable about both Judaism and Hinduism to appreciate the subtle interweavings of these cultures in the life of the Cochin Jewish community. Therefore, detailed background information has been supplied about Jewish practices for those not familiar with them, especially Hindu readers, and about Hindu culture, particularly for the Jewish audience. We realize that it may be somewhat tedious for scholars of Jewish studies to read so many details about Jewish observances, but we have targeted this work at non-Jewish Indians who know very little about Judaism. The converse is also true: Indologists may grow weary reading so much elementary information about India, but this is new terrain for many other readers.

In consideration of our non-academic readers, scholarly transliterations of Sanskrit, Malayalam and Hebrew words have been avoided in favour of more readily recognizable (and pronounceable!) renderings. Specialist readers will be familiar with the original languages in any case.

We are acutely aware that the Jewish community of Cochin is on the verge of extinction. Once there were 2,500 Jews in Kerala and 300 in Jew Town. Today, their numbers have dwindled to around 60 and 20 respectively. In no small measure, we have written this book for them. It is intended as an affectionate requiem for the Cochin Jews, and we bear that responsibility with seriousness and respect.

In the study of culture, the researcher should 'be guided by projection of his own human qualities into the situation to be understood', as anthropologist Robert Redfield perceptively commented.[5] So it was for us. Not only was participation in the religious and social life of the community the essence of our approach, but also the effect upon us of living in this community for the better part of a year was profound personally. The style of Indian observance was entirely new to us, and simply being able to follow prayers in the Cochin Synagogue was something of an achievement, as any visitor can attest! Working on this project has enhanced not only our commitment to Judaism, but also our admiration for Indian culture.

The project has also modified our understanding of India. Both of us are 'India-wallahs', Westerners who make a living by writing and lecturing about India. Nathan first visited India in 1969 and has studied, worked and lived in South Asia for nearly a third of the three decades since. In America, he taught Hinduism and Buddhism for over thirty years. One of Ellen's career steps as a journalist was reporting from South Asia for *The Christian Science Monitor*. Despite extensive study in the field and in libraries, and many years of personal involvement with Hindus and Buddhists, until we lived as members of the Cochin community and became accepted by Indians as somehow belonging there, our understanding of the culture was hindered by a distance so fundamental as to seem ontological in nature. This distance disappeared with the adoption of an identity which was recognized by Indians as Indian. Living in Raymond Salem's home, eating at Jacob and Sarah Cohen's table, praying in the Cochin Synagogue, joining the community in their social interactions with non-Jews—all this conferred membership in an Indian community, a membership which is impossible for the Western scholar studying Sanskrit or the Western journalist writing about politics. Despite decades of study in Indian and American universities, it was as though we saw India for the first time from Jew Town, seeing it from within, as it were, as '*pukka* Cochinites'.

We hope that this book will serve as one more small link between Hindus and Jews. May the long overdue establishment of ambassadorial relations between India and Israel herald a new era of mutual cooperation and respect which builds upon the millennia of affection which this book documents.

NATHAN KATZ
ELLEN S. GOLDBERG

Miami Beach
January 2005

NOTES

1. Sartre, *Anti-Semite and Jew*, pp. 94-5.
2. Lily Koder, October 1986.
3. Sartre, *Anti-Semite and Jew*, pp. 94-5.
4. Jacob Cohen, March 1984.
5. Redfield, 'Relations of Anthropology to the Social Sciences and to the Humanities', p. 733.

CHAPTER 1

Rituals and Identity

INTRODUCTION

In any discussion of the Cochin Jews, the question inevitably arises: 'Are they Jewish *or* are they Indian?' The following discussion of the Cochin *minhag* (traditions, customs and observances) will demonstrate that this question is inappropriate.

In *A Jewish King at Shingly*, the concern was about *place*. For the Jews of Kerala, 'place' had a double connotation: the symbolic intertwining of Jerusalem and Cranganore. Place also involved *time* because long-standing residency (Cranganore) as well as ancient, foreign origin (Jerusalem) each conferred status, a 'double-*yichus*'. Status was vital for the Cochin Jews' place in Hindu society and, therefore, for their economic and political well-being.

Thus, as will be discussed in Chapter 6, there was a sibling-like rivalry between the Paradesi and Malabari Jews over who were the rightful heirs of the line of Joseph Rabban—Cranganore *yichus*. At the same time, the Paradesis and Malabaris clashed over the latter's claim to Jerusalem *yichus*.

In this book, place is to be understood as social position—a position which is never simply a given, but which must be established ritually. Cochin observances, especially the unique and exotic aspects of their *minhag*, served to locate the Jews within Kerala's complex caste system.

One of the distinguishing features of Indian civilization in general is the twin polar sources of social prestige, position and power. Ever since the fourth century codification of social law, the *Dharmashastra* by the archetypal brahmin, Manu, the priestly brahmins and the nobility (usually the kshatriyas, but in Kerala the nobility comprised the Nayars) derived status from separate sources—the ascetic and the royal, respectively.

The brahmins derived their power from their purity, and they were distinguished by their pure food, their white clothes, their ascetic lifestyle, and their self-distancing from such sources of pollution as animal carcasses and meat, lowly-born people and agriculture. This distance was maintained through an intricate system of social interdependences, customs and taboos. Such purity was deemed an essential prerequisite for the efficacious re-enactments of ancient rituals—the brahmins' means of livelihood.

The nobility enacted their power by ritually displaying the symbols of conquest and wealth. Not the homespun white cotton of the brahmin, but fine silks and jewels adorned the maharajas. Unlike the brahmin's chaste, polytheistic rituals, the Nayars' religion was riotous, colourful deity processions. Rather than worship an abstract metaphysical concept, their God was Krishna, the life-embracing, erotic warrior, and their Goddess was Bhagavati-Bhadrakali, the demanding nature goddess.

The Cochin Jews foregrounded the symbols of purity and royalty inherent in Judaism, at the same time adapting some of the priestly and royal symbols of Hinduism in their *minhag*, making for one of the most exotic systems of Jewish observance found anywhere in the diaspora. They managed their acculturation judiciously so as not to contravene *Halakha* or Jewish law. The notable exception was the apartheid-like divisions within the community: by organizing themselves into endogamous subcastes in emulation of Indian social structures, the Cochin Jews breached *Halakha*.

Halakha is the ethical and ritual norms which have defined Jewish practice since the establishment of the rabbinic academy at Yavneh following the destruction of the Second Temple. *Minhag* is the way *Halakha* is observed according to local customs, and *minhagim* vary from place to place. There is some overlap between *Halakha* and *minhag*, but for general purposes a distinction should be maintained. For example, the basic requirement to wear fringes (*tzitzit*) is given in *Halakha*, but the design of a *tallit* (fringed prayer shawl), the fabrics—silk, wool, cotton, synthetics—from which the *tallit* is made, whether the stripes on the *tallit* are black, blue or multicoloured, these are matters of *minhag*.

Halakha is incomplete without *minhag*. Jewish law is not sufficiently specific and detailed to serve as a guide for many Jewish observances, especially the life cycle rituals. *Halakha* provides the framework, but one would be unable to celebrate a *brit milah*, a *bar mitzvah*, a wedding, or a funeral unless one relied upon the local *minhagim*.[1] To express this by using a traditional metaphor, *Halakha* as Oral Torah is God's imperative, and *minhagim* are creative, human responses to that imperative.

Judaism's adaptations to various cultures went beyond these *minhagim*. Like all truly ancient religions, Judaism is extremely complex, comprising diverse threads over centuries and millennia. Unique among the world's religions is Judaism's diasporization: Jews have lived as guests—welcome or otherwise—among all peoples of the world. Since Jewish tradition is so multidimensional, depending upon the host culture differing aspects of Jewishness became the foreground and other aspects receded into the background. In Protestant America, Judaism's prophetic threads came to the foreground, and according to some Jews, Judaism is reducible to ethics. In Hindu India, however, it was the Jewish priestly-ascetic and noble-kingly threads which were emphasized, and the fiery ethical imperatives of the prophets became less central. Certainly, no Indian Jew would understand the prophetic threads as in themselves constitutive of Jewishness, but an American Jew might.

We may speculate: if American Judaism and Indian Judaism could be characterized as prophetic and priestly/royal respectively, what of Judaism in a Catholic, or a Muslim, or a Confucian nation?[2] In the context of Catholicism, did Judaism foreground its ritualistic and priestly threads? In Muslims lands, did Jews emphasize patterns of social organization and community leadership? Were ancestor rites and the pursuit of social harmony central to the Chinese Jewish practice? Moreover, how did remote Jewish communities assimilate these diverse symbols and practices while maintaining *halakhic* integrity? The answer is that Judaism already possessed the symbolic and ritual resources to make these adaptations possible, within the *halakhic* framework.

Judaism had ample resources to appropriate the brahmanic ascetic's power. These resources included (*a*) a hereditary priesthood of *kohanim*, paralleling the brahmins; (*b*) a fastidious system of dietary regulations; (*c*) complex laws governing family purity; and (*d*) ascetical tendencies characterizing certain holidays, especially Passover, Yom Kippur and other fasts. At the same time, Judaism's noble kingly resources included: (*a*) the royalty symbolism (*malkhut*) of the High Holy Days; (*b*) the resemblances between the Torah processions (*haqafot* or rodeamentos) of Simchat Torah and Hinduism's deity processions; and (*c*) the royalty symbolism traditionally ascribed to brides and bridegrooms. Having concentrated on Jewish social structure as reflective of Hindu norms, we will analyse the Cochin *minha* in terms of its adaptation to these two poles of power in Hindu society.

It is important to bear in mind that the Cochin Jews' adaptation of high caste Hindu ritual behaviours and symbols into their observances was a very serious matter, for it served to integrate them into the society in which they lived. Susan Bayly made a similar observation about Kerala's Syrian Christian community:

These and other customs which the Syrians shared with caste Hindus must be seen as much more than superficial borrowings from Hinduism—mere 'accretions' as the European missionaries maintained. In fact they were rites which safeguarded the Syrian's corporate substance and guaranteed their status within a shared moral order which was defined in terms of gradations of ritual purity and pollution. It was through adherence to these standards that the Syrians had come to be classed as *savarna*, persons of clean caste and standing in the Hindu moral order. [3]

Invariably, Western people misapprehend the Cochin Jews' identity. Because visitors to Jew Town are largely either Western Jews with little appreciation of India, or Indians with little knowledge of Jewishness, no one has yet described Cochini identity as both *fully* Indian and fully Jewish. In part, this problem is due to the disciplinary fields of study pursued in Western universities, fields which inelegantly divide the world into East and West. Academically, the Cochin Jews have been approached from the perspectives of both Jewish studies and South Asian studies. However, for the people of Jew Town, Indianness and Jewishness were not neatly bound fields of study, but together they formed a seamless universe of meanings, customs, aesthetics and rituals. Through this study of their observances, they will be represented as both Jewish and Indian, and both fully so.

What is being described is the admixture of religious symbols and practices across cultures. When a people relocate from one culture to another, their religion typically acquires aspects of the religion of the new host culture. As Bayly notes in *Saints, Goddesses and Kings*, her excellent study of south Indian Christians and Muslims, it is not the case that a guest religion 'must obliterate all pre-existing beliefs and social ties amongst its new affiliates'.[4] But how does this process of cultural adaptation work? How does one religious tradition borrow symbol complexes from another without compromising its unique identity? What are the patterns for interaction between the host and guest religious cultures?

Without doubt, the Cochin *minhag* contains many elements borrowed from local Hinduism, as will be described and analysed later. Jewish borrowings from Hinduism were too judicious, primarily the outcome of reflection and deliberation, to have simply 'happened'. The data from Cochin suggest a process of cultural adaptation which was guided by Jewish tradition. Aspects of Hindu behaviour and symbolism were adjudged to have been acceptable by the standards of *Halakha*, or not. When acceptable, they were matched with indigenous, Jewish symbol complexes and thereby became a part of the Cochin *minhag*. If a Hindu practice was found to be unacceptable by those standards, it was rejected, with the notable exception of the social structure.

Thus, the unique Cochin Jewish identity was fully Jewish, implying that their practices adhered to normative Jewish standards, at the same time that it was fully Indian, meaning that it embodied Indian cultural values to the extent they could be accommodated within the *halakhic* framework. The Cochin Jews' fine balance between the worlds of Judaism and Hinduism reflects serious ritual and symbolic strategies for a religious community's survival in a new cultural environment.

This study begins with the Jewish calendric holidays. First is the autumn cycle of Rosh Hashanah, Yom Kippur, Sukkot and Shmini Chag Atzeret/Simchat Torah, followed by the spring cycle centred around Passover. A brief account of Shabbat in Mattancheri will be presented, as also the minor observance of Chanukkah, Purim, Tisha B'Av and Lag B'Omer. Last, the life cycle rites—circumcision, *bar mitzvah*, marriage and burial—will be considered. This chapter, however, does not offer a complete treatment of the Cochin *minhag*; this work will consider the Cochin Jews' *minhag* as it served to integrate them into the Hindu social context.

There is more to this study than an ethnographer's cataloguing of exotic customs, charming as that undertaking may be. The fascination of studying an Indian-Jewish community implies a reconsideration of Judaism in its better known contexts. Fresh and important questions arise. From the perspective of Jew Town in Hindu Cochin, for example, American Judaism looks very Protestant and very American. This is because it is never simply the 'other' that is the object of scholarship, but always self-understanding.

NOTES

1. Chill, *The Minhagim*, p. vii.
2. To see how Judaism was reconfigured in China, Katz, 'The Judaisms of Kaifeng and Cochin'.
3. Bayly, *Saints, Goddesses and Kings*, p. 252.
4. Ibid., p. 1.

THE RELIGIOUS LIFE OF THE JEWS OF COCHIN

CHAPTER 2

The Royalty of the Autumn Sacred Cycle

CALENDRIC RITUALS

The rhythms and cycles of the lunar Jewish calendar dominate Jew Town. Time flows from Shabbat to Shabbat, from Tisha B'Av to Yom Kippur, from Pesach to Shavu'oth, from new year to new year. A calendric year is one in a cycle, and the Jewish calendar was neither a beginning nor an end. Curiously, the Jewish new year falls on the first day of the seventh month,[1] and the spring festival of Pesach occurs six months later during the first month. The festivals are interconnected, revealing a structuring of time that simultaneously remembers the past as it anticipates the future. Yom Kippur is preceded by forty days of penitential prayers, prayers which set the mood for the new year and the new purity of the Day of Atonement. Rosh Hashanah also anticipates Simchat Torah, the dramatic conclusion of the fall cycle, especially in Cochin. Similarly, Pesach commemorates the exodus from Egyptian slavery, just as it prepares for the annual re-receiving of the Torah during Shavu'oth. In Cochin, the conclusion of Chanukkah marks the beginning of preparations for Pesach, some three months later. Solemnity and exuberant joy, chaste purity and riotous nobility, asceticism and sensual enjoyment, past and future—all were bound together in annual rhythms.

THE ROYALTY OF THE HIGH HOLY DAYS

The liturgical theme of the Jewish High Holy Days is God's kingship or *malkhut* in Hebrew. One of the most popular prayers is *Avinu Malkenu*, 'Our Father, Our King'. Beginning with the morning service on Rosh Hashanah and continuing through Yom Kippur, it is God's attribute of kingship which is the focus of prayers.

In Cochin, indigenous songs enhanced this symbolism, as did the unique manner of displaying Sifrei Torah and joyous afternoon processionals on Simchat Torah. Royalty, one of the two symbolic metaphors by which the Jews' place in Kerala society was ritually established and celebrated, was the *leitmotif* of the autumn holy days.

One month before Rosh Hashanah, spiritual and material preparations for the new year began.

S'LICHOT: SPIRITUAL AND MUNDANE PREPARATIONS FOR THE NEW YEAR

At the spiritual level, thirty days before Rosh Hashanah, beginning with the first of Elul, the *shofar* (ceremonial horn) was sounded. The shrill notes heralded the dawn of the new year. According to Saadia Gaon (882-942), the *shofar* is a herald announcing God's majesty, just as an earthly king is preceded by trumpets. [2] The sounds call Jews to repent before man and God. Following Sephardi *minhag*, they call the Jews to forty days of *s'lichot* prayers (pronounced *seliyot* in Cochin) at 4 a. m. each morning until Yom Kippur (simply 'Kippur' in Cochin). As God's compassion (*rachamim*) is believed to be most accessible during this *s'lichot* period, it is a local custom to name boys born at this time Rachamim. [3] During the pre-dawn darkness the sexton's Christian assistant, Jamie, walked up and down Synagogue Lane and tunefully called each Jew by name to the synagogue. The traditional forty days of penitence was reduced to just two in 1984, due to dwindling numbers and broken spirits. [4]

On the more mundane level of preparations, the huge houses of Jew Town became a whirl of activity. A new year meant a fresh start, and each home was thoroughly scrubbed. Of course, the cleaning prior to Rosh Hashanah paled in comparison with Pesach cleaning, as will be described later, but it was frenzied nevertheless. In recent years, the elaborate preparations for festivals became all the more difficult. Higher wages for Indian workers in the Persian Gulf states lured servants away and dramatically increased the wages of those who stayed. Servants, who had been a mainstay of the Indian middle class, were hard to come by and even harder to retain. Hence, the burden of semi-annual cleaning and scrubbing lay on the women of Jew Town.

All during the week preceding Rosh Hashanah, every house was filled with the sweet aroma of cakes and cookies in the ovens. A Rosh Hashanah specialty was delicious 'wedding cakes'. To mix the rich batter of semolina, eggs, sugar, ghee (clarified butter), nuts and raisins, Sarah Cohen used a large bowl known as a *kangaalam*. According to south Indian tradition, a *kangaalam* was used only by the Nambudiri brahmins to mix special holiday sweets made of jaggery and coconuts, [5] a high caste behaviour emulated by the Jews. The individual-size cakes were distributed among neighbours, and especially among non-Jewish friends. The exchange of 'emblematic' foods at festival time was an important identity-generating activity for the Cochin Jews, and a steady stream of Gentile friends stopped by to pick up the eagerly awaited rich cakes.

Other baked goodies at Rosh Hashanah were made of semolina as well, there being an association of unknown origin between semolina and the new year. Unlike their Malayali neighbours, the Cochin Jews used the Persian word, *suji* to refer to semolina. Perhaps their choice of words reflected a borrowing from the Persian custom of distributing sweetened *suji* for their springtime new year celebration, *nawroz*.

Their busy but joyous anticipation of Rosh Hashanah was tinged with dread about the future. As she baked, Sarah Cohen commented sadly, 'I don't know if we'll ever see any more weddings or festivals, or the kind of celebrations we used to have. It was so beautiful in the old days.'[6]

The women made three new *kippot* (Hebrew skull caps; singular *kippa*; 'cap' in Cochin; *yahlmolke* in Yiddish) for each man in their household: a white one for Rosh Hashanah and Yom Kippur, a green one for Sukkot, and a 'shiny' one for Simchat Torah (called Shmini in Cochin), usually made of a brilliant brocade of gold, red, or pink. In the synagogue, everyone dressed in colours coordinated for each of the holidays: embroidered white for Rosh Hashanah and plain white for Kippur were an added distinction. The synagogue was decorated similarly. There was a white *parochet* before the *aron hakodesh* and a white mantle for the *tebah* for the High Holy Days, and a green one for Sukkot. For Shmini, the synagogue was utterly transformed with a riot of colours, fabrics and flowers.

Another feature of the autumn festivals was the presence of Sattu and Gladys Koder in Jew Town. During the rest of the year, the elderly couple resided in a stately house in Fort Cochin. But for the festival season, the Koders spent the month with their daughter, Queenie, and her husband, Samuel Hallegua, in their large house in Synagogue Lane. As the community's undisputed leader, Sattu Koder stood in the line of Joseph Rabban and Ezekiel Rahabi—Jewish 'royalty' returned to Mattancheri. It was a sign that virtually all 'normal' activities were to be suspended as the community as a whole, much as its members individually, looked inward during sacred time.

ROSH HASHAṆAH

Rosh Hashanah observances began with the lighting of the *teriya*, a lamp made of seven brass circles, in each home. A glass container filled with coconut oil and a wick was placed inside each circle, and the lamp was suspended from the ceiling. In the past, the *teriya* was used for all observances. But the rising cost of oil and the difficulty in obtaining wicks restricted its use to Rosh Hashanah and Shmini. The word *teriya*, according to I.S. Hallegua, [7] is the Cochini pronunciation of *t'reychah*, Hebrew for 'trouble'.

On Rosh Hashanah the synagogue assumed an ethereal appearance. White silks covered the *tebah*, and a white *parochet* embroidered with pure gold threads hung in front of the *aron hakodesh*. The Jews, freshly bathed and dressed entirely in white, seemed almost angelic as they prayed in awe. Their coreligionists from Ernakulam joined them for the High Holy Days, as they had been doing ever since their synagogues closed down. A huge *shofar* in the Yemeni style was sounded by Yosef Hallegua, but as the festival coincided with Shabbat that year, the *shofar* sounding had to be delayed until the festival's second day.

Hearing the sound of the *shofar* is one of the central commandments for observing the Jewish new year. Mandelbaum witnessed Rosh Hashanah in Cochin in 1939, and commented:

> The blowing of the *shofar*... delighted the children. When it was taken down from the balcony to be sounded for the last time (it had previously been blown from the upper lectern), the boys crowded around to observe the technique of its use with minute attention. For hours thereafter, blasts from the thirty inch spiral erupted from every house in which there was a shofar, as the boys practised on the instrument. [8]

After prayers, Synagogue Lane bustled with people wishing each other a happy new year: 'May you be inscribed in the Book of Life'. For a brief moment, the tiny street resembled the 'little Jerusalem' it once was. Then they returned to their homes for a festive meal. To ensure a sweet year, it was customary for them to eat sweet dishes on Rosh Hashanah. Among many Ashkenazim, after sanctifying the wine (*kiddush*), an apple is dipped into honey and two prayers were offered—one over the fruits growing on trees, and the other known as the *shehecheyanu*, over the first instance of any seasonal event, or at any joyous occasion—before the sweet was tasted. The Cochin *minhag* was far more elaborate. Every seasonally available fruit had to be served and blessed, and more than a dozen dishes of cut fruits covered the table, which was elegantly laid with folded napkins and cutlery which were removed as soon as the guests sat down to eat. Where a Western Jew would expect honey, *meruba* was found, a syrup made of wild pears boiled with sugar. Like their Western coreligionists, the Cochin Jews began with homemade wine and then dipped and blessed an apple, but there the similarity ended. Next came fresh pineapples, bananas, oranges, green and red grapes, pomegranates, a huge grapefruit-like fruit known as *bamblamus*, guavas, melons, zappotas (*chicu* in Cochin), tinned cherries, followed by dried figs, dates and several varieties of raisins. Each fruit had its own blessing. For example, to the pomegranate blessing was appended, 'May the Heavenly Judge find us as filled with good deeds as this pomegranate is filled with seeds.'[9] If there was no specific prayer for a fruit, then the multipurpose *shehecheyanu* blessing was intoned. Small dried fish were blessed: 'May Israel be as fruitful and multiply like the fish in the seas', and eaten, as were other fertility symbols, such as legumes, since the Hebrew for peas, *rubiya*, is derived from *rav*, 'abundance'.[10] Green pumpkins were also eaten because the Aramaic word for pumpkin, *kara*, means to tear, and the prayer was: 'May any unfavourable verdict against us be torn up at the last moment.'[11] In some homes, leeks were blessed, because 'the Hebrew word for leek is *karti* . . . (which is) similar to *karet* which means cut off, excise. With this food we pray that God will eradicate our enemies.'[12]

The main meal comprised two kinds of chicken curry, coconut curry served with a steamed bread made from semolina, and a plethora of vegetable and rice dishes. In many places in the world, Jews make it a point to eat fish on festivals; the Ashkenazi *gefilte* fish is well known in the West as a starter course. Except for the symbolic dried fish, the Cochen family specifically avoided fish on Rosh Hashanah, in conformity with Baghdadi *minhag*. In their custom, fish was avoided on festivals because the Hebrew for fish, *dag*, is too similar to *d'agah*, worry. [13] On the other hand, the Koders, whose ancestors may have hailed from Germany, enjoyed both fried fish and fish curry before their chicken.

The next morning began with pre-dawn *s'lichot*, followed by a breakfast of semolina cakes and coffee. Then the morning prayers were offered which included the unique Cochin 'Shingly tunes'. According to local tradition, these haunting melodies were popular during the Second Temple era, tunes which have been uniquely preserved in Cranganore and brought to Cochin. The Shingly tunes were intoned only for specific prayers on particular holidays. During the second day of Rosh Hashanah and at the second Passover Seder, they could be heard, but they were especially prominent on Simchat Torah.

In fact, not only the melody but also the pronunciation of their Hebrew had changed. The qamatz vowel, usually pronounced by the Sephardim and in Israel as **a** (as in f**a**ther), was transformed into a Yemeni-like **aw** sound, as in **awe**. Curiously, this is how the vowel is pronounced by East European Jews as well, a coincidence which led several observers to infer Ashkenazi influence.[14]

Ethnomusicologist Joanna Spector studied these Shingly tunes and found no traces of the Spanish-Portuguese Sephardi melodies, but very strong influences of Yemen, Babylonia (Iraq), Kurdistan and, to a lesser degree, indigenous Indian musical motifs.[15]

Cochin Jewish music, of which Shingly tunes comprised a very specific and delimited festival component, evidenced a diversity of influences as well as antique origins. According to Spector, 'Cochin cantillation (Torah reading) is based on European Sefardic cantillation, brought in the 15th century from Spain, with elements of Yemenite and Kurdish cantillations, both considered older than the Sefardic.'[16] Writing in *Musica Judaica*, Israel Ross summarized the range of music of the Cochin Jews:

> the examples of cantillation, prayer, semi-religious song, and folksong reveal the strands of influence comprising the integrated musical style which we may now call the Cochin tradition. The core of this style is Baghdadi (Babylonian), but elements of the Yemenite, Sephardic-Portuguese, and Central European traditions, as well as the inevitable influence of local Indian practices of ornamentation and rhythm, may be detected.[17]

At the conclusion of the afternoon Rosh Hashanah prayers, the congregation strolled across a dilapidated park once maintained by the synagogue, to a spot on the water next to the maharaja's private jetty. There they performed *tashlikh*, the symbolic casting away of sins.

YOM KIPPUR

Between Rosh Hashanah and Kippur lie the *yomim nora'im*, the ten days of awe. It is believed that on Rosh Hashanah, God opens his record books, and during these ten days each person is inscribed for life or death. During this period, traditional Jews seek to make amends with neighbours as well as with God. In Jewish tradition, it is only the offended party who may forgive an offence. God cannot forgive an offence against a human, and the converse is believed to be true as well. Those who merit forgiveness will pass under God's gate to life. But who will earn forgiveness is not known until the end of the Kippur service, and the penultimate prayers are known as the closing (*ne'ilah*) of the gate of repentance.

With such deep concern for repentance, asceticism found its way into many Jewish observances associated with Kippur. In Cochin, preparations for the holiest day included a practice known in Hebrew as *malqut*, and in Malayalam as *thakka adi*. *Thakka* means something which is deserved, and *adi*, is to strike. On the evening before the holiday, two bamboo poles would be erected in the synagogue courtyard. Men would remove their shirts and their hands would be tied across each other onto the poles. Then they would receive fifteen lashes on each side of the back and nine across the front, delivered with a leather thong. This practice died out about fifty years ago, according to Sattu Koder.[18] Mandelbaum commented in 1939 on the demise of this practice: 'the white Jews have recently given up ceremonial scourging on the day before Yom Kippur, but among the black community (whom Mandelbaum thought were more religious) this rite is still faithfully performed.'[19]

The expiatory practice known as *kapparot* (a word sharing the same root with Kippur) was not seen in Cochin in 1986. The ritual was usually held the night before Kippur. A white fowl was swung over the family members' heads with the father reciting: 'This is my atonement; this is my ransom; this is my substitute. ' The fowl was then ritually slaughtered and given to a poor family as charity. When Jacob Cohen was asked about the practice, he replied with a twinkle in his eyes: 'Why should an innocent chicken die on account of my sins? That's not fair.'[20]

For *Kol Nidre*, the prayer which annuls all unfulfilled vows of the previous year (for Ashkenazim, of the coming year) on the eve of the holy day, the synagogue was lit by candles and oil lamps only. The Jews dressed entirely in white. White is traditional for two reasons. First, as the entire day is spent in the synagogue, there is no opportunity for a Jew to commit any sins on Kippur. If a person does not sin, then he is like an angel, and angels are dressed in white. The second reason is that white is reminiscent of a funeral shroud, which 'should stir us to even greater efforts in prayer and repentance'.[21] 'Women tie up their hair in a tight knot', Mandelbaum wrote of a Cochin *minhag*, 'for should a single strand be broken during the day, its wearer's life would be snapped forthwith'.[22]

The mood was subdued as the 26-hour fast began. Prayers began the next morning with *s'lichot* at 4:30 a.m. as a pink hue from the rising sun tinged the Jews' white clothes in a subtle glow. Prayers continued, with a 90 minute break early in the afternoon for a nap, until the *shofar* was sounded around 8 p.m. The women, many in their 70s, *stood* throughout the day; the men were more casual. As Mandelbaum observed of Kippur services: 'Everyone, from the tottering children to the tottering aged, is in the synagogue. It is this totality of mutual participation that explains the shatterproof cohesiveness of the group.'[23] Highlighting the afternoon

Kippur liturgy was the *Avodah* service, when the hereditary priests blessed the congregation. After washing at the ornate brass laver kept in the vestibule, the *kohanim* ascended the *dukhan*, a spot in front of the *aron hakodesh*. Placing their *tallitot* over their heads and arms and making the priests' sacred gesture with their fingers, the blessing was intoned. Congregants placed their handkerchiefs on the floor and prostrated themselves, their faces touching their handkerchiefs, the underlying belief being that no one may look upon the hands of a *kohen* as he performed the *dukhan* rite. A handkerchief was used to honour the Biblical verse, 'Neither shall you place any figured stone in your land, to bow down to it.'[24] As the floors of the synagogue were often made of stone, and especially since the Paradesi Synagogue's floor was covered with figured tiles, the handkerchief covered the possibly offensive floor.[25]

'Chazak! Chazak! (Strength! Strength!)' everyone proclaimed as the *shofar* was sounded and the synagogue's famous 22-karat solid gold kiddush cup was used for the blessing over wine. The synagogue emptied into the street, and everyone broke their fasts with *ural*, a mild wheat pudding. After bathing, everyone enjoyed a hearty meal.

SIMCHAT KOHEN

A little known *minhag* which may be practised only in India is Simchat Kohen. In the days of the Temple, Kippur was characterized by intense ritual activity on the part of the priests. They practised day-long sacrifices. In the *Avodah* service, the high priest would enter the holy of holies, pronounce the Ineffable Name, and return to the people to bless them (the origin of the *dukhan* rite).

According to Jacob Cohen, Simchat Kohen was the celebratory feast of the *kohanim* after their physically and spiritually arduous activities associated with Kippur. I.S. Hallegua added that Simchat Kohen celebrations were indicated in Livorno, Italy, editions of the *Machazor* (High Holy Day prayer books), but not in the American Sephardi ones.[26] The *kohanim* would host a feast for the people, and to commemorate the Temple custom, Indian *kohanim* would organize a party for their friends the day after Kippur. Cochin's four *kohanim*—Jacob, brother-in-law Shalom, and cousins Jackie and Sassoon Cohen, as well as a visiting *kohen* from America—were hosts to the town. Whiskey, rum and mixers flowed freely, tables were laden with savoury snacks, and songs were sung lustily as the entire Jew Town, joined by a few Gentile friends, revelled at the Cohen house.

SUKKOT

Immediately after Kippur, the 'booth' or *sukkah* was erected in the synagogue. This temporary structure, covered with fronds (*skakh*), was open to the elements. Jews are commanded to 'dwell' in such booths for the week-long festival, which usually meant that they ate some of their meals in a *sukkah*, or at least visited one and made blessings, sang a hymn, and drank a cup of wine. As tradition dictates, Biblical 'guests', *ushpizin*-Abraham, Isaac, Jacob, Joseph, Moses, Aaron and David—are invited to enjoy the *sukkah*.

A few of the Jew Town families continued the tradition of erecting a *sukkah* in the courtyards of their homes, but most were satisfied with visiting the community's *sukkah* at the synagogue, which was gaily decorated with coloured glass lamps, twinkling electric lights, fruits and flowers. During the 'good old days', each family erected its own *sukkah*, as was observed by Lowell Thomas during a visit to Cochin in the late 1920s. He wrote,

> Among both groups (i.e., the Malabari and Paradesi Jews), the Feast of Tabernacles is the most important event of the year. During this festival a temporary pandal with a flat roof covered with plaited leaves of cocoanut-palm and decorated with tropical flowers is erected outside each house. The families gather in the huts to observe the feast.[27]

The Jews scoured Ernakulam's vegetable market for a ritually proper citron, known as an *etrog*. There were lively discussions on which *etrogim* were kosher—they had to be replete with stems (*pittum*) and unblemished. Prestige accrued to the one who bought the best *etrog* at the most reasonable price. Palm fronds, willow and myrtle were gathered and tied to form the *lulav*. The *lulav* and *etrog*, which were blessed and waved in six directions, were the central symbolic ritual objects of Sukkot.

The last day of Sukkot is known as Hoshana Rabba, 'the great day of the call for help'.[28] On each day of Sukkot, the *Hoshana* prayer was read, but on Hoshana Rabba it was the focal point of the service. At the conclusion of the additional (*Musaf*) morning service, one Torah scroll was removed from the ark and placed on the *tebah* downstairs. The *chazzan* then led the congregation in circumambulating the *tebah* seven times, beating willows on the ground and tossing them over their left shoulders, dolefully intoning the *Hoshana* prayer. The entreaty for God's salvation was chanted in a particularly moving, plaintive tune. The scroll was returned to the *aron hakodesh*, and the *chazzan* then chanted the *Eiyn Kaloheinu* ('There is None Like Our God') in Shingly melody.

SHMINI ATZERET/SIMCHAT TORAH

Immediately following Sukkot is the two-day festival of Shmini as it is known in Cochin. Synagogues in the Diaspora observe two separate festivals: Shmini Chag Atzeret and Simchat Torah. In Israel, Shmini Chag Atzeret and Simchat Torah are celebrated together on the same day, the second day of the festival being a diaspora observance. Shmini Chag Atzeret commemorates the additional sacrifices offered after Sukkot at the Temple, and Simchat Torah is a non-Biblical celebration of the conclusion of the yearly cycle of Torah reading, and the beginning of the new cycle.[29] In Cochin, Shmini has enormous significance, arguably the community's most distinctive autumn observance.

People dressed in their finest and gleaming clothes for Shmini. Strolling down Synagogue Lane for evening prayers, one came across a 'tree of light'—a 12-foot metal 'tree' whose branches supported blazing oil lamps. I.S. Hallegua observed that the tree supported 82 lights, representing the 82 families of Jew Town listed by Roby.[30] In the past, the Jews quickly reminded their guests, there were 'trees' before each of Synagogue Lane's three synagogues. At the base of the clock tower was a similar contraption in the shape of a Star of David. The overall effect was brilliant; Shmini in Cochin was a very special occasion.

But the festive air outside the synagogue paled in comparison with the splendours inside. The synagogue, brilliant and colourful at any time, on Shmini was utterly dazzling.

The whitewashed walls and dark wooden benches were covered with golden satin. The effect of the shimmering walls reflecting the blazing oil lamps encircling the *tebah* suffused the dainty prayer hall with a light which bordered upon the supernal. All around the upper half of the walls were *parokhets*—in green, gold, blue, red and white embroidered silks. The impact was enhanced by the fragrance of freshly-plucked jasmine flowers which were hung from the many chandeliers and oil lamps.

The most striking decorations transformed the *aron hakodesh*. A special, temporary ark was constructed. Sitting atop the Haile Selaisse carpet just before the ark, a temporary structure stood between two tall, silver pillars. The platform was covered with gold-embroidered, red Benarsi silk. All seven Sifrei Torah, replete with gold, jewel-encrusted crowns and finials, were proudly displayed. The effect was com-pleted by a canopy of red and gold silks, topped off with the cover of the synagogue's famous, solid gold Kiddush cup, the one which was used to break the fast on Kippur, and which sanctified every bride and bridegroom of Cochin for centuries. The synagogue became a vision of eternity.

The prayer for rain (*Geshem*) is chanted on Shmini with a special earnestness. In Kerala, the fall monsoon usually carries rain at that time of the year, rain which not only brings sustenance but also lowers temperatures. In an elaborate rite just before the Torah scrolls were replaced in the ark, several *chazzanim* and the day's Torah reader led the heartfelt petition for rain, after which the additional morning service (*Musaf*) began.[31]

Simchat Torah prayers increased in intensity during the course of the festival's service. On the first evening they were most subdued. The synagogue was crowded for *Arvith* (evening) services: Indian Jews from as far as Bombay, Trivandrum and Madras, not to mention Ernakulam and Alwaye, were present as also Jewish travellers from Switzerland, South Africa, England, Israel and America. As the seven *haqafot* (circumambulations around the *tebah* with the Torah scrolls) commenced, song books were produced and the synagogue was filled with haunting Shingly tunes. There was much dancing, jumping and clapping. Bottles of rum, brandy and whiskey were placed in the corners and recesses of the building as well as in the women's section.

By *Shacharit* prayers the next morning, the mood became more festive. The high spirits were boosted by the 'petrol' drunk to enliven the steps of the younger men, who carried then Sifrei Torah, as well as by the chanting of the older men and women. As the men paused to catch their breath after each round of the *tebah* with the heavy, metal-encased scrolls elaborately bedecked with crowns and *rimomim*, a fellow celebrant invariably tapped his shoulder with a naughty grin on his face, and invited him to share 'Petrol! Petrol!' The scroll was passed to other, eager hands, and the two escaped to the crowded apartment of the *shamash*, next to the synagogue. Jackie Cohen's dining table was covered with bottles of liquor, as well as boiled potatoes and eggs to ease the absorption of the spirits.

The Jew Town folk reminded their guests that contemporary festivals paled in comparison with 'the good old days' when all of 'the gang' was still in Cochin. A favourite of Simchat Torah festivities in the past was Sassoon Hallegua. Every year, Sassoon concocted an infamous milk punch, which of course contained no milk but arrack and other spirits. By dawn, Sassoon visited each house on Synagogue Lane armed with several bottles of milk punch, and insisted that his friends drank it while they were still drowsy. Jocularly, Raymond Salem recalled when Sassoon called on him to share some milk punch while Raymond was in the middle of his morning toilette. Undeterred, Sassoon invaded Raymond's privacy and refused to leave until he had poured a healthy swig down Raymond's throat![32]

Apart from the seven *haqafot*, the focus of the morning prayers was on reading from the Sefer Torah. On this festival, the final lines of the Torah dealing with the death of Moses were immediately followed by lines which described the creation of the world, *b'reshit*. Jews allow no time to elapse between the conclusion of one annual cycle of Torah reading and its recommencement, because Satan may then argue before God: 'Lord, behold Thy favorite children. They finish the study of the Torah and have no desire to continue with it.'[33] All men were called upon to recite the blessings over the Torah, and for many years this was the only such festive occasion for manumitted slaves, *meshuchrarim* to receive the honour.

Symbolically, every Jew is wedded to the Torah, and the one who reads the concluding verses of *D'varim* is known as *Chatan Torah*, the bridegroom of the Torah. The one who reads the first lines is referred to as *Chatan B'reshit*, the bridegroom of Genesis, and in the Cochin *minhag* he should be the most recent groom among the community.[34]

Another intriguing Cochin *minhag* involved the Torah reading that day. Two readers ascended to the *tebah* for the sixth portion. I. C. Hallegua read a Hebrew line from the Sefer, and Jacob Cohen chanted the verse in Aramaic translation. The practice was repeated for the Haftarah on the first day of Pesach. No one had any knowledge about the origin of this *minhag*. Sattu Koder believed that it may have been a Yemeni custom.[35] Another possible explanation was that it was a remnant from the ancient traditions of Cranganore, where Aramaic was believed to have been the spoken language. Perhaps Torah and Haftarah readings were routinely translated into a readily understandable language, although why only the sixth *aliyah* on Simchat Torah and the Haftarah for the first day of Passover should be singled out remained a mystery. [36]

The *Haftarah* (prophetic reading) for Simchat Torah was sung in Shingly cantillation and pronunciation, as were its blessings—an especially beautiful chant. The popular Sephardi songs, *Imre na* and *Mi sepharad hikakhti*, were also chanted with Shingly melodies.

After the morning prayers, the entire community enjoyed a lavish banquet (*se'uda mitzvah*) at Sassoon Hall, the massive residence of bachelor Isaac Ashkenazy. The old building was once the home of a branch of the Hallegua family which had been wiped out, according to Raymond Salem, due to a curse by a Hindu merchant who felt he had been wronged in a commercial transaction.[37] Ashkenazy, a quiet man who resembled the actor Peter Lorre, lived alone in the house since his sisters had emigrated to Israel. In the past, the cavernous rooms had been the site of hundreds of Simchat Torah banquets and innumerable wedding feasts, some of which were described by Yaakob Sapir during his visit to Jew Town more than a century ago. The hall was large enough to accommodate as many as 600 guests at one sitting, so Isaac's lone residency there was incongruous.

For the first time in five years, the tradition of community banquets was revived in 1986 in honour of foreign guests, it was said. In the past, there were numerous such celebrations, but many observances deemed less essential had been abandoned. Gamliel Salem, his energetic son Kenneth, and Sarah Cohen, the unofficial leader of women, had been engaged in preparations for weeks. Everyone played a role: young people collected chairs and set up long tables. Women prepared their favourite festival dishes. Men made seemingly endless trips to liquor stores.

About sixty guests sat down to a lavish meal—nineteen fowls were laid out on the table, not to mention huge trays of steaming yellow rice, buriyanis, vegetables and other specialties. Bottle after bottle of 'petrol', most of it imported, made the rounds as the building shook from the thunderous singing, stomping, jumping and clapping. The elders—Sattu and Elias Koder, Jacob Cohen, Raymond Salem, Samuel Hallegua and P.T. Aron—led the festivities from the head of the table, and occasionally younger members burst into a modern Hebrew song. Selections included the old Malayalam songs, Cochini Hebrew *shirot*, Sephardi tunes, and modern Israeli *horas*. It was probably a mere shadow of the years gone by, but it was surely an impressive event! It seemed as though the many ghosts of Jew Town joined their few descendants for the fleeting moment—a window into the past, a glimpse of what Jew Town was for so long.

After the banquet, the uniqueness of Cochini observances of Simchat Torah became even more evident. The three afternoon *haqafot* in the courtyard, outside the synagogue building, were unique in the world.[38] A red coir carpet was laid around the synagogue. The younger and stronger men carried the scrolls while the older men sprinkled rose water on them. There was concern whether there were enough young and able bodies to complete the circumambulations with the heavy scrolls, but in the past there was concern whether there would be enough rounds to give everyone a chance to carry the beloved scrolls! Mandelbaum commented on the children's eager participation:

> The younger men try hard to have the honor of carrying them. There are two small scrolls which are carried by boys. I noticed one little fellow tearfully pleading with his father that he might have the privilege of bearing the *sefer*. The privilege must be purchased, and when the father finally nodded his assent, the boy went bounding off in an about face of emotion, to tell his friends of his luck.[39]

All men, women and children lustily chanted unique Cochini Hebrew songs proclaiming their love of Torah. According to local tradition, the entire liturgy for the afternoon *haqafot* was composed in Cranganore.[40]

The elder men led the procession, walking backward as they sang, facing the scrolls, carrying handwritten song books. Women, dressed in brilliant saris and kerchiefs, sang no less enthusiastically. This festival was the only time women freely entered the main hall of the synagogue.

There were many 'petrol' refuelling stops for both men and women. By the afternoon, the 'petrol-discourse' became more nuanced: rum was referred to as 'petrol', brandy as 'high octane petrol', and whiskey was known as 'aviation fuel'. Abigail Elias of Ernakulam wielded an open whiskey bottle, forcing some of the more reticent women and men to drink. Revelry and reversal permeated the atmosphere. As Sarah Cohen put it, 'During Simchat Torah, everything is allowed!'[41]

After the *haqafot*, almost everyone left the synagogue and headed home for a rest. During the 1930s, Cecil Koder introduced yet another festivity to Simchat Torah observances: water fights. Reminiscent of the riotous Hindu festival of Holi, Synagogue Lane on Simchat Torah afternoon was transformed into a jocular battleground. Pails of water were poured over any and every unsuspecting head, followed by rotten eggs which were hidden away and painted with Hebrew festive greetings. Some elders secured their doors, but most accepted a rotten egg and pail of water as their due. There was enough time for a shower before *Minchah* prayers. Mandelbaum aptly commented upon the seemingly chaotic merriment:

> On this day the tears in the social fabric are mended. All quarrels are supposed to be patched up on *Simchat Torah*, and many dissensions really are smoothed over in the general merry-making. The least of the congregation enjoys the honor of reading the blessings before the Law together with the most distinguished. Women are allowed to come into the synagogue hall to kiss the sacred books. At noon the young people dine in houses other than their own. Wine and arrack flow copiously and some men become gloriously tight. Like drunken men the world over, they crack muddled jokes and bawl out catchy tunes. But in Cochin the tunes that they sing in their groggy animation are synagogue melodies, hymns and paeans to the Lord of Israel.[42]

After having rested, the Jews returned to the synagogue for *Minchah* prayers at 6:30 p.m. There is documentary evidence that the Cochin Simchat Torah *Minchah*, a unique and highly significant service, dates back to Cranganore itself, just as the Cochin Jews claimed. Baltimore Hebrew University Hebracist Arthur M. Lesley discovered three documents from or about Shingly, dating between 1494 and 1504.[43] A letter dated 1503 by Moshe ben Abba Mori of Shingly reads:

And there is with us a custom and the second holy day of Shemini Atzeret, after they pray the additional morning service (*musaf*) and bring out eight Torah scrolls in precious coverings, and chains. . . and golden pomegranates (finials? *rimomim*), outside the synagogue, and utter song and praise and thanks in a loud voice and circle three times and pray the afternoon (*minhah*).[44]

So significant was this service that when Yaakob Daniel Cohen established a Hebrew-Malayalam printing press in Jew Town in 1877, his first publication was a liturgy for this occasion.[45] The service included the liturgy for the three *haqafot*[46] as well as the longest *kaddish* in the world.[47]

Arvith prayers followed the unique *Minchah*, and then there was another unique and intriguing Cochin observance. The Sifrei Torah were placed on chairs and benches, and as men, women and children sang *shirot* in the synagogue hall, the congregation dismantled the temporary ark. It was demolished ritually and methodically: the Benarsi silks were carefully removed, followed by the silver pillars. Finally, the wooden planks were disassembled. During the process of dismantling, the people sang *shirot*, and when it was over the young people sang and danced an Israeli *hora*. On the completion of the task, the Israeli national anthem, *Hatiqvah* ('The Hope'), was sung.

Once again, the Jew Town folk walked from the synagogue to the tiny street, this time with measured steps and restrained demeanour. Past the blazing 'tree of light', the slow steps of Sattu Koder set the pace. The entire community escorted the eldest member to his house, sneaking longing glances at the metal-and-fire tree. The restraint of this final ritual act of the fall cycle was a striking counterpoint to the animated dismantling of the ark and *hora* dancing.

As the community stood outside Sattu's door, he blessed everyone. His brief remarks were cutting. Like virtually all Jews, the Jew Town folks loved Israel, but their love was tinged with ambivalence because emigration to Israel had reduced Kerala's Jewish population from nearly 3,000 in the early 1950s to less than two dozen. Sattu's remarks meld resentment with bravado.

He recalled the antiquity and singularity of Cochin's observances, and expressed his joy that these traditions had survived till 1986. He was full of praise for all those who had participated: the young men who carried the heavy scrolls, people who worked hard to organize the banquet for the first time after many years, Bene Israel guests from Mumbai and foreign guests came from distant lands. Everyone was singled out for praise. He also mentioned some guests from Israel who had informed him that virtually no one in Israel was religious. 'I know that's an exaggeration', he said, 'but that's how it's perceived here in Cochin'. Sattu was scornful about the 'Jewish culture' prevailing in the Jewish state. As if to defy history, continued:

What kind of Jewish culture are they developing if they don't fast on Kippur, if they don't observe Shabbat, if they don't believe in God? What kind of Jewish culture is that? At least in some parts of the Diaspora, like here in Cochin, we fast on Kippur and we observe Shabbat. Real orthodox Judaism continues, at least here in the Diaspora. . . . Our prayers and songs go back to the days of the Temple. I don't know if that is true, but that is our belief. . . . We should be proud that here the old ways continue and, God willing, the old ways will continue for many years yet.[48]

Having instilled pride in the congregation, Sattu asked the elders and guests to make a few comments, and then everyone sang the Indian national anthem, a counterbalance to *Hatiqvah*. Before entering his house Sattu proclaimed with a wave: 'God bless everyone', and the people gathered replied in one voice: *L'shanah ha-ba'ah b'Yerushalayim* ('Next year in Jerusalem!'). Someone decided to adapt the Hebrew adage to better fit their circumstances and shouted *L'shanah ha-ba'ah b'Cochin* ('Next year in Cochin'), a rallying cry which echoed along Synagogue Lane until everyone retired to their homes, exhausted after month-long festivities.

HINDU-JEWISH PARALLELS

In every culture, Jewish worship resembles that of the host community. It is a tautology that British Jews are British in style and that Afghan Jews are Afghan. Mindful of preserving *halakhic* integrity, Jews have been free to adapt themselves to their contexts, and authorities have generally been liberal in permitting localized *minhagim* to flourish. Nevertheless, Western Jews have looked askance at local customs pervading the so-called 'exotic' Jewish communities. This disdain reflects a provincial attitude, at best.

Three singular aspects of the Cochin *minhag* for Simchat Torah—displaying the Sifrei Torah on a temporary ark, adding afternoon *haqafot* outside the synagogue building, and ritually dismantling the ark—were creative responses to the Hindu environment prevailing in Malabar.

In a similar way, Hinduized symbols and behaviours of priestly purity were adapted in the Cochin Pesach *minhag*, as will be discussed later.

Hindu practice is always defined by a particular community of Hindus, determined by caste, geography as well as other factors. There is no one normative version of Hinduism, but a dazzling array of local traditions. The metaphors and symbols of royalty and nobility, therefore, are those practised by the royalty of the region, i.e. the Nayar caste in Malabar and the Perumpadappu family in Cochin.

Like most of the royal families, the Perumpadappus are devotees of Lord Krishna, and of the goddess Bhagavati, who is associated with Parvati, the consort of Lord Shiva. The maharaja's temple which abuts the Paradesi Synagogue is known as the Pazhayannur Shri Krishna Temple, and it is not surprising that most Hindus prefer to worship a God who rose from their own community. Warriors and rulers in traditional India occupied the same station in life.

South India's warrior-kings relied upon the brahmins to sacralize their rule. This was done, in part, by constructing and patronizing temples, Hindu or otherwise. As Bayly put it, 'the support and protection of temples was one of the defining acts of south Indian kingship'. [49] But such benefaction amounts to conquest, and results not only in the religious legitimation of the king, but also in the kingly coronation of the temple's deity. 'It will be remembered', Bayly added, 'that the god of a great temple was himself conceived of as a king: from his *kôvil* (a term for temple which also meant 'royal palace') he ruled over a realm of his own. . . . '[50]

What enables the Jews to adapt to a royal Hindu God are their own metaphors of God's royalty (*malkhut*), the dominant liturgical theme for the High Holy Days. What is required is a foregrounding of ritual themes inherent in Judaism, not the adoption of alien symbols. In virtually every country in which they live, Jews adopt 'additional observances' (*hiddur mitzvot*) to those required by *Halakha*. These 'additional observances' allow for creative adaptations to host cultures, and in Cochin, essentially the Jews adapted royalty themes in the autumn and ascetical themes in the spring.

Each Hindu temple has its own deity and an annual festival is held for that deity known as an *utsavam*. Typically, the image (*murti*) of the deity is removed from the *garbhagriha* (holy of holies, *sanctum sanctorum*) and placed in a *mandapa* (caparison) atop a cart or chariot (*ratha*).[51] At the end of many of these festivals, the *murti* is ceremoniously discarded either into a river or the ocean; at Puri, the processional icon is destroyed only once in twelve or seventeen years.[52] Alternatively, the *murti* is returned to the *garbhagriha* and the *mandapa* is dismantled.

These three elements—display, procession and dismantling—characterized Simchat Torah in Cochin. Like the Hindu *murti*, the Sifrei Torah were removed from their usual, holy abode (the *aron hakodesh*, paralleling the Hindu *garbhagriha*) and displayed on a temporary structure or ark (paralleling the Hindu *mandapa*). Like the *murti*, the scrolls were carried through a public area, the synagogue courtyard. Like the *mandapa*, the temporary ark was dismantled ritually. Through these three unique aspects of the Cochin *minhag* royal Hindu religious behaviours were adapted and Judaized.

The ingenuity of these adaptations is an instance of the adaptive cultural genius of the Jews. How to participate in the gentile world while maintaining allegiance to Jewish observance has been a challenge facing Jews in all four corners of the diaspora. In India, a culture not merely tolerant of religious diversity but also affectionately supportive of it, Jews adapted to Hinduism while adhering to normative Judaism's standards. Theirs was a perfectly balanced, ritually established identity.

Beyond these ritual symmetries of the Jews and the Nayars, there were social, 'attributional' similarities as well. The most significant were the economic patterns of the Jews and the Nayars. Both groups were large landholders, the defining characteristic of a 'dominant caste'. They were also among Kerala's greatest warriors.

Other parallels may be drawn between the Nayars and the Jews. One features was particularly striking: the power and independence enjoyed by the women of Jew Town. Many of them were professionals—physicians, professors, office managers and merchants. They were extremely well educated in Hebrew traditionally and, since the early twentieth century, in secular subjects as well. Besides, they have always been respected members of the community. These patterns were particularly striking when contrasted with either traditional Jewish or Hindu patterns of gender arrangements. The independence of women partly reflected their contact with the matrilinear traditions of the Nayars. In Nayar tradition, once a 'primary marriage' was contracted with a Nambudiri man, Nayar women enjoyed autonomy in selecting sexual partners. While Jewish women's sexuality was strictly limited, their autonomy was more generalized and was particularly evident in religious education and professional achievement.

Day-to-day social interactions between women and men were strikingly egalitarian, and this equality could not be attributed to modernization because it predated and in some respects exceeded it. For example, there were few gender barriers in social interactions. Men and women 'mixed freely' and openly expressed affection. The people of Jew Town were not impressed with the practice of some orthodox Ashkenazim for men and women to avoid any physical contact, including a casual handshake. According to Lily Koder, 'In Cochin, we are pleasantly religious; we're not fanatics.'[53] Raymond Salem, too, was perplexed. 'There is nothing in *Halakha* to prevent men and women from shaking hands', he said, and added after some reflection, 'That must be borrowing from Muslim culture which some Jews picked up. It's certainly not Jewish.'[54]

A coincidence between the Jewish and Nayar marriage customs was observed by Johnson: 'Jewish law permits both cross-cousin and parallel-cousin marriages, unlike many South Indian groups which encourage cross-cousin but prohibit parallel-cousin alliances. The Nayars of Central Kerala permit both.'[55]

Examples of parallels between the Jews and the Nayars (and Nambudiris) can be extended, all of which count as evidence from the perspective of an 'attributional' approach to the study of caste. In his definitive work on the subject, *Homo Hierarchicus*, Louis Dumont summarized this approach: 'The theory of attribution is that a caste's rank derives from the characteristics of its way of life, high or low according to the criteria of collective purity.'[56] In the other approach to caste ranking known as the 'interactional' approach, 'castes are ranked according to the structure of interaction among them . . . (especially in) the ritualized giving and receiving of food... 'Emphasis in this system of ranking is not on qualities, but on transactions. . . . '[57] Both perspectives will be employed in considering aspects of the Cochin's Pesach *minhagim*, and both demonstrate the Jews' remarkable attainment of high status in a system designed by and for Hindus, especially brahmins.

To summarize how the autumn High Holy Days—Simchat Torah in particular—served to integrate the Jews into Malabar's Hindu social order: traditional Jewish metaphors and symbols of royalty, judiciously merged with borrowings from Hindu practice, connected Jews with one of India's twin poles of power. During Passover, Jews emulated the ascetical, purity-conscious Hinduism of the brahmins, as will be discussed later.

WINTER INTERLUDES: CHANUKKAH AND 1 JANUARY

The infinitely recoverable sacred time of October passed and ordinary, secular time returned. A slight drop in the temperature was counterbalanced by a rise in the tedium of life in a dying community.

In the past, the *chanukkiyot* (Chanukkah lamps) burning to the right of each doorway heralded a special time for children. But there were no children in 1986, and Chanukkah without children was scarcely Chanukkah. Inside the synagogue, the beautiful, old oil lamp was dutifully lit after *Arvith* prayers each day, to the tune of unique Cochini Hebrew songs. In most homes, the lovely *chanukkiyot* were no longer seen: the Jew Town folks recounted the tale of an unscrupulous American rabbi who conned them out of their heirlooms, exchanging the centuries-old, Sephardi nine-wicked oil lamps for a few rupees and cheap, contemporary Israeli candle holders.

The first day of Chanukkah also marked the death anniversary of Nehemiah Mota, the sixteenth century Qabbalist. Considered a minor festival among the Malabari Jews, the Paradesis allowed the event to pass unnoticed.[58]

The monsoon rains did not follow the *Geshem* prayer, and the area depended entirely upon hydroelectricity. Power shortages and blackouts were common occurrences. One evening, electricity failed during the chanting of *Arvith* songs, plunging the synagogue into darkness. Despite the fact that the congregation was intoning songs specific to that holiday, not a beat was missed. Everyone knew their *shirot* so well they remained undeterred—even though they had no use of the song books they carried![59]

The Western new year's eve, simply referred to as 'the 31st night' in Cochin, was an occasion for the Jews to mingle with their gentile friends. Dressed in their finest safari suits and saris, they visited private clubs in Ernakulam, or the officers' club at the naval base, for an evening of vegetarian dining and dancing.

On 1 January, a recent tradition was enacted: Mr. Isidore, the only Christian resident of Synagogue Lane, customarily invited the people of Jew Town for dinner—strictly *kosher*, of course. Isidore bought live chickens and Jackie Cohen 'cut the fowls', as *sh'chita* was known. Isidore borrowed cooking pots and dishes from Jewish homes, and hired the Jews' servants, to ensure that he offered *kosher* foods to his friends. And eat they did! Among Isidore's ornate, Syrian crosses and statues of Jesus and Mary, all of Jew Town boisterously cheered their favourite in curry-eating contests. More than a little liquor was drunk, too.

Another midwinter diversion was the conversion of Prem Doss Swami Doss. A native of Trivandrum, Prem's grandfather had converted from Hinduism to Anglican Christianity. Demonstrably talented, he studied theology in England and became a pastor of the leading church of his area. Prem's father followed in his footsteps, and Prem was expected to receive the mantle of leadership in the church.

Prem narrated his story: he so deeply loved Jesus that he wanted to know everything about him. He studied his life, and was startled to learn that Jesus was a Jew. Eventually, he visited Cochin to meet his saviour's coreligionists. The more he studied, the more he was convinced that Jesus was a Pharisaic rabbi who had been totally misunderstood by Paul and his followers. In 1981, Prem went to Israel where he studied in an Ashkenazi *yeshiva* for *ba'alei t'shuvah* (a school for Jews who wish to observe Judaic law but who possess little background). He produced a book about his experiences, *Israel as Seen by an Indian*.[60]

He led the life of a Jew. His family's small house outside Trivandrum became a veritable shrine to Israel. Prem conspicuously erected a Maghen David above the doorway, and the sitting room was decorated with pictures of Bethlehem, Jerusalem, various rabbis, David Ben-Gurion, Anne Frank, Golda Meir and Meir Kahane. His family, however, remained Christian, but his mother was careful to prepare his vegetable and fish dishes in separate pots instead of those she used for the rest of the family.

The Jew Town folk were suspicious of converts, and they reiterated that anyone who became a Jew because of marriage was not a proper Jew. Such conversions, they reasoned, were *asur* or forbidden, because they were undertaken with ulterior motives. Prem's conversion was clearly the proper type in their view, and he was welcomed into the community wholeheartedly. Visiting Cochin for Chanukkah, he elected to undergo ritual circumcision. Because of pain due to the operation, Prem had to forego his usual trousers and had to don a *mundu* until his wound had healed—a matter which evoked more than a little teasing. Eventually, the *miqveh* at Isaac Ashkenazy's house was cleaned—all the *miqvehs* in Jew Town had fallen into disuse as there had been no ritual need for them for some years—and Prem immersed himself (*t'vilah*) and was called by his proud, new name, Prem Doss S. Yehudi ben Avraham, to bless the Sefer Torah.

An interesting Cochin custom took place on Shabbat *Parashat Vayichi*, when the portion of the Torah containing the patriarch Jacob's blessings to his twelve sons was read. In Cochin, the oldest man who was not a *kohen* read the section. In 1987, the honour fell upon Raymond Salem.

Another diversion was the birth of Gamliel and Reema Salem's grandson in Canada on 3 January 1987. After *havdallah* in the evening, fruits, eggs and boiled potatoes were blessed and eaten, and the newborn Cocha Nathan ('Little Nathan') was toasted. The *brit milah* (called *bris* by Ashkenazim, *milah* by Cochinim) on the eighth day after birth was heartily celebrated. Unique *milah* songs were sung, and great-uncle Raymond Salem's house was crowded with friends and well-wishers, Jewish and gentile. Predictably, his table was laden with drinks, chicken curries, rice and snacks.

As early as the end of Chanukkah, the calendric rhythm in Cochin began to anticipate the year's next focal point, Pesach. On 15 January, a basket of tamarind for Passover use was delivered to Sarah Cohen's home, 'Now the work begins for Passover',[61] she sighed as she commenced to clean them. It was difficult for the visitor to imagine what to anticipate.

NOTES

1. Lev. 23: 24.
2. Chill, *The Minhagim*, p. 190.
3. Cowen, *Jews in Remote Corners of the World*, p. 204.
4. Gamliel Salem, 2 October 1986.
5. A. Surangam, 4 July 1989.
6. Sarah Cohen, 30 September 1986.
7. I.S. Hallegua, personal communication, 1990.
8. Mandelbaum, 'The Jewish Way of Life in Cochin', pp. 455-6.
9. Chill, *The Minhagim*, p. 186.
10. Ibid., p. 186.
11. Ibid., p. 186.
12. Ibid., p. 186.
13. Ibid., p. 185.
14. For example, Reinman, 'Masa'oth Shlomo b'Kogin', p. 22, Rabinowitz, *Far East Mission*, p. 109.
15. Spector, 'The Music of the Cochin Jews', pp. 181-3.
16. Spector, 'Shingli Tunes of the Cochin Jews', p. 26.
17. Ross, 'Cross-Cultural Dynamics in Musical Traditions', pp. 65-6.
18. Sattu Koder, 14 April 1987.
19. Mandelbaum, 'The Jewish Way of Life in Cochin', p. 442. Cf. Stritzower, *Exotic Jewish Communities*, p. 120.
20. Jacob Cohen, 8 October 1986. Most modern Hindus would express similar disdain for animal sacrifices which played a large role in their classical traditions.
21. Chill, *The Minhagim*, p. 205.
22. Mandelbaum, 'The Jewish Way of Life in Cochin', p. 456.
23. Ibid., p. 456.
24. Lev. 25: 1.
25. Chill, *The Minhagim*, p. 212.
26. I.S. Hallegua, personal communication, 12 July 1989.
27. Thomas, 'The City of Black and White Jews', p. 38.
28. Chill, *The Minhagim*, p. 233.
29. Ibid., p. 236.
30. I.S. Hallegua, personal communication, 28 July 1989.
31. The autumn festivals fall during the Hebrew month of Tishrei, which corresponds to the Tamil month of Margashrisha. It is during this time that the Hindus, too, perform an annual prayer for rain. Dennis Hudson, personal communication, 1991; cf. Dehejia, *Antal and Her Path of Love*, pp. 103-6.
32. Raymond Salem, 26 October 1986.
33. *Ta'ame ha-Minhagim*, cited by Chill, *The Minhagim*, p. 238.
34. Jacob Cohen, 8 October 1986.
35. Sattu Koder, 14 April 1987.

36. While vernacular translation of Torah readings is an ancient custom, dating from the beginning of the diaspora, the retention of this tradition in Cochin is puzzling. It has been suggested that it may reflect the Hindu Bhagavata custom, the form of Hinduism practised by Cochin's royal family. At Tamil Nadu's Srirangam Temple during the Vaikuntha Ekadashi festival, which falls at the same lunar times as does Simchat Torah, the chanting of the Vedas in Sanskrit is followed by the recitation of a vernacular, Tamil translation. Dennis Hudson, personal communication, 1991.
37. Raymond Salem, 15 October 1986.
38. Hallegua, 'Simchat Torah in Cochin', p. 6.
39. Mandelbaum, 'The Jewish Way of Life in Cochin', p. 458.
40. A recent discovery by Lesley tends to corroborate the Cochin Jews' tradition. See just below.
41. Sarah Cohen, 26 October 1986.
42. Mandelbaum, 'The Jewish Way of Life in Cochin', pp. 457-8.
43. Lesley's discovery was announced in 'Shingly in Cochin Jewish Memory and in Eyewitness Accounts'.
44. Lesley, 'Shingly in Cochin Jewish Memory and in Eyewitness Accounts', p. 16.
45. Cohen, ed., *Seder Minchah Simchat Torah*, published in 5637/1877.
46. Ibid., pp. 13f, 16f, 25f.
47. Ibid., pp. 35-40.
48. Sattu Koder, 26 October 1986.
49. Bayly, *Saints, Goddesses and Kings*, p. 56.
50. Ibid., p. 59.
51. Sometimes these carts are enormous, as the most famous cart at the Shri Jagannath Temple of Puri, Orissa. More than a million Hindus participate in Shri Jagannath's annual festival, pulling the 300-foot tall cart down Puri's main road. The English word 'juggernaut', something which rolls over everything in its path, is an Anglicization of the deity's name, since his cart rolls over everything on Puri's main avenue, including an occasional devotee.
52. Tripathi, 'Navakalevara', p. 223.
53. Lily Koder, March 1984.
54. Raymond Salem, 11 April 1987.
55. Johnson, '"Our Community" in Two Worlds', p. 427, fn. 2.
56. Dumont, *Homo Hierarchicus*, p. 90.
57. Marriott, 'Interactional and Attributional Theories of Caste Ranking', pp. 96-7.
58. Samuel Hallegua, 16 May 1987.
59. Field notes, 29 December 1986.
60. Yehudi, *Israel as Seen by an Indian*.
61. Sarah Cohen, 15 January 1987.

CHAPTER 3

Spring Rites: An Ascetic Passover

The subtle interconnections between the festivals and holy days of the Hebrew calendar provided the rhythm for life in Jew Town. Almost imperceptibly, the autumn cycle led to Chanukkah, just as Chanukkah anticipated Purim and especially, Pesach. If Simchat Torah and Pesach were the anchors of Jew Town time, then the other festivals were the counterpoints.

PURIM

In 'the good old days', Purim was celebrated heartily in Cochin, especially by children. They would receive silver rupees from all the adults. An effigy of Haman, the archetypical anti-Semite of the *Megillat Esther* (Book of Esther), was burnt,[1] and gala fancy dress parties were held for young and old alike. Little girls dressed as the beautiful Queen Esther, and boys donned the royal robes of the buffoonish tyrant, King Ahashverot, or the Persian silks of the wise Mordecai. A grand festive meal, the Purim *se'uda*, was held, similar to the banquet on Simchat Torah. However, all these joys had passed into memory.

Purim coincides with the riotous Hindu festival of Holi. A celebration of the defeat of the demoness Holika at the same time as it is a celebration of Lord Krishna's dalliances with his girlfriends in the forests of Vrindavan, an erotic Hindu Eden, Holi is a festival of social reversals and 'saturnalian carousing. . . . [E] ach person plays and for the moment may experience the role of his opposite', observed McKim Marriott in a well-known article,[2] and during this festival the most lowly may harass the highest with impunity. Coloured water (and worse) is thrown on one and all, poor women kick their landlords' shins and youngsters revile brahmins—all in an attempt at social levelling in the context of a society characterized by strict hierarchy.

Indian Jews adopted some of the tamer forms of celebration, as Holi and Purim share beyond a lunar date an atmosphere of reversal and revelry. Not too long ago, Synagogue Lane would be awash with the reds, oranges, blues and yellows the youngsters tossed onto the heads of one and all.

In 1987, Purim was subdued. The *Megillat Esther* itself instructs Jews to observe the festival in four ways: (*a*) the reading of the *Megillah*; (*b*) giving charity; (*c*) giving gifts of food to others; and (*d*) a festive meal.[3] These four acts, the rudiments of Purim observance, were performed.

Most of the men of Jew Town carried their own *Megillot* to the synagogue. Sattu Koder's was encased in a beautiful silver holder. Others were simple calligraphed pieces of parchment. Samuel Hallegua read the text, together with special Cochini blessings appended to the usual three. It was believed that these unique blessings were composed by Jew Town's greatest mystic, Nehemiah Mota. Every time the name of the wicked prime minister, Haman, was read, benches were pounded with wooden mallets, shoes and fists in order to 'blot out the remembrance of Amalek',[4] as Haman is believed to have descended from the Biblical enemy of the Jewish people, who himself was a descendant of Esau, Jacob's estranged brother. Depending on events outside India, at times the names of Hitler and Nasser were substituted for Haman's.

As part of the ritual of giving on Purim, coins and foods were exchanged. Each person in the community received a shiny, new five rupee coin from Gladys Koder, and fruits and cakes were in evidence. On Purim, servants were also given coins by all the folks of Jew Town as well as new saris by their employers. Local beggars were well aware of the custom and several of them lined Synagogue Lane.

The communal festive meal had been reduced to drinks and snacks, although everyone participated enthusiastically and a jovial spirit prevailed.

The festivities associated with Purim were conducted in the shadow of preparations for Pesach, preparations which began just after Chanukkah.

PASSOVER, ASCETICISM AND CASTE

According to *Halakha*, Jewish communities are free to institute and practice 'additional observances' (*hiddur mitzvah*), 'those which express the Jew's love of the *mitzvot* by embellishing them'.[5] Passover preparations in Cochin were striking; in certain ways they were more fastidious than those found in other Jewish communities, even orthodox ones. The question is: *Why* did the Cochinim 'exaggerate' their Passover observances? *Why* did they add these 'additional observances'?

The answer is complex, and it involves the values attached to ascetical behaviour in Hindu society. If one pole of power in India is the noble, the other is the priestly. In order to emulate the brahmins' concern about purity the Jews foregrounded their own parallel traditions; nowhere in Jewish tradition is purity more emphasized than in a disdain which borders on the obsessive for leavening and that which might come into contact with leavening (*chametz*) prior to and during the eight-day Passover festival. In order to contextualize the observances and meaning of Passover in Cochin, some observations about asceticism in general, as well as about the ethos of Kerala's brahmin caste, the Nambudiris, need to be elaborated.

The Cochin Jews maintained a fine balance between the worlds of Judaism and Hinduism, as substantiated by their *minhag* for Simchat Torah. This balance was also exemplified in their observances of Passover, where a form of asceticism which served to integrate them into Kerala's caste system was added to normative Jewish practice. In addition to its usual Jewish 'meaning'—as a celebration of the Exodus story, as a commemoration of Temple sacrifices, and as a springtime agricultural festival—Cochin's Passover offered another layer of 'meaning': by means of exemplary group asceticism and a period of liminal separation from the non-Jewish world, this 'additional meaning' was the reassertion of the group's high caste status.

According to anthropologist Victor Turner, a marginal position affords fresh and enlivening perspectives on familiar structures.[6] Discussing the importance of the study of Judaism for understanding Western civilization, Jonathan Z. Smith,[7] a historian of religion, underscored the Jews' interstitial position: 'This tension between the familiar and the unfamiliar, at the very heart of the imagining of Judaism, has enormous cognitive power.' Indeed it has, but how much greater this tension becomes in the case of Jew Town, whether viewed from a Jewish studies or a South Asian studies perspective, a place especially 'close, yet distant; commonplace, yet exotic'.[8]

The Cochin Jews remained marginal in several senses: as India's most microscopic minority, as a cultural and commercial bridge between the East and West, and as falling at the interstices between the usual academic disciplines. They were doubly marginal as Jews in the context of India and as Indians in the context of world Jewry. Their marginality affords an occasion to look afresh at such familiar issues as asceticism, caste and Passover.

Asceticism is a topic familiar to scholars of religion. However, a perspective from Jew Town raises the question of whether standard treatments of the subject have not been overly spiritualized. By exclusive concern with its spiritual orientation, have we perhaps failed to recognize asceticism's very down-to-earth meanings and rewards?

Dumont's influential study of caste as defined by a hierarchy of purity and pollution has been complemented in more recent scholarship by systematic attention to social interactions between castes. We shall employ both analytic tools, which Marriott called the interactional and the attributional approaches,[9] to address the issues surrounding the formation of castes by and within non-Hindu Indian communities.

In general, there has been a tendency to view caste apart from its Hindu 'sacred canopy' of textual sacralization and ideation as somehow eccentric, somehow to be understood as a *version* of Hindu caste formation. But are these the questions we should be asking? Does the way the question is formulated perhaps restrict our understanding of the Cochin Jews' integration into Kerala's social structure? The story of Indian Jews poses the broader question of whether there is something 'Indian' that is not reducible to 'Hinduism'?[10] The problem may be in the assumption of a monolithic Hindu canopy rather than a set of localized—in terms of both region and caste—canopies. In any event, considering the case of the Cochin Jews and the complex ways in which they as a group related to Kerala's social structure, forces a re-examination of presuppositions about the ideological framework of caste.

Finally, the interstitial position of the Cochin Jews calls for a reconsideration of Passover and the meanings usually associated with its observance. The austerity of Passover celebrations in Cochin, where it is known as 'the fasting feast', were striking. What is joyous and intergenerational elsewhere was somber in Cochin, with no special roles for children. Women worked to the point of exhaustion, purity was stressed as nowhere else in the Jewish world, the usual warm relationships with non-Jews were held in abeyance for the period of the festival, at the Seder (ritual meal) there was no raucous ransoming of the *afiqoman*, and children did not ask the traditional four questions, which were instead chanted in unison, as in the Baghdadi *minhag*. The mood of 'Pesah work' was frantic, whereas it was subdued in the case of the Seder. Of course, the usual symbols lay on the Seder table, and the Passover text, the *Haggadah*, was the same as found elsewhere. But the mood was quite other.

The absence of specific roles for children at the Cochini Seder was striking. The four questions, the starting point for the recitation of the narrative, elsewhere are asked by the youngest son. Maimonides even recommended ruses, such as snatching away the *matzah*, to trigger youthful curiosity.[11] Also, there was no cup of wine for the harbinger of the messiah, Eliahu Hanabi. Interpreting these aspects of the Cochin *minhag* is risky; nevertheless, it is intriguing that both customs truncate those themes in the Seder most closely associated with redemption: children and

Eliahu. Could it be that the ease and security of life in India made redemption a less pressing issue that it was in less hospitable regions of exile?

To sum up, this study of asceticism and caste in the Passover celebrations of the Cochin Jews makes contributions to three parallel discussions of: (*a*) the overall orientation of ascetic practices; (*b*) how we understand caste and its ideological base; and (*c*) the 'meaning' traditionally associated with Passover. Such broad implications are mandated by such an interstitial perspective, one which would be straitjacketed intellectually if approached from within the usual, provincial disciplinary boundaries.

ASCETICISM AND STATUS

Scholarship on asceticism revolves around two issues: (*a*) the ideational framework for asceticism, which treats motives and purported rewards for ascetical practices; and (*b*) forms of ascetic practices. Each of these two theoretical issues must be considered separately. The data from Cochin do not contest asceticism's forms, but rigorously challenge what is understood as its 'ideology'.

Virtually all studies of asceticism echo the long-standing view of Hall: 'Primarily asceticism consists in the contradiction of natural desires under the mandate of some higher, or supposed higher, ideal set by the will before the life.'[12] In the interim between Hall's entry in Hasting's classic *Encyclopedia of Religion and Ethics* and the contemporary *Encyclopedia of Religion* edited by Eliade, there has been little development in thinking about asceticism's theoretical framework. In the latter work, Kaelber defined asceticism 'as a voluntary, sustained, and at least partially systematic program of self-discipline and self-denial in which immediate, sensual, or profane gratifications are renounced in order to obtain a higher spiritual state or a more thorough absorption in the scared.'[13]

There are innumerable variants of these definitions, and the point under consideration is the goal for which asceticism is understood to be practised: a highly spiritualized, other-worldly goal. Whether it is Kaelber's 'absorption in the sacred', or Rader's 'initiation or maintenance of contact with divinity, or some supranatural or transcendent being',[14] all asceticism is believed to have 'a moral purport, and is based on the eternal contrast of the proposition, 'This is right,' with the proposition, 'That is pleasant.'[15]

While no one would deny that extremely high spiritual motives—such as 'absorption in the sacred'—are often involved in ascetic practices, it appears that insisting upon any unidimensional goal for asceticism does not do justice to the complexity, nuance and overdetermination of human motivation and behaviour. In religious studies in particular, we must guard against simple, univocal answers. What observations of Passover in Cochin demand is recognition that *status* is a very important motive in religious behaviour. And what immediately becomes apparent from this observation is that it is by no means unique to the Cochin Jews. Status is an equally important motivating force in the ascetic life of the Hindu *sadhu*, the Buddhist *bhikshu*, the village brahmin and the Jaina layman.

Regarding the forms of asceticism, Kaelber[16] listed: '(1) fasting, (2) sexual continence, (3) poverty, under which may be included begging, (4) seclusion or isolation, and (5) self-inflicted pain, either physical . . . or mental . . .'. Cochin Passover observances include all but sexual continence; fasting and isolation are primary. Fasting may involve either total abstention from food or from particular foods.[17] In Cochin, the fast was partial.

Often it is an individual ascetic who is secluded, the hermit ideal. However, a group may undergo a period of temporary, liminal seclusion which often precedes rituals of status elevation.[18] In Cochin, where caste status comprised an integral component of Passover rituals, the community as a whole became isolated from its normal context prior to and during the festival. As will be discussed later, this isolation was a crucial component for the ritual establishment and celebration of their status in the context of Hindu Kerala.

Of course, Passover practices throughout the Jewish world involve a modified fast in the abstention from leaven and that which might have come into contact with leaven, or *chametz*—pronounced *hamas* in the sweet-sounding Hebrew of Cochin. Fasting is often connected with purity, purification and pollution, and the avoidance of *chametz* is the origin of spring cleaning, associated with Easter in Christian communities and simply with springtime among secularists. However, the Cochin *minhag*—especially regarding cleaning, separation and purity—went beyond standard *halakhic* requirements to a marked degree and in uniquely Indian ways. This 'excess' will be traced to the dynamic interplay of asceticism, diet and caste in Kerala, and the need of the Cochin Jews, as 'foreign' meat eaters in a society which valorizes vegetarianism, to reassert periodically their high caste status.

According to *Halakha* Pesach preparations should begin thirty days before the festival,[19] i.e. they should begin just after Purim. In Cochin, however, the Chanukkah candles had barely cooled down before 'Pesah work'—as it was called—began to warm up. First was the cleaning of tea, chillies, tamarind and spices to be set aside for use during Passover.

'Now the work for Pesah begins', said Sarah Cohen on 15 January, when she brought a basket of tamarind for Passover cleaning. 'Everything must start afresh for Pesah', she added, combining the motifs of special preparations and cleaning with the traditional understanding of Pesach as a 'second new year', coming as it does during the first month of the Jewish lunar calendar.

'Pesah work' increasingly dominated life in Jew Town from the beginning of the month of Teveth until the middle of Nisan, i.e. nearly a hundred days. So important was 'Pesah work' to the Cochin community that, it was believed, if a woman made even the slightest mistake in Passover preparations, the lives of her husband and children would be endangered. 'The legend is that they won't make it to the next Pesah. That's why women are more orthodox than men.'[20] In a similar vein, the Jews' gentile servants believed that if they brought any *chametz* into their masters' homes, even inadvertently, they and their families would perish.

Special rooms for storing items for Passover were scrubbed, followed by all utensils, pots and crockery. Houses were painted or whitewashed soon after Purim, a custom not found elsewhere—except among the Beta Yisrael Jews of Ethiopia and among some Yemeni Jews. Hindu homes are often whitewashed in preparation for the Diwali festival. Yet whatever was done in 1987 paled in comparison with observance in the past. Sarah Cohen recollected, 'The elders would scrape off all paint from the previous year, using coconut fiber, and then repaint everything. They say *hamas* would be there, too, so they would scrape it off.'[21]

Wells were drained and scrubbed, lest they be polluted by a crumb of bread.[22] Each grain of rice to be used during the festival was examined to ensure that it was free from defects, after which it became 'Pesah rice'. Cushion covers and curtains were replaced with special ones for the occasion. Wooden furniture was stripped and repolished. Many of these observances are documented in anthropologist Barbara Johnson's doctoral dissertation,[23] and all of them evidence the traditional Jewish concern for avoiding any contact with *chametz*, carried to a remarkable degree of fastidiousness.

Making wine—either the fermented *yayin* or the fresh *mai*—was a major undertaking in Jew Town. *Yayin*, Hebrew for wine, is made from fresh grapes and sugar sealed in a container and stirred daily for twelve days, then strained and bottled. Around 1 kg of grapes is needed to make a bottle of wine, which is slightly fermented and quite sweet and tasty.[24] The word *mai* is of unknown etymology, although it may have been derived from the Hebrew *mayim*, water. It is simply grape juice which is strained through a cheesecloth.[25]

Winemaking is an instance where *halakhic* and Cochini concerns for purity perfectly overlap. Judaism's abhorrence of idolatry is manifest in severe restrictions on wine. As wine was used to consecrate pagan idols, any wine which *might* be so used is forbidden to the Jew. Therefore, only wine made by Jews is considered *kosher*. These restrictions resembled Hindu taboos on food preparation when they went further: if this wine was *touched* by a gentile, it became forbidden because, as *Halakha* assumes the gentile to be religious, he or she would likely dedicate some of the wine to the gods.[26] The Cochin Jews went a step further: if even the shelf or table upon which the wine was placed was touched by a gentile servant, the wine became taboo.

Similar scrupulous restrictions governed *matzah*, pronounced *massa* in Cochin. After grains of wheat had been obtained, many hours were spent inspecting each grain for cracks or breaks which might indicate leavening due to contact with water, or into which *chamtez* might havè become embedded. This inspection was done thrice: first by non-Jewish servants, then twice by Jewish women (and, rarely, by a Jewish man). On the completion of the third inspection when all the questionable grains had been removed, neither the wheat nor its containers nor the shelf on which it was placed could be touched by non-Jews. As in the case of wine preparation, it is this extra prohibition which marks off Cochin observance from *halakhic* norms.

Grinding of the wheat was traditionally done at home, but in recent times due to the dwindling numbers of Jews in Cochin, some modifications were introduced. In 1987 wheat was ground in the nearby, Hindu-owned Kanchana Flour Mill, which had been specially cleaned the previous evening by the compliant proprietor. Jewish women brought the wheat early the next morning and then cleaned the milling machinery again. To ensure that there was no contact between the wheat and non-Jews, the miller touched only the machinery; the women themselves poured in the wheat kernels and collected the flour, which was subsequently sent to Jew Town for sifting.

The climax of 'Pesah work' was '*massa* day'. Early on that day women and young people gathered in the courtyard of Queenie Hallegua's vast home. The only job which was assigned to gentile servants was to tend to the fire of coconut husks (charcoal was mixed with the husks as an innovation in 1987), which was used to heat flat iron griddles, and to scour special mixing bowls called *legen* with 'a bit of clean new coconut fiber and the soapy substance from a small green soapnut fruit, which the Jews use only for Passover washing, because it is thought to be particularly pure'.[27]

Water, which had been drawn from a purified well and cooled by standing overnight in special earthenware jugs kept solely for this purpose, was used to knead the flour.[28] The *massa* was then rolled out with *kozhali*, hollow brass cylinders filled with metal beads, used only for this purpose and which produced a sweet, bell-like sound. Blessings were chanted over each household's batch of flour, usually around 2 kg, and the obligatory *chalah* (the portion of the dough which during Temple days was set aside for the *kohanim*) was thrown into the fire. The whole process was accompanied by the sounding of the *shofar* and the chanting of Passover songs and sections from the *Haggadah*.

It is well known that the purity associated with the *kohanim*—hereditary priests—in the Temple cult was transferred to all Israel as 'a nation of priests', especially but not exclusively regarding the system of food purity known as *kashrut*.[29] The table (*shulchan*) in every home replaced the altar (*mizbayach*) in the Temple. Restrictions on food, in many ways analogous to the brahmin's concerns about food purity, remained identity markers for both groups. The preparations of 'emblematic' foods during the partial fast of Passover—*massa* in particular, but wine and other consumables as well—exceeded *halakhic* norms at crucial points, points which resembled high caste Hindu taboos about possible pollution by contact of *kaccha* (cooked) food. As Yosef Hallegua put it, 'Pesah is the *cleanest* holiday.'[30]

Jokes and complaints tended to reinforce this ascetic quality of Passover preparations and observances in Cochin. Recalling that the ascetic's self-infliction of pain may be psychological as well as physical, such banter should not be dismissed as insignificant. Despite the fact that dinner tables were laden with steaming buriyanis and curries, the meals were believed to be too meagre to sustain life—'the fasting feast' theme. 'Bread fills up the holes in a diet', complained Jacob Cohen.[31] Gamliel Salem, the community's most unabashed sceptic, joked: 'Just because Moses did these things so long ago, we all have to suffer now. What rotten nonsense!'[32] Meals at the brahmin-run Krishna Cafe were often recalled with an exaggerated fondness. As will be discussed, this particular form of banter which opposed brahmin (or Jaina) food with Jewish food during Passover was particularly closely connected with the status that accrued to the ascetic in India.

An intriguing variant of seclusion and isolation, common ascetic practices, was seen among the Cochin Jews. Usually very gregarious, they became increasingly isolated from their non-Jewish friends during a month or two prior to Passover, culminating in an almost total isolation during the eight days of the festival itself. Thus, Passover served to define the boundaries between one *jati* and all others, just as many village festivals in south India defined a community's boundaries.[33] Passover also distinguished between Jews and gentiles, and during Passover gentiles were equated with *chametz* or pollution. Nevertheless, the loss of their usual connectedness with their Hindu neighbours was missed. In 1987, Passover coincided with the local Hindu festival, *Vishu*, the Malayalis' national holiday. Sarah Cohen complained, with a real sense of loss: 'It's too bad that *Vishu* falls during our Pesah this year. Otherwise we would all go to the (Hindu) temple and mix with our Hindu friends and take our lunch with them.'[34]

Their gradual and increasing isolation became apparent by the festival of Purim, a month before Passover, by which time 'Pesah work' became so dominating and consuming that there was little time for interactions outside of the community. Cochin Jews enjoyed sharing food and conversation with their Hindu, Christian, Jaina, Muslim and Parsi friends on any occasion. In fact, the inter-communal exchange of special foods, such as the special Rosh Hashanah cakes, was particularly enjoyed—but not during Passover.

It was believed that the only way to ensure the avoidance of *chametz* was by avoiding non-Jewish friends. 'For eight days I cut off everything. If I see my friends', Isaac Ashkenazy said, 'they may offer a cup of tea or some food. Actually, Pesah is a very hard time for us.'[35] Sarah Cohen warned: 'Don't go outside (of Jew Town). You might make a mistake and eat or drink something you can't have.'[36] While they normally enjoyed visiting friends or going to the local brahmin restaurant, these were scrupulously avoided: 'The main thing', according to Reema Salem, 'is that we take nothing from outside.'[37] During the festival, the universe of the Cochin Jews was confined to Synagogue Lane.

Only one family regularly invited 'outsiders' to their Seder: Sattu and Gladys Koder, the leaders of the community who traditionally bore the responsibility for the group's external relations. It was commonly believed that the presence of a non-Jew at the Seder table 'pollutes' the ritual.[38] This exclusion was in sharp contrast to the group's usual gregarious instincts. A compromise had on occasion been effected by aligning two dining tables under one table cloth, such that the ritual separation of tables was maintained while being kept, quite literally, under cover so as not to offend their gentile guests.[39]

A celebratory reaggregation into Kerala society culminated this period, which resembled the 'liminality' observed in African coming-of-age rites by Turner,[40] a liminality which temporarily suspended normal societal interactions, which were of necessity hierarchical in Kerala, only to reaffirm that hierarchy after a ritualized reaggregation in a charming '*hamas* party' hosted by D.B. Khona, an influential Jaina businessman who was also the lay leader of the local Jaina temple. Thus, the ritually-bounded separation and isolation of the Cochin Jews were both temporary and communal.

As mentioned earlier, a more obvious instance of ascetic, self-inflicted pain was performed just prior to Kippur. Nevertheless, there was a degree of self-inflicted pain involved in the Passover of Cochin, although this pain was more psychological than physical—at least for the men. Passover was anticipated with dread. Cochin men bemoaned Passover as 'the fasting feast' and 'a nuisance festival' when there was '*nothing* to eat'. Interestingly, leaven was overvalued prior to and during Passover. Protestations of a need for 'a cold beer'—something only rarely drunk in this community—were repeatedly heard. Discussions of what desired foods were forbidden increased as Passover drew nearer, often accompanied by vigorous protests. The fact that all these complaints were made in half-jest did not diminish their psychological effect.

Women underwent more physical suffering as they had to prepare their large homes for the festival, a pain exacerbated by the unbearably high temperatures of the pre-monsoon months. The very real pain associated with 'Pesah work' was verbally reinforced: 'Cleaning the wheat—a backbreaking job', said Sarah Cohen. Summing up, she added: 'During Pesah you die from the work, and then there is no food to eat!'[41]

Four of Kaelber's five general forms of asceticism[42] were found in the Cochin Passover: fasting, in the modified form of avoidance of leaven, which went beyond normative Judaism; a temporary, isolation of the community from non-Jewish Cochin, a separation which functioned along Turner's 'liminality' paradigm; self-inflicted psychological and perhaps even physical pain; and a degree of expense that created real financial difficulties for many in the community, approximating the theoretical concern with poverty. Missing from among these forms was sexual abstinence, or at least this was not observed to be the case.

CASTE

Against this background of the actual practices of the Cochin Jews, the crucial question of how they established their caste status through their rituals may be approached. First, we must ascertain in which ways they resembled a caste, or emulated caste behaviour. Of necessity certain methodological questions about caste must be considered: What do we mean by caste? Is caste a function of Hindu sacralization, a somewhat idealized view, or does caste reflect the material more than the religious realities of South Asia?

Second, we must consider where to place the Jews within Kerala's caste system. Here we need to distinguish between 'attributional' approaches to caste and 'interactive' ones. The case of the Jews is a notable exception to the 'rule' of caste behaviour promulgated by Dumont: 'there are two main avenues whereby a foreign group could enter a territorial set of castes. One is at the level of the Untouchable. . . . The other possible avenue into a caste system is at the level of dominance.'[43] In fact, the Jews' position lay somewhere between the dominant groups and untouchability, although they were considerably closer to the dominant Nayars and brahmin Nambudiris.

One of the most significant ways in which the Jews emulated caste behaviour was by proliferating into endogamous subgroups. Typically, a Hindu caste (*jati* in Hindi) becomes 'subdivided at least once and often several times, and marriage, for example, takes place only within one of the subdivisions. In fact there is no end to this subdivision.'[44] So did the Jews, as will be discussed later.

What is a caste? Linguistically, the term *jati* derives from *ja*, 'to be born'.[45] It conveys the sense of 'nature', 'character', or 'class' in the biological sense.[46] According to accepted scholarly analysis, castes can be distinguished on the basis of three characteristics:

> Separation in matters of marriage and contact, whether direct or indirect (food); division of labour, each group having, in theory or by tradition, a profession from which its members can depart only with certain limits; and finally *hierarchy*, which ranks the groups as relatively superior or inferior to one another.[47]

The Cochin Jews approximated caste behaviour in their separation, which was maintained through endogamy and dietary restrictions. The observances of *kashrut* distinguished them from other meat-eating groups, which tended to be low caste. When outside of Jew Town, that is when 'in public', they frequented brahmin restaurants which were strictly vegetarian and therefore acceptable to both high caste Hindus and Jews.

As for hereditary occupation, adequate evidence is not available to reach definitive conclusions. In modern times they have been professionals (attorneys, professors, engineers, teachers, physicians), merchants (large and small) and clerks. We know that in the past, from the sixteenth century until the vigorous land redistribution policy undertaken by Kerala's government in 1957, most of the community's income was derived from coconut estates owned by the synagogue and by leading Jewish families. Landholding was the main criterion by which a caste, such as the Nayars, was considered 'dominant'. They were also international spice merchants. What meagre evidence exists about their life prior to their fleeing from Cranganore suggests that they were primarily agriculturists and warriors. In general, however, occupation did not play a major role in the Jews' identity, at least as they understood it. 'Work, for many of them . . .', noted Mandelbaum, 'was necessary and even meritorious in its proper time and place, but was a practice that should not stand in the way of ritual devotion or pleasure.'[48]

Finally, we come to the issue of hierarchy: How has the group been perceived by other groups within the dynamics of Kerala society? We will turn our attention to this point.

Dumont reduced these three components of caste—separation (endogamy and food), division (occupation) and hierarchy (status)—into one overarching principle of purity and pollution.[49] As has been indicated, the Cochin Jews' concern with purity at Passover was excessive by normative Jewish standard, and this 'excess' is best understood as a function of the Cochin Jews' 'Indianness'.

Any group which has its own ritual language, food restrictions, calendar and endogamous marriages, and which is accepted as Indian , ought to be considered a caste. But there has been some scholarly squeamishness because the Jews followed a foreign religion and claimed a foreign origin. Some hold that the caste system is a unique manifestation of Hinduism, sacralized in the *Rig Veda* and expounded in the *Dharmashastras*—such as the *Manusmriti*—as the basis for society.[50] This view stresses the uniquely *Hindu* nature of caste, and non-Hindu groups such as Muslims, Sikhs, Christians and Jews were considered more as *variants* of the caste system rather than as castes proper. In any case, their behaviour was seen as problematic and eccentric. In fact, Mandelbaum is the only early scholar to refer explicitly to the Cochin Jews as a *jati*.[51] How, it is asked, could such egalitarian religions adopt such non-egalitarian—which is to say hierarchical—practices? Our data suggested that this is a wrong question to ask.

As the archetypal brahmin, Manu articulated in his writings a specifically brahmin ideology of caste. His concern is the establishment of a sacred social order with his community at the apex. To do so, he employs a specifically religious ideology, one rooted in texts which are associated with Hinduism. It would be uncritical to believe that all segments of Indian society accept Manu's vision of a sacred social order, or to hold that caste is rooted only in ancient texts. Such a textual view of a civilization can be highly misleading.

Further complications arise from foreign perceptions of India. As striking as it may seem, the very term 'Hindu' is what misleads us. It is a highly reified and non-Indian concept. In origin, the term is geographic and not religious. It was first coined by the eleventh century Muslim invader, Mahmud of Ghazni, to refer to the inhabitants of the land beyond the River Indus, which he crossed en route from Afghanistan to the Punjab. In short, 'Hindu' is the Muslim invaders' perception of India, not an Indian self-perception.

Similarly, the concept of 'Hinduism' is a British construction. Just as 'Hindu' is a Muslim concept, the construction of 'Hinduism' is the British attempt to impose order, first conceptual and later bureaucratic, upon a world alien to them. The suffix 'ism' implies a doctrinal system, a unity of thought, which is not found among the diverse religious practices of the subcontinent. Taken together, these three ideas—Manu's textual approach of caste, the misapplication of the Muslim geographic conception, and the pseudo-system implied in the British construction of 'Hinduism'—coalesce to present the common sense view of the caste system as a uniquely Hindu, sacred, textual society.

Therefore, to look for an overarching, *Hindu* ideological basis for caste is to look in the wrong place. India's religious and caste practices are local in character. We need no overarching sacralization to explain cultural assumptions about 'the differentiation of all living beings into general groups . . . each of which possesses a defining code of conduct carried in its bodily substance'.[52] While 'substance' and 'behaviour codes' complexly interact in the maintenance of caste identity, the point is that though Manu's writings may well articulate a specifically brahmin ideology of caste, it would be reading history in an extremely idealistic way to claim that such textuality could explain everything. Setting aside the pseudo-issue of 'Hindu' sacralization, it becomes much easier to account for the obvious fact of caste formation among non-Hindu groups, something which would otherwise remain puzzling or eccentric at best.

JEWS AND NAMBUDIRIS

The Cochin Jews adopted many Hindu practices, yet scrupulously ensured that their acculturated religious patterns did not violate Jewish legal or ethical principles. In so doing, they did what Jews everywhere have done:

to maintain a distinct identity while adapting creatively to their cultural milieus, whether in Baghdad, Kai-fêng, Berlin, or Miami. Some of these borrowings include their proliferation into four subcastes; the ritual use of Hebrew, paralleling the Hindu use of Sanskrit; dietary restrictions of *kashrut*; removing footwear in the synagogue; etc. Some of these practices such as dietary codes; a sacred language; the concern for family purity, entailing avoidance of menstruating women; and endogamy reflected coincidences between Jewish and Hindu values. Others evidenced more specific borrowings. In some cases, these borrowings were from the Nambudiris.

For example, the town planning of the various Jew Towns of Kerala—whether in Mattancheri, Parur, Mala or Chendamangalam—followed that of the various 'Brahmins' Towns known as *agrahâram*. In each case, their street ended in a cul-de-sac at the town's synagogue or temple. The Jews and the brahmins lived adjacent to their sacred complex, be it a straight line, as in Mattancheri and Mala, or in a cluster, as in Chendamangalam and Parur. Both the Jews and the Nambudiris aligned their houses in such a way as to ensure that the front doors, hallways and rear door were in a straight line. Similarly, many Jews' and brahmins' houses were interconnected on the second storey.[53]

More significant were the similarities in the economic organization of the communities. In each case, individuals depended upon the synagogue or temple which held vast estates. The corporate identity of the group known as the *yogam*, or congregation, is a term used to translate the Hebrew *qehilah*, the usual Jewish communal organization.

In a similar vein, both the Nambudiris and the Jews evidenced an awareness of the significance of networks which extended beyond the local chiefdom or *nad*. 'Only the superior castes had an internal organization which extended throughout the *nad* and beyond,' noted Dumont, 'though not beyond the frontiers of the kingdom. Only the Nambudiri Brahmans transcended political frontiers.'[54] So did the Jews, who remained connected with their fellow Jews around the world.

The Jews resembled the Nambudiris in their emphasis on purity of descent (*yichus*), an issue of great import for the neighbouring Knani Christians as well; in their close association with the Cheraman Perumal emperors of Cranganore;[55] in their relatively fair complexion and the importance attributed to their foreign origin (*yichus* from ancient Israel); in the use of a series of paintings in the synagogue, temple, or church to narrate the community's 'sacred history';[56] and in the custom that 'only women and men of the higher castes were allowed to cover the upper part of their bodies'.[57]

Plate 1: Sarah Cohen prepares 'Rosh Hashanah cakes' for the New Year.
(Photo by Ellen S. Goldberg, 1986.)

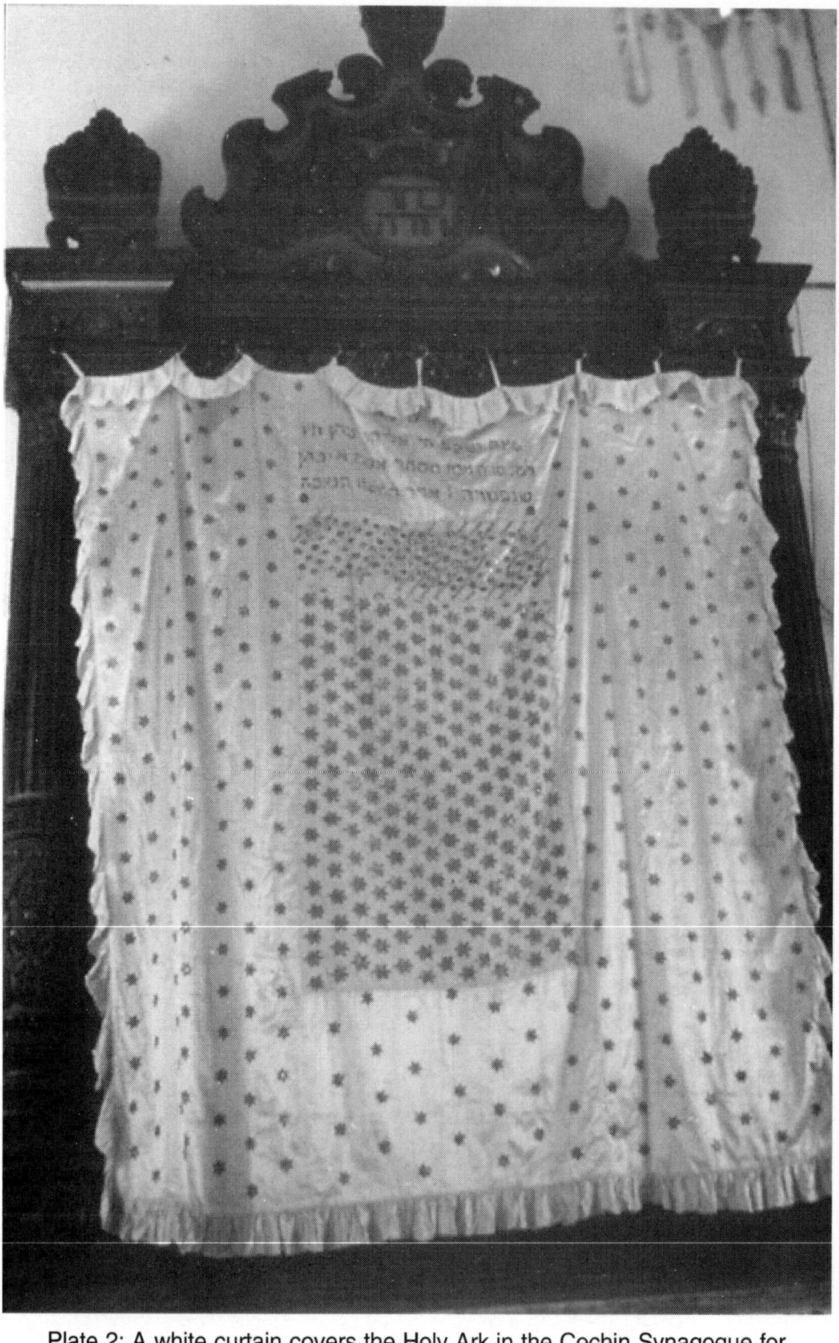

Plate 2: A white curtain covers the Holy Ark in the Cochin Synagogue for Rosh Hashanah. (Photo by Ellen S. Goldberg, 1986.)

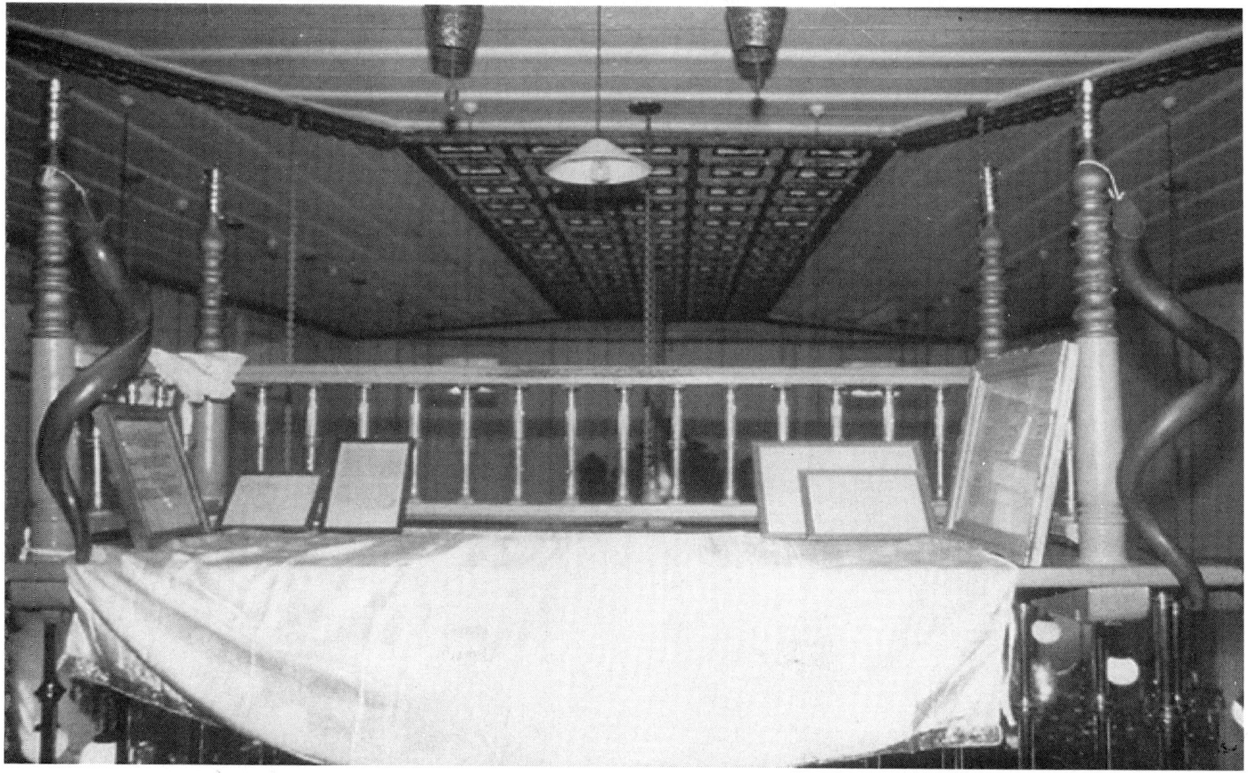

Plate 3: White silk covers the upstairs *bimah*, where the Torah will be read on Rosh Hashanah in the Cochin Synagogue. (Photo by Ellen S. Goldberg, 1986.)

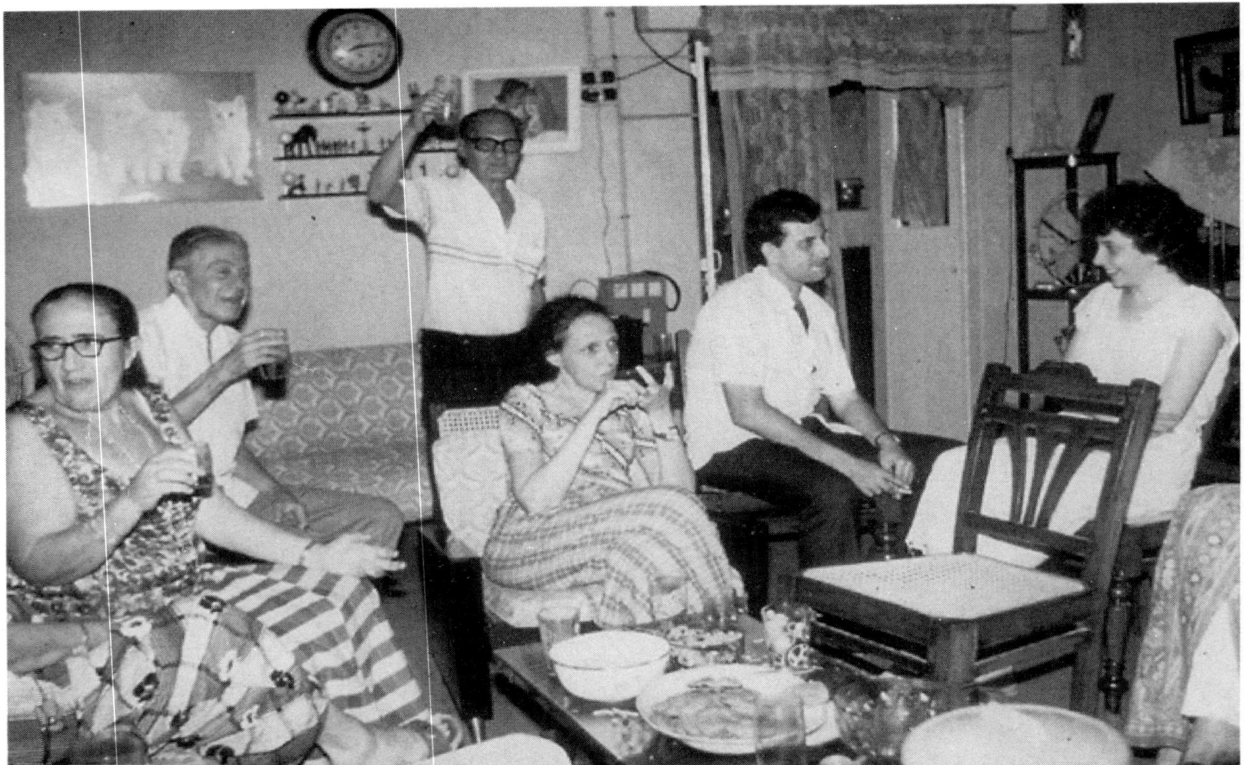

Plate 4: Hereditary priest Jackie Cohen raises his glass to toast Simhat Cohen, a unique Indian Jewish observance. (Photo by Ellen S. Goldberg, 1986.)

Plate 5: A *lulav* (bundle of myrtle, willow and palm branches) and *etrog* (citron) on the downstairs *bimah* in the Cochin Synagogue. (Photo by Ellen S. Goldberg, 1986.)

Plate 6: Raymond Salem blesses the *lulav* and *etrog* in the Cochin Synagogue. (Photo by Ellen S. Goldberg, 1986.)

Plate 7: A 'tree of light' blazes before the Cochin Synagogue to proclaim the holiday of Simhat Torah. (Photo by Ellen S. Goldberg, 1986.)

Plate 8: The Cochin Synagogue decorated for Simhat Torah. (Photo by Ellen S. Goldberg, 1986.)

Plate 9: Afternoon Torah procession in the courtyard of the Cochin Synagogue.
(Photo by Ellen S. Goldberg, 1986.)

Plate 10: Shalom Cohen and Raymond Salem kindle the Hanukkah lamp in the Cochin Synagogue. (Photo by Ellen S. Goldberg, 1986.)

Plate 11: Sattu Koder's Scroll of Esther. (Photo by Ellen S. Goldberg, 1987.)

Plate 12: Workmen clean out the well in the Salem home, also part of Passover preparations. (Photo by Ellen S. Goldberg, 1987.)

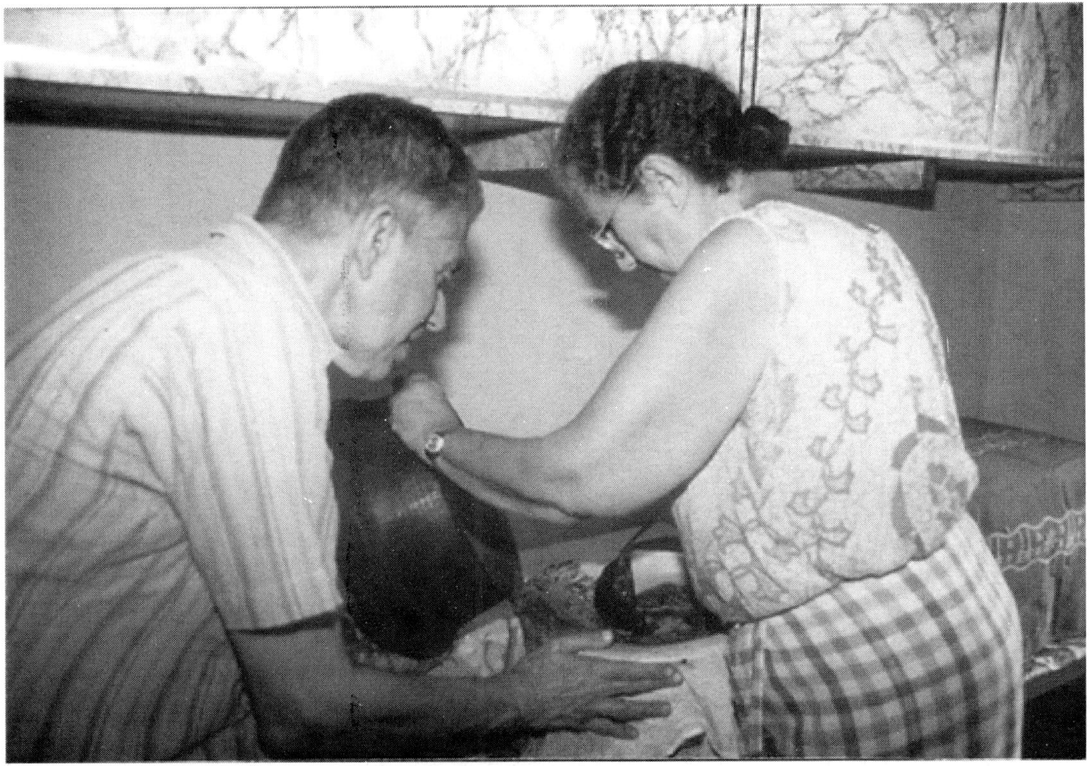

Plate 13: Shalom Cohen helps his sister, Sarah, make wine for Passover.
(Photo by Ellen S. Goldberg, 1987.)

Plate 14: Sarah Cohen cools an earthen jug of water that will be used to make'*matzah* for Passover. (Photo by Ellen S. Goldberg, 1987.)

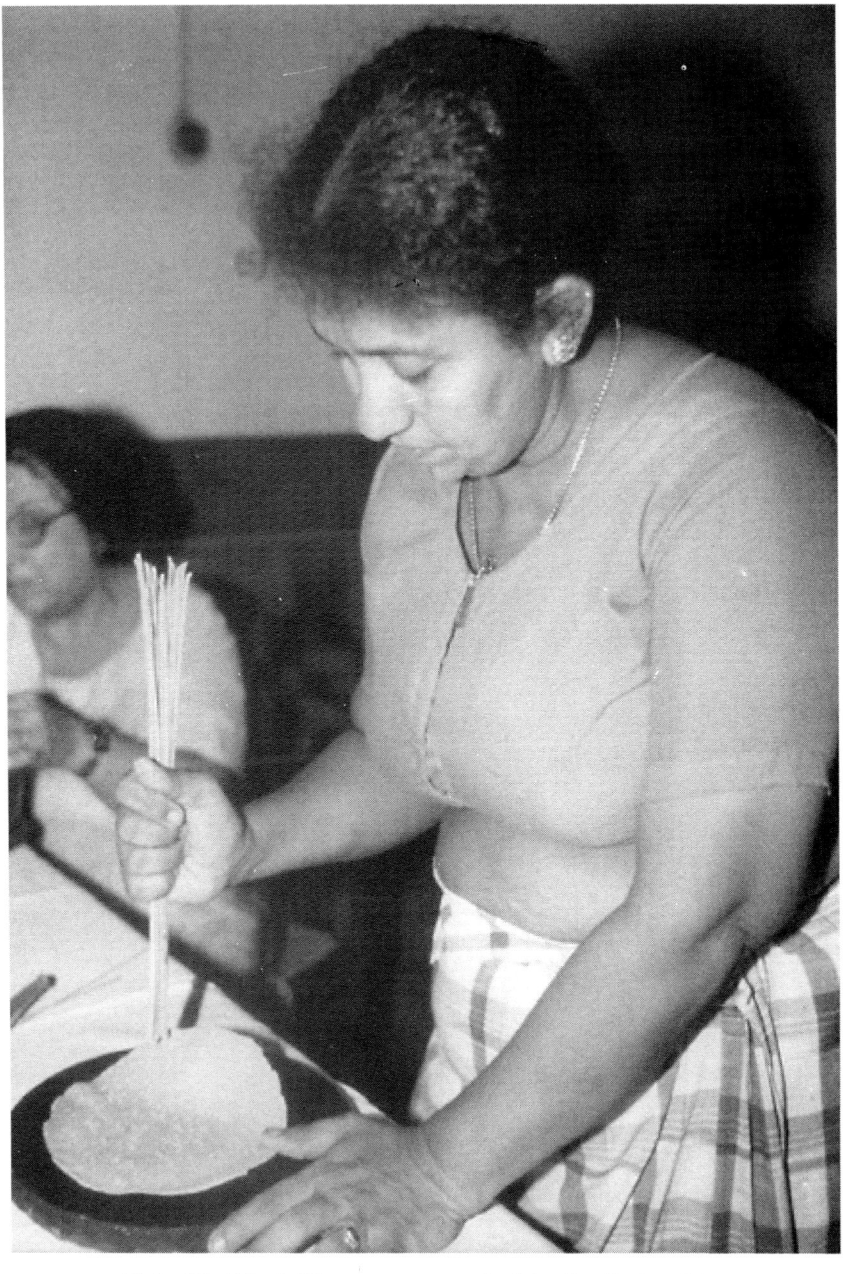

Plate 15: Abigail Elias prepares *matzah* for the Seder plate.
(Photo by Ellen S. Goldberg, 1987.)

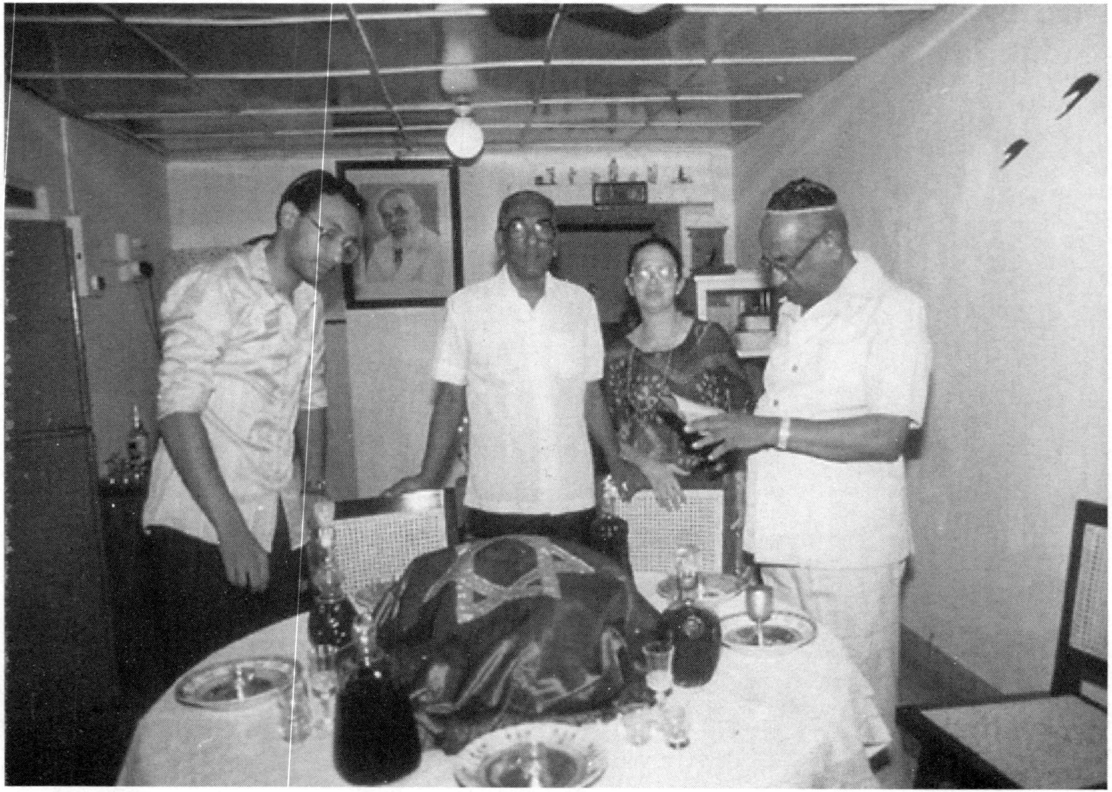

Plate 16: The Salem family's Seder. (Photo by Ellen S. Goldberg, 1987.)

Having surveyed the Jews' adaptations of high caste behaviours, we will adopt an 'interactional' approach to caste as well. By this method, 'castes are ranked according to the structure of interaction among them . . . (especially in) the ritualized giving and receiving of food. . . . Emphasis in this system of ranking is not on qualities, but on transactions.'[58] Such interactions will be discussed in terms of Jew Town prior to and during Passover in 1987.

THE DRAMA OF ASCETICISM AND CASTE STATUS

Cochin Jews relished jokes. Practical jokes were carefully planned and continued to amuse in their retelling for years. Whether at the expense of a long-suffering community member or their own, the folks of Jew Town admired a ready wit second only to Jewish learning. Jokes were not only a source of entertainment but also conveyed serious information. Passover brought with it its own humour, offhand comments which reflected such serious issues as the community's place in the larger society of Cochin. And place, as Smith noted, is 'not simply in the sense of environmental generation, but also in the sense of social location, of genealogy, kinship, authority, superordination, and subordination'.[59]

For example, there was an exaggerated desire for a snack at the Krishna Cafe (and for *chametz* in general). In India, the south in particular, there are brahmin-run restaurants in every town. The dietary rule of thumb is that 'the cook must be as pure as the eater',[60] so one implicitly acknowledged another's equal or greater purity by the simple act of accepting food from him. Brahmins followed the strictest dietary regulations of any caste in India, except for the Jainas. The fact that anyone could eat food cooked by a brahmin is a corollary to the brahmins' highest caste status.

Jews were in a somewhat ambiguous position as regards their dietary practices or *kashrut*. The very existence of a strict and complex dietary code bestowed high status. On the other hand, the inclusion of meat in their diet was akin to a low-caste practice. However, meat was eaten only at home, as it was the only place where *kosher* meat was available.

To joke about missing a Krishna Cafe *dosha* is to point out that for the duration of Passover at least, even this pure brahmin food was not 'pure' enough. The special requirements for avoiding *chamtez* during Passover added a layer of food taboos which *ipso facto* carried high status. As Dumont succinctly put it 'superiority and superior purity are identical'.[61] This drama of purity and status was played out nightly in Jew Town.

On a typical week night in Jew Town, a car pulled up to Elias Koder's house at 7:30 p.m. sharp, as it had done for more than fifteen years. The car belonged to D.B. Khona, a Jaina businessman whom everyone called 'Bapusait', carrying his usual array of stainless steel tiffin carriers filled with snacks. A few minutes later, Koder's Jewish neighbours, Jacob Cohen and I.C. Hallegua, arrived. Dr. Panikar, a Hindu surgeon, was usually the last to arrive from a nearby hospital. Occasionally V.K. Hamza, a Muslim lawyer, dropped in, as did the Syrian Christian newspaper editor, P.M. Jussay, to complete the scene. All 'members' of the drinking club took their places around a huge table.

A teetotaller himself, Koder nonetheless made sure there was plenty of rum, whiskey and mixers. As the drinks continued to flow, so did the conversation on business, politics, risqué jokes, gossip and, quite often, religious matters.

Bapusait played the role of provider for the group because as a Jaina, he was subject to the most stringent dietary regulations, exceeding even those of the brahmins. Whatever came from his kitchen was pure enough for anyone. But it appeared that more than such reasoned practicality was at stake in the issue of who provided the food.

Given the Jews' isolation from non-Jews during Passover, we expected the drinking club to be suspended during the festival. But it was not, and analysis revealed the symbolic importance of maintaining the club's nightly meetings during this period.

As Passover drew closer, the conversation became increasingly centred on the festival's dietary requirements. Of course, whiskey and beer were taboo. Brandy made from grapes was considered acceptable, because it is made from grapes rather than a suspicious grain. Discussion ensued. Indian brandy is also a grain product, flavoured to resemble its European model, and therefore should be avoided. Samuel Hallegua suggested that they drink only French cognac during Passover, an idea that was lauded until someone mentioned the exorbitant price a bottle of imported brandy fetched on the Ernakulam black market, more than US $50. Despite religious scruples, it was decided to make do with the Indian variety.

As the discussion shifted from drinks to snacks, Bapusait's curiosity was aroused. 'Could you eat parched corn? How about flat rice pancakes?' he pursued the issue. When he learnt that flat rice pancakes were acceptable, he offered to bring some. 'No, because we don't know what else is in your kitchen, what has been cooked in your pots, where *hamas* can be found', Jacob Cohen replied.

But Bapusait remained undaunted: 'I will buy new pots to cook your pancakes, and will only carry them on new plates. Could you eat it then?'

At this point everyone around broke into laughter. 'We just can't take anything from outside', the Jews said, and Bapusait was crestfallen. Eventually, he satisfied himself by bringing delicious mangoes (Passover falls during the mango season in Kerala), as fresh fruit is *kosher* for Passover.

The fact that the discussion was enjoyed by all did not diminish its significance: by 'out-brahmining the brahmin', the Jews' status during the period of liminality was established. Even the purest Jaina food was not considered pure enough during that period.

Passover celebrations culminated at Elias's house in a '*hamas* party' hosted by Bapusait. He carried *iddlis*, *puris*, sweetmeats, and other temporarily forbidden dishes. The Jews especially relished the *chametz*—Gamliel Salem yearned 'to eat *hamas* like hell' for days—thereby demarcating their period of abstaining from certain foods and from contact with their non-Jewish friends. At the same time, Bapusait resumed his role as provider, ritually reintegrating the Jews into Kerala society and hierarchy. Thus, the Jews' high status ritually re-established, they returned to and reaffirmed the society in which they had lived happily for so long.

SUMMER RITES

Although the festivals which came after Pesach paled in comparison, there were some intriguing *minhagim* in the Cochini observances of Lag B'Omer—known as Bar Yochai—Shavu'oth, and Tisha B'Av.

BAR YOCHAI

The period of forty-nine days between the second day of Pesach and the day before Shavu'oth is known as the *Omer*. During *Arvith* prayers each evening, these forty-nine days are ritually counted, and the counting is blessed.

The term *omer* means sheaf, as the first sheaves of the annual barley crop would be ripened—and ready to be offered at the Temple—by the second day of Pesach. Similarly, the first of the wheat crop would be ready the day before Shavu'oth, when two loaves of bread from the first wheat would be offered. These two agricultural sacrifices connect Pesach with Shavu'oth in the Jewish calendar.

The two major festivals are also linked by history. Pesach commemorates the exodus from slavery in Egypt, and Shavu'oth marks the giving of the Torah at Mount Sinai. The liberation of Israel from bondage is understood as the necessary precondition for the Revelation, for nationhood. These two most significant events in the history of the Jewish people are linked through the ritual counting of the *omer*.

In the Jewish calendar the first thirty-four days of the *omer* period (thirty-three days for Ashkenazim) were likened to a period of mourning. No marriages, festive meals, music, or even haircuts were arranged during this period because, it is said, 24,000 students of the great sage, Rabbi Akiva, died during the *omer*, soon after the destruction of the Second Temple. Other tragic events which occurred during this time, such as the Crusades and various pogroms, were commemorated with dirges and *piyyutim*.[62] The period of semi-mourning ends on the thirty-third day, or Lag B'Omer, which falls on the 18th of Iyyar.[63] (Many Jewish children participate in sporting competitions, and families organize picnics and enjoy nature.)

In many Sephardic communities, Lag B'Omer is known as Bar Yochai, named after the greatest of all Qabbalists, Rabbi Shimon bar Yochai, who died on the 18th of Iyyar. Like many great Jewish mystics, he directed his disciples to observe his death anniversary as a feast day. Tradition attributes the *Zohar*, the central book of the Qabbalah, to Bar Yochai. His tomb in Tsfat is visited on this day; candles are lit and *piyyutim* were sung.

Bar Yochai was controversial in Cochin. Several people, especially Sattu Koder and Yosef Hallegua, believed that the observances closely resembled the saint worship which Jews are enjoined to avoid, but which is virtually universal among Kerala's religions.[64] Most of the Jews attended the synagogue that evening, each carrying a packet of 'St. Mary's Superior Candles' which were placed on the steps before the *aron hakodesh* and atop the brass rail encircling the *bimah* and lit. A special *shir* (song) for Bar Yochai was chanted.

Bar Yochai is a patron of vows, and the Jew Town folks—especially women—often made a secret pact with the saint. In return for some boon, the saint was honoured with a festive meal on his death anniversary. In 1987, Queenie Hallegua hosted a gala party in fulfilment of a vow she had made, and the party became an occasion for a heated discussion on Bar Yochai, saint worship and mysticism.

Yosef Hallegua maintained that these observances were *asur* as saint worship. Jacob Cohen agreed, but added that it was a useful *minhag* for the 'common people.' Samuel Hallegua was more tolerant, and likened the practices associated with Nehemiah Mota with those of Bar Yochai. The discussion turned to Bar Yochai's purported magnum opus, the Zohar, the Book of Splendor. Jacob Cohen admitted that he had tried to read some parts of the *Zohar* but could not understand it. Samuel Hallegua emphatically asserted that he had no interest in mysticism whatsoever, except to read some on occasion! Apparently, the *Zohar* was once popular in Cochin. When Yaakob Sapir arrived in time for Lag B'Omer in 1860, he enjoined that the community elders would remain awake the entire night reading the *Zohar*![65]

SHAVU'OTH

Shavu'oth is best known as the commemoration of the giving of the Torah at Mount Sinai. It is also one of the three agricultural Biblical pilgrimage festivals, when all the Jews of ancient Israel would go on a pilgrimage to Jerusalem. There they would offer two loaves made from newly-harvested wheat, immediately followed by offerings of the first fruits of the harvest (*chag ha-bikurim*). It derives its name from the 'feast of weeks' (*chag ha- Shavu'oth*), as it marks the conclusion of the forty-nine days of the counting of the *omer*.

We missed Shavu'oth in Cochin in 1987, and no extensive descriptions are available. According to informants, the synagogue, the Sifrei Torah, and Jews' homes were decorated with flowers and special *shirot* were sung. During *Shacharit* prayers, the eldest man in the community ascended to the upstairs *tebah* and proclaimed loudly and solemnly the ten commandments to the standing congregation.

A unique Cochin observance was the congregational reading of *Azharoth* by Eliahu 'Adeni after *Musaf* prayers. In most observant communities, selections from the Torah and the Talmud are studied throughout the night; this custom is called *tikkun leil Shavu'oth*. Among the Sephardim, portions from the Qabbalah are studied as well, in Cochin to the accompaniment of these *azharoth*, which are liturgical poems based on the 613 *mitzvot*. The eldest member of the congregation chanted the first two *azharoth* verses, the second eldest, the next two, and so on down to the young boys. Elders loudly corrected any mistakes the boys made in reciting and they were often rebuked even when they made no error! The Book of Ruth was read after *Minchah* services in the same manner, each congregant chanting two verses.[66]

TISHA B'AV

The most mournful day in the Jewish year is the ninth day of Av, Tisha B'Av. Historically on this day numerous tragedies befell the Jewish people, including the destruction of both Temples and their expulsion from Spain.

Like elsewhere in the Jewish world, in Cochin it was a day of fasting and mourning. *Eikhah*, the Book of Lamentations, was read in the darkened synagogue as barefooted Jews sat on the floor—a sign of mourning—and recollected past tragedies. Liturgically, Tisha B'Av anticipates the next calendric fast day, Kippur.

The Cochin Jews called the fast *siriya* for reasons unknown. Rabbi Aaron Greenbaum, a *shaliach* (emissary) from Israel in 1969, conjectured:

> The first *Kinah* recited on Tish'ah B'av. . . is attributed to Eleazar Kalir and is found in ancient orders of lamentations in the Ashkenazy rite to this day, which may thus be referred to a *Seereh* (after the second word of prayer). . . . The word has either undergone mutations, or the community deliberately retained the Ashkenazy pronunciation .[67]

Near the end of the *Kinot* (elegies) is the oft-repeated phrase *k'mo eshah v'tsireha*, 'like a woman in the pangs of birth'.[68] The last word would be pronounced *siriya* in Cochini, and this is likely the origin of the name.

A unique Tisha B'Av custom was a board game for men. It was played on 'a wooden board balanced on four legs; the playing pieces were coloured cowrie shells'.[69] Known as 'the royal game of Ur', it is believed to date back to the Babylonian captivity.[70] Sattu Koder donated his to the Israel Museum.[71]

NOTES

1. Apparently, this is a very old custom, dating back to Cranganore. See Lesley, 'Shingly in Cochin Jewish Memory and in Eyewitness Accounts', p. 11.
2. Marriott, 'The Feast of Love', pp. 210-12.
3. Chill, *The Minhagim*, p. 261.
4. Exodus 17: 14.
5. Chill, *The Minhagim*, p. xx.
6. Turner, *The Ritual Process*: *Structure and Anti-Structure.*
7. Smith, *Imagining Religion*, p. xii.
8. Ibid., p. xii.
9. Marriott, 'Interactional and Attributional Theories of Caste Ranking'.
10. Speaking at the Cochin synagogue's quarter centenary celebrations, Prime Minister Indira Gandhi indicated an 'Indianness' which is not reducible to 'Hinduness' (*Hindutva*). She said, 'The Indian nation is such a rich mosaic of people, of dress and diet, of cultures, of languages and faiths. Yet, this diversity is encompassed within an intangible quality of Indianness', Gandhi, 'Great Heritage', p. 6.
11. Maimonides, *Rambam Mishneh Torah Hilchot Chametz U'Matzah*, pp. 132-6.

12. Hall, 'Asceticism (Introduction)', p. 63.
13. Kaelber, 'Asceticism', p. 441.
14. Rader, 'Fasting', p. 286.
15. *Encyclopedia Britannica*, 'Asceticism', vol. II, p. 717.
16. Kaelber, 'Asceticism', p. 442.
17. Rader, 'Fasting', p. 289.
18. Turner, *The Ritual Process*.
19. Zalman, *Shulchan 'Arukh Orech Chayyim*, ch. 3, p. 1; cf. Fredman, *The Passover Seder*, pp. 12-13; Berman, *Popular Halacha*, p. 148.
20. Jacob Cohen, April 1987.
21. Sarah Cohen, April 1987.
22. Ganzfried, *Kitzur Shulcham 'Arukh'*, vol. 3, p. 43.
23. Johnson, '"Our community" in Two Worlds'.
24. In the past, apparently as recently as 1983, it had been made from cleaned and chopped raisins which were soaked, drained, mixed with the liquid, and stirred every day for between thirteen and twenty-two days. It was then pressed, strained and bottled. Johnson, '"Our Community" in Two Worlds', p. 240.
25. Earlier it had been made 'by boiling raisins in water and squeezing the juice through a cheesecloth . . . shortly before the Seder so that it will not have a chance to ferment' (Johnson, '"Our Community" in Two Worlds', pp. 240-1). The cost of raisins had risen so sharply in recent years that their use became prohibitive. Sarah Cohen estimated that to make *yayin* in the traditional way would cost around Rs. 100 per bottle, since one *maund* (approximately 30 lbs) of raisins would yield only fifteen bottles of *yayin* (Sarah Cohen, April 1987).
26. Zalman, *Shulchan 'Arukh Orech Chayyim*, vol. 2, pp. 53-107 and 504ff; cf. Cohen, *The Royal Table*, p. 128.
27. Johnson, '"Our Community" in Two Worlds', p. 237.
28. See Zalman, *Shulchan 'Arukh Orech Chayyim*, vol. 3-4, p. 1025.
29. Neusner, *The Idea of Purity in Ancient Judaism*, pp. 66-7.
30. Yosef Hallegua, 25 March 1987.
31. Jacob Cohen, April 1987.
32. Gamliel Salem, 17 April 1987.
33. Whitehead, *The Village Gods of South India*, pp. 73, 74, 100-1, 102-5.
34. Sarah Cohen, 15 April 1987.
35. Isaac Ashkenazy, 25 March 1987.
36. Sarah Cohen, 11 April 1987.
37. Reema Salem, 1 April 1987.
38. Cf. Schneerson, *Haggadah for Pesach*, p. 43, fn. a.
39. Johnson, '"Our Community" in Two Worlds', p. 163.
40. Turner, *The Ritual Process*.
41. Sarah Cohen, 8 May 1987.
42. Kaelber, 'Asceticism', p. 442. The numbering here follows Kaelber's.

43. Dumont, *Homo Hierarchicus*, p. 193.
44. Ibid., p. 34. See also pp. 61-2.
45. Whitney, *The Roots, Verb-Forms and Primary Derivatives of the Sanskrit Language*, p. 52.
46. Edgerton, *Buddhist Hybrid Sanskrit Dictionary*, p. 240.
47. Dumont, *Homo Hierarchicus*, p. 21.
48. Mandelbaum, 'A Case History of Judasim', p. 226.
49. Dumont, *Homo Hierarchicus*, p. 43.
50. Dutt, *The Dharma Shastra.*
51. Mandelbaum, 'The Jewish Way of Life in Cochin'.
52. Anonymous, 'Caste', p. 4.
53. Salem, *Eternal Light of Jewtown Synagogue*, p. 32.
54. Dumont, *Homo Hierarchicus*, p. 154.
55. Johnson, 'The Emperor's Welcome', pp. 164-5.
56. Ibid., p. 162.
57. Johnson, '"Our Community" in Two Worlds', p. 170.
58. Marriott, 'Interactional and Attributional Theories of Caste Ranking', pp. 96-7.
59. Smith, *To Take Place*, p. 46.
60. Dumont, *Homo Hierarchicus*, p. 139.
61. Ibid., p. 56.
62. Berman, *Popular Halakha*, p. 189.
63. Dobrinsky, *A Treasury of Sephardic Laws and Customs*, p. 259.
64. Bayly, *Saints, Goddesses and Kings*, pp. 32-4.
65. Sapir, 'Ha Yehudim b'Kogin', p. 21.
66. I.S. Hallegua, personal communication, 18 July 1989.
67. Greenbaum, 'The Cochin Jewish Community', p. 90.
68. Rosenfeld, *Seder HaYom l'Tisha B'Av*, p. 176.
69. Brafman, 'Field Work in India among Jewish Communities', p. 98.
70. *Dateline World Jewry*, December 1990.
71. Acquisition no. 315. 84.

CHAPTER 4

A Shabbat Interlude

In the Cohen household, Shabbat preparations occupied a large part of Thursday. Accompanied by her compliant brother, Shalom, Sarah Cohen boarded a crowded bus for the hour-long trip to Ernakulam. Shopping baskets under their arms, the two made their way through the town's market. Smiles were intermixed with cajoles and threats, as Sarah made sure that she got the finest vegetables, fruits, fish and fowl at the best price for Shabbat. Having patronized the same fishmonger for years, she was shown only those fish with scales and fins, i.e. which were *kosher*. With Shalom trailing behind her in the heat, Sarah made her purchases: snake gourds, tomatoes, garlic, onions, fresh coriander, long grain rice, pomfret fish, spices, bananas and grapes. Their last stop was Elias Hai Elias' house, where she bought several chickens and chatted with Elias' mother. Eventually Jacob arrived, performed *sh'chita* (ritual slaughter), had a cool drink, and they headed back to Mattancheri—by taxi, if tax attorney Jacob met a client whom he could charge, or by bus or ferry if he could not.

Returning home, the hens were cleaned and dressed by the servants, and Sarah got into her weekly frenzy of Shabbat preparations. Her huge, Dutch-period house had to be scrubbed. Brass menorahs were polished to a dazzling sheen. As no cooking was allowed on Shabbat, three 'proper meals' (*pukha khana*) had to be prepared in advance. After Friday lunch, Sarah made sure that a beggar woman, who had been patiently waiting, received her only hot meal of the week. Local beggars were all too aware that Jews were generous before Shabbat. It was a frantic battle against time, waged with a broom in one hand, a soup spoon in the other.

By the time the sun's last rays had dipped below the palm fronds and the men headed towards the synagogue, the women had finished their chores. They had bathed, dressed, kindled the Shabbat lights and, at last in the uncommon quiet, chanted Hebrew prayers for the health of their families. Sarah stole a few minutes to enjoy her Malayalam newspaper, sitting in her window seat, aching feet stretched out before her. Then the women gathered outside their homes to discuss the day's work. The air was filled with camaraderie as they complained and commiserated about the hectic work, the ever-rising prices in Ernakulam, difficulties with servants, or the erratic electric supply. There was also an unmistakable sense of relief and pride that a duty to God had been fulfilled for one more week.

As soon as the men returned from their prayers, wine was sanctified in every house. A social hour ensured; Samuel and Queenie Hallegua's parlour was a popular meeting place, and the Jew Town folks exchanged visits. Two bachelors, Issac Ashkenazy and Raymond Salem, went from house to house, jokingly in search of 'the perfect pastel'—a pastry filled with chicken or egg, a special Shabbat treat. Pastels were served with a coriander sauce called *hulba*, a Yemeni preparation. Pastels, known as *borekas* in Israel, were an emblematic food of the Cochinim, and in 1987 were made precisely as described by Sholmo Reinman more than a hundred years earlier. Rice flour was mixed with coconut milk, filled with spiced meat or cheese, folded, fried lightly, and then baked.[1] After a few drinks and a discussion on politics, religion and cricket matches, people meandered to their homes where a hearty meal was served, often including the Baghdadi treat, *kubah*, a vegetable-stuffed dumpling in tomato sauce, at least two chicken preparations and rich buriyanis.

After a light breakfast of cheese *borekas* and coffee, people made a beeline for the synagogue for the Shabbat prayers. It was often touch and go whether the required ten men would show up. Depending on who was out of town and who was ill, there was often a long wait on the steps of the synagogue. At times, one of the community's few non-religious members had to be roused, and complaints could be heard as the quorum assembled.

Standing at the downstairs *tebah*, Raymond Salem chanted tuneful psalms. A *minyan* was not required for the preliminaries, and men picked up a prayer book—Pool's Spanish-Portuguese rite *siddur* was used—and a *Chumash* (Pentateuch) on their way to their fixed places, often directly under the whirring electric fans.

When the quorum had been reached the eldest member made a call to prayer, and Samuel Hallegua led the *Shacharit* service—if he was not in Trivandrum; otherwise brother Yosef assumed the *tebah*. Chirping birds and fluttering bats flew through the open windows. Occasionally, *pujas* conducted at the Krishna temple next door could be heard. In Sephardi style, the men and women gently rocked from side to side, rather than the characteristic back and forth movement of Ashkenazim. To honour God with their bodies as well as their voices, the congregants rocked on the balls of their feet, following the prayers' rhythms and meanings. Clearly, the Cochin Jews enjoyed praying; it was far more than a religious obligation for them. Women sang even more lustily than the men, at times calling to the *chazzan* downstairs to chant more loudly so they could hear better. Even the young girls covered their heads in the synagogue. Prayers were regularly punctuated by hushes from older women, usually directed at their daughters and nieces.

As the men intoned their haunting melodies, an occasional, sweet smile brightened their faces. Some prayed rapidly—Yosef Hallegua was occasionally chided for chanting too fast, 'like an express train'. Others savoured each word and each note. For all, prayers—especially in the synagogue—were one of life's greatest pleasures.

The dramatic highlight of Shabbat morning services was reading from the Torah. Kenneth Salem, the levantadore, removed the scroll from the *aron hakodesh* and opened the hinged case of the Sefer to display the parchment text to the congregation, who responded by lifting one fringe (*tzitzit*) of their *tallit* in reverential salute, chanting: 'This is the Torah which Moses set before the children of Israel. A Law Moses commanded us, a heritage for the congregation of Jacob.'[2] Several of the women raised a corner of their saris. Kenneth then ascended to the upper *tebah* with the scroll, and the reading began.

As each man who had been called upon to bless the Sefer climbed the stairs to the upper *tebah*, he was cheered with shouts of 'Kavod!' ('Honor!'). A *kohen* read the first two blessings. When a visiting *levi* was found, he chanted the second. The *kohen* and the *levi* were followed by five Israelites, as demanded by tradition.

Many of the men were expert Torah readers; others needed to practice their reading during the week. As in any observant synagogue, there was concern that each of God's words be pronounced correctly, and when a reader made an error, there were shouts to promptly correct him. It was indeed striking that Jacob Cohen, the community's most proficient reader, called out corrections with no *Chumash* on his lap—entirely from memory.

At the end of the blessing and reading, cries of 'Chazak! Barukh!' ('Strength! Blessing!') welcomed the man back to his place. As he returned to his seat, the honoree extended one fringed corner of his *tallit* to each elder fellow congregant, who touched it with the fringe of his own *tallit*. The honoree replied 'Barukh U'Mivorakh!' ('Blessings! May you be blessed!'), and each kissed his fringes. In this way, the honour of blessing the Sefer Torah was shared among all the men.

The additional morning service (*Musaf*) was centred around the priestly blessing (*dukhan*). At a specific point during the repetition of the *Amidah* prayer, the *kohanim* absented themselves to the antechamber and washed their hands at the antique, brass laver reserved for that purpose. If a *levi* tourist was present, he was recruited to pour water over the hands of the *kohanim*—as required by law, but often to the foreign *levi*'s confusion. The *kohanim* then covered their head and hands with their *tallitot* and, standing on the Haile Selaisse carpet, intoned the ancient, threefold blessing.

After the morning services, *kiddush* (the blessing over wine) was recited in each home, followed by a rich meal. A favourite dish was *hamin*—Arabic for 'hot'—a chicken and rice preparation from Baghdad which had been prepared the day before and left on stoves or in ovens to keep warm, the Indian counterpart to the Eastern European *cholent*.

The afternoon was spent in Torah study, reading and a nap. Afternoon card games were once popular. Tables were placed in the middle of Synagogue Lane, oblivious to the vehicular, animal and pedestrian traffic which had recently intruded upon Jew Town. Scores were kept with brass counting devices, avoiding the proscribed activity of writing on Shabbat. The required 'third meal' (*se'uda shelishi*), usually snacks, was served before the men returned to the synagogue for *Minchah* and *Arvith* prayers.

In the slightly cooler evening air, the women sat on the doorsteps reading newspapers or quietly conversing as they awaited the ritualized closure of Shabbat observance. When they saw the synagogue lights turned on, they knew the weekly festival was over, and they were then permitted to switch on the lights in their houses. In the past, the *shamash* would carry a taper which had been lit from the *ner tamid* to every home to light the brahmin-like stone oil lamps beside each doorway.[3] When the men reached their houses, the *havdallah* ('separation' of Shabbat from the weekdays) rite was performed, and the evening's social activities and dinner commenced.

NOTES

1. Reinman, 'Masa'oth Sholmo b'Kogin', p. 39.
2. Pool, *Seder HaTefilot*, p. 210.
3. Johnson, '"Our Community" in Two Worlds', p. 178.

CHAPTER 5

Life Cycle Rituals: 'Every Bridegroom is Joseph Rabban'

Some religious rituals follow the calendar, commemorating and/or celebrating the rhythms of nature: the 'first fruits' aspect of Shavu'oth and the *Geshem* prayer for rain on Shmini, for example. Other calendric rituals commemorate historical events such as the Exodus on Pesach and the destruction of the Temples on Tisha B'Av; or mythical themes, such as the creation of the world, which structures Rosh Hashanah and Shabbat observances. Other rituals which follow the rhythms of an individual's life are called life cycle rituals, rituals of status elevation, or *rites de passages*: the 'hatch, match, and dispatch' rites, as jaded clergy call them, events surrounding the birth and naming of a child, his or her education, weddings and funeral observances. There are also specific rituals which are performed at times of crisis, and in India these often involve protection, pilgrimage and vowing.

Weddings are the most distinctive and elaborate of the Cochin rites, using the symbolism of royalty—as do Simchat Torah in particular and the High Holy Days in general—and emphasizing the community's double *yichus* from Cranganore and Jerusalem.

Birth rituals in Cochin are the same as those found throughout the Jewish world—circumcision or *brit milah* (for Ashkenazim, *bris*; in Cochin, *milah*) for a boy, and a naming ceremony for a girl.

Education rites, all of which are for males but which are crucial in asserting the mother's status as well, assumed unique forms: (*a*) earliest in a boy's life is his first public reading of the Haftarah, usually at the age of seven or eight; (*b*) this is followed by the *bar minyan*, elsewhere known as the *bar mitzvah*, a rite wherein the boy's religious status is elevated to that of an adult; and (*c*) there is the lay *chazzan* (cantor's) ordination known as *pattankaran*.

Funeral rites are similar to those of the Sephardim of the Middle East.

MARRIAGE

Nowhere is it more true than in Cochin that 'The most elaborate ceremony in Judaism, and the one which abounds in customs more than any other religious observance, is that of marriage.'[1] According to the Cochin Jews, a person must witness three observances in order to understand Jew Town: Simchat Torah, Pesach, especially '*massa-day*', and a wedding. There were no weddings during 1986-7, but vivid, first-hand accounts are scattered in various journals and publications—Shlomo Reinman's[2] and Yaakob Sapir's[3] of a hundred years ago, Rabbi Louis Rabinowitz's[4] of the early 1950s and Ida Cowen's[5] of late 1960s are the most descriptive. In addition, A.I. Simon[6] analysed the Malayalam wedding songs of Cochin women, Mishael Maswari Caspi[7] studied Cochini wedding texts, and Marcia Walerstein[8] compared Malabari weddings in India and Israel. The account which follows is a composite of all of these, as well as reminiscences by Cochin Jews. Minor divergences between the Malabari and Paradesi communities have been ignored.

The *halakhic* requirements for the wedding ceremony are relatively modest, so Jews everywhere, wanting to celebrate this joyous event as fully as possible, have been free to embellish their weddings with customs borrowed from their host cultures. For example, in the West one routinely finds flower girls, bridesmaids, ring bearers and ushers at Jewish weddings. All these customs have no basis in Jewish practice; they have been borrowed from the Christian host culture.[9] In Cochin, customs were borrowed from the Nayar nobility.

Jewish wedding customs include both Judaic rites and general celebrations. Both the rites and celebrations are unique in Cochin, but it is in the latter that Hindu practices are most evident. The most obvious borrowing is the very scale of Cochini weddings. Reinman provided detailed descriptions of weddings a century ago, when they involved fifteen days of celebrations. So many guests were in attendance that on each day, forty cattle were slaughtered to feed all of them—and the groom's father bore a considerable cost for the meat and the wine.[10]

Matches, of course, are arranged, conforming to both traditional Jewish and Indian practice. After the bride's family accepts a proposal from the groom's, all the community's elders and relatives—in effect, all of Jew Town—summon the young couple. The eldest member of the community asks the groom whether the match meets his own desires, to which he replies: 'The desire of my parents is my desire.' If his parents are no longer alive he simply says: 'I desire her.' The *chazzan* then poses the same question to the bride, and receiving the same reply, he blesses a cup of wine and toasts them with it. Sweets and coffee are served.[11] Singing Malayalam wedding songs, women bake sesame cookies as a symbol of fertility. The event is known as 'sesame evening' or *til manda*.[12] The groom's parents present the bride with a small ivory casket filled with jewels, and the wedding date is announced.[13]

Then the preparations begin. First, the couple's wedding costumes have to be stitched. A tailor is summoned to the groom's house to make his set of white clothes. As the tailor prepares to make the first cut in the cloth, he is showered with sweets.[14] Ten days prior to the wedding, the bride's father begins to stock the required foods. Sassoon Hall is whitewashed, oil lamps hung, and decorations are made for Synagogue Lane.[15]

In accordance with tradition, weddings are held on Tuesdays, although of late Sundays have became popular in Mattancheri. On Thursday before the wedding, women conduct the nuptial bed ceremony. Singing wedding songs in Malayalam, they raise and lower the canopied bed.[16] In the Shingly *minhag*, the word *chuppah* does not refer to the temporary canopy erected for the wedding ceremony found in most of the Jewish world. Rather, it retains its older sense of a nuptial chamber, the canopied bridal bed.[17] These women's songs, preserved in handwritten notebooks or *kolas*, utilize the symbolism of royalty, comparing the groom to Joseph Rabban and the bride to Queen Esther. This theme is recurring in Malayalam and Hebrew wedding songs of Cochin.[18]

The Shabbat before the wedding is known as *Nadakannu* Shabbat, or 'the Shabbat of Coming'. During services, the groom is summoned to the Torah and receives the community's blessings. Following services, he hosts a banquet for all the men—the bachelor party of Cochin.[19] After the feast, the community proceeds to the bride's house to escort her to her uncle's home, reflecting the Nayar patterns of family descent.[20] Coffee and snacks are served. At the conclusion of Shabbat, drummers and trumpeters carrying torches fill Synagogue Lane. The bride is escorted from her parents' home to the house in which the young couple will reside. In the street men and women dance until midnight, although the bride and groom are excused from the evening's revelry.[21]

To the accompaniment of 'timbrels and dancing',[22] on the day before the wedding the bride immerses herself in the *miqveh*. While some of the houses have their own *miqveh*, the well in the synagogue courtyard is preferred for the prenuptial immersion because 'it is accepted that she will give birth to a son the same year if she dips herself in the synagogue enclosure.'[23] A bamboo ladder is used by the bride to reach the purifying waters.[24]

The bride makes her last visit to the synagogue as a virgin. As she leaves her door, everyone around throw coins for luck. She then 'kisses the knees' of all the elders of the community.[25] It is a Yemenite custom that the groom 'kisses the knees' of his mother—an act symbolic of asking forgiveness—just before his wedding ceremony;[26] a version of this expression of respect is enacted in Cochin. This kissing is performed 'in token form, that is to say, she touches the knees with her hand, then raises her hand to her lips'.[27] As she enters the Synagogue, the community breaks out into a wedding song, *Yafah Ca Levana*, or 'Oh Beautiful as the Moon', the moon being a traditional south Indian symbol for a woman's beauty.[28]

> Oh, beautiful as the moon,
> Like a dove in her nest,
> Rejoice, for the Lord
> Hath built thy city.
> Arise, shine,
> For the light hath come.[29]

The bride then approaches the Sefer Torah, which has been unrolled to the Ten Commandments and, her eyes covered, kisses it seven times.

In the evening a banquet is held at the bride's parents' home. At a relative's house she wears a white dress with gold embroidery and the groom and his friends escort her to the dinner. The young men walk backwards along Synagogue Lane, clapping and singing to the accompaniment of drummers.[30] This meal, known as *ainni*, possibly reflects the Moroccan Jewish custom of the *k'anni*, a testimonial banquet.[31]

According to the Jews, Tuesday is 'a day of good augury',[32] and Cochin weddings are so scheduled. By 3:00 a.m. the women of Jew Town assemble at the bride's home to help her prepare. Singing Malayalam songs to the bride, the party parade down Synagogue Lane, which is gaily decorated for the big event, with a brass and drum band, proclaiming the wedding day. The women prepare a sweet rice dish in a huge pot known as a *chambi*, these early morning rites are known as *chambidikale*.[33]

By 5:00 a.m., the women return to the bride's house for breakfast.[34] A goldsmith arrives at the bride's home to take her ring size and fashions a ring on the spot.[35] Preferably, a gold rupee coin from Ahmedabad is used to make the ring.[36]

Meanwhile, the groom and his friends go for a haircut. Upon his return to Jew Town, it is his turn to 'kiss the knees' of the elders.[37] He hosts another banquet luncheon at which only fish, a symbol of fertility, is served.[38] The Cochin Jews do not observe a fast for the bride and groom on their wedding day, and the avoidance of meat at this luncheon may be interpreted as a token fast. There is much lusty singing at the banquet, of course. Rabinowitz attended a Jew Town wedding in 1952 and was struck by the amount of singing. He commented: 'The Jews of Cochin are the most tuneful of Jews I have ever met. They break into song at the slightest, or indeed without any, provocation.'[39]

As the groom enters the dining hall, the community recites from the Book of Esther, comparing him to Mordecai. Then they intone God's promise to Abraham ('I will make thee a great nation') and to Jacob ('The Lord Almighty make thee fruitful and multiply thee; and I will make of thee a company of peoples'), followed by Psalm 91. At the end of the festive meal, a 'rather florid' version of the *birqat hamazon* (grace) is recited.[40]

On Tuesday afternoon the *tali* ceremony is held, a purely south Indian custom. The *tali*, a golden ornament shaped like a hook, is suspended around the neck by seven threads. It is conjectured that it represents the tiger's tooth pendant worn by men as a symbol of their hunting prowess, as described in the *Shilappadikaram*.[41] While among most south Indian castes the *tali* is given by the husband, among the Cochin Jews the groom's sister presents the *tali* to the bride, which, according to Walerstein, reflects Nayar matrilinear heritage.[42]

The significance of the *tali* ceremony has not been fully explored in the literature on Cochini weddings. It symbolizes deep, underlying beliefs about women, men and marriage, and its presence in Jewish marriage customs underscores their acculturation into south Indian culture.

Tamil tradition classifies women into six categories: virgin, unmarried mother, married woman, barren woman, woman who dies during childbirth or pregnancy, and widow.[43] Of these, the married woman, or *cumankali*, is the most powerful; unlike the other groups, she is fully benevolent. 'The ideal woman in Tamilnadu', observed Reynolds, 'is the *cumankali*, literally, "she who is auspicious". This auspiciousness is predicated upon two factors: possession of a husband and of children.'[44]

A woman's power, spiritual or procreative, is referred to as *shakti* (energy) in Hindu culture. The concept of *shakti* has been divinized as the female consort associated with a male deity and, unlike in the ancient Near East, the Indian goddesses are perceived as the power or energy of the male god; thus the aphorism, 'Shiva (the quiescent god) without Shakti (the energetic goddess) is a corpse'.

A woman's power, or *shakti*, is a function of her *cumankali* status, and *shakti* is the power 'to control and alter the course of events in order to save their husbands from death and to provide their families with wealth, health, and prosperity'.[45] When Jacob Cohen remarked that a woman's lack of diligence in Passover preparations could endanger the lives of her family, he was referring precisely to this south Indian view of the *cumankali*'s *shakti*.

Two sources of a married woman's *shakti* illustrate this pervasive, female power. One is *karpu*, which is usually glossed as 'chastity', but which 'means more than sexual fidelity, it means following the husband through thick and thin, however weak or cruel he may turn out to be. It means above all the power of patience . . . and endurance . . . and this is the real power.'[46] The other, interrelated source is *tapas*, which denotes self-sacrifice, austerity or asceticism. Some dimensions of the power which derives from *tapas* were obvious in Cochini Passover observances. According to Margaret Egnor,

> The power acquired through suffering and servitude, is a special case of the Hindu theory of *tapas*, whereby through certain forms of self-denial (called *tapas*), the individual accumulates a certain internal heat (also called *tapas*). . . . It is common for Tamils to say that a woman has born a particular child by the strength of her *tapas*, for childbirth is regarded as one of the most terrible forms of suffering.[47]

Reynolds connected *shakti* with *cumankali* status and with the *tali*:

> *Cumankali* status is symbolized by the *tali*, which . . . (is) tied around the neck of the bride by the groom at the time of marriage and never to be removed until the marriage bond is dissolved or the husband dies. The act of tying the *tali* is the one that confirms the marriage, legitimates sexual relations, binds the procreative capabilities of the wife to the husband, and makes the woman auspicious.[48]

The *tali* ceremony is followed by the Judaic aspects of the wedding ceremony. The groom is dressed in white clothes topped by a gold-embroidered white *kippa*, wrapped in his *tallit*, and bedecked with a fragrant flower garland. In olden times, the groom and *chazzan* wore Baghdadi-style silk kaftans and the groom wore a white turban.[49] Two best men—*shushvinim*—as well as 'leaping and gesticulating' dancers and musicians, accompany him to the synagogue to await his bride.[50] The repeated processions along Synagogue Lane, with drummers, dancers, torch-bearers, and salutes, are a very important expression of the Jews' quasi-noble status in Malabar. As Walerstein demonstrated, in their wedding and *brit milah* processions the Jews re-enact the 'seventy-two privileges' granted to Joseph Rabban by the Cheraman Perumal emperor.[51]

A special chair to the right of the *aron hakodesh* is set up for the bride, over which an iron hoop is hung, and suspended from it is a linen canopy known as a *killah* or *manara*, under which she sits during the ceremony. Placed on a table in front of the ark are the marriage contract (*ketubah*), the synagogue registry, and a silver pen and inkstand for signing both. [52]

Jewish wedding rites have three components. First is the betrothal ceremony or *erusin*—the 'acquiring' of a wife by a groom, also known as *kiddushin*—the 'consecration' of a match. Second is the wedding itself, known as *nissuin*, or 'elevation'. This rite enacts the couple's new status, and a canopy (*chuppah*) is used to symbolize the newly-wedded couple's home.[53] Finally, there is the *yichud*, the 'seclusion' of the couple. In modern times, this 'seclusion' offered them a moment together during which they broke their fast in solitude. In the past, however, the marriage would be consummated at this time.[54]

After *Minchah*, the entire congregation fetches the bride, who is accompanied by *musicians*, and her brother escorts her to the synagogue.[55] She is dressed in a white bridal costume known as a *marante deldpud*, with heavy gold ornaments and a heavy veil. As she enters the synagogue, a chorus of ululations (*kuruva*) greets her, followed by the chanting of the Psalm 136 in Shingly tune. As she takes her special seat under the canopy, the *erusin* ceremony begins.

The Cochin *erusin*, according to Rabinowitz, is 'remarkable . . . unique . . . (which) exists nowhere else in the world.'[56] Instead of a rabbi or *chazzan* reciting the seven betrothal blessings, the bridegroom himself does it. Rabinowitz enthused over this custom: 'I (cannot) find any authority for it, but it seems to be so essentially correct that it adds considerably to the meaning of the well-known blessings. . . . (H)ow much more impressive it is for the *bridegroom* to say (the blessings) . . . than it is for the officiating Minister.'[57]

After the blessings, the groom places the wedding ring in the famous gold kiddush cup, and along with the congregation chants in Shingly tune:

Bridegroom: 'By your leave.'
Congregation: 'By leave of Heaven.'
Bridegroom: 'By leave of our Masters.'
Congregation: 'By leave of Heaven.'
Bridegroom: 'Give thanks unto the Lord, for He is good.'
Congregation: 'For His mercy endureth forever.'
Bridegroom: 'May joyous occasions multiply in Israel.'
Congregation: 'As on this day in Jerusalem, rejoicing and glad of heart at the building of the Sanctuary. May Elijah

> the Prophet and the Messiah, son of David, come in our lifetime.'[58]

After having recited the seven betrothal blessings in Hebrew and Aramaic and tasted the wine, the groom hands the gold cup to the bride and chants in Aramaic, 'This is thy *keddushin*', to which the congregation replies, 'May it be a good sign'. Using a string to retrieve the ring, the groom places it upon the bride's finger, repeating: 'This is thy *keddushin*', to which the congregation again replies, 'May it be a good sign.'

To commence the *nissuin* or 'elevation' rite, the *ketubah* (marriage contract) is chanted, usually by the youngest male member present—another Cochini innovation. Elsewhere in the Jewish world the officiating rabbi reads the *ketubah*. In Cochin, the terms for the union are read by a male child, thus ritually connecting the husband with his future children, the two sources of a *cumankali*'s *shakti*.

In the middle of the chanting of the *ketubah*, the *chazzan* interrupts with the words: 'From the mouth of the holy and sanctified one, according to the law which was given in testimony on Sinai, "her food, her raiment, her conjugal rights, he shall not diminish" (Ex. 217).' The groom, solemnizing his vows by clutching the fringe of the *chazzan*'s *arba kanfot* (a four-fringed garment, or *tzitzit*, which elsewhere is worn beneath a man's shirt, but which the Cochin *chazzan* wears on the outside for the wedding ceremony), assents to these specific obligations, and the *chazzan* asks three times 'Thou hast undertaken this?' The groom affirms his vow thrice: 'An undertaking taken before heaven and earth', and the congregation witnesses his vows, exclaiming: 'Blessed is he who sanctifieth Israel.'[59] After the chanting of the *ketubah*, it is signed by the two *shushvanim* and the groom, and then presented to the bride as the groom proclaims in Aramaic: 'Take thy *ketubah*, thy document, in thy hand, with it all that is written therein. It is thine, thy property, in the presence of witnesses, and the rabbis, according to the law of Moses and of Israel. Here is thy *ketubah*.' Cochin women keep their *ketubot* rolled in silver or gold cases. The congregation responds: 'May it be an auspicious moment', and sings:

> The bridegroom in his garments
> And the bride in her *kiddushin*.
> He is worthy among men
> And she is pleasant among women.
> Sanctified by the holy ones,
> Hallowed on Mount Sinai.

Finally, the groom removes the bride's veil and sings 'Oh Beautiful as the Moon' again. Two cups of wine are blessed, the seven blessings are recited, the *chazzan* drinks one cup and the bride and groom share the other, and the *nissuin* ritual is completed.[60] The couple are wrapped in the groom's *tallit*, and they proceed to their *yichud*, seclusion, where they eat *payudee*, a light cereal used to break fasts.[61]

The ceremony included several unique *minhagim*, the most striking of which is that the groom himself 'performs' the marriage by reciting the seven blessings. The reading of the *ketubah* by the youngest male is also noteworthy, as are some of the liturgical details, songs and Shingly tunes. Conspicuous by its absence is the breaking of a glass, an act closely associated with Jewish weddings elsewhere. Instead, the Cochini bride and groom have ashes smeared on their foreheads, which is interpreted as a sign of mourning for the Temple.[62] It may also be reflective of the Hindu custom of wearing *vibhuti* or sacred ash on the forehead. The couple does not stand under a *chuppah*, instead the bride sits under a white, circular piece of linen suspended from a hoop.

The newlyweds, along with drummers, musicians and torch-bearers, lead a community procession to the wedding feast, which is usually held in Sassoon Hall. The seven blessings are repeated, and there is great joy, revelry, dancing and, of course, drinking and singing. According to Reinman, the musicians at this banquet played violins, and men and women danced together.[63] During the festivities, the bride and groom are not called by their given names, but by the Malayalam honorific words for bride and groom, *manamatee* and *manamarlen*. The reason for this is that 'like a king and queen, who are not called by their proper names, so the couple were now not called by their names. He who made the mistake and injected familiarity, as guests sometimes did deliberately, was fined a small sum or a bottle of whiskey.'[64]

Wednesday, referred to as *polichu paduna* or 'the day of homage and singing' has been described by Simon in the following:

> . . . the main characteristic of the celebration is the singing of songs . . . by women, sitting in a line on either side of the bride and bridegroom . . . , representing the latter as 'King and Queen', especially the bridegroom who is represented as the descendant of Chirianandhan (Shri Anandan) or Prince Joseph Rabban. It is to my mind a day of 'national glorification', compared with which even the actual wedding day pales into insignificance.[65]

The Shabbat after the wedding is known as *Porapeddunne Shabbat*, 'the Shabbat of going', or *Chatan Shabbat*, the bridegroom's Shabbat. The groom is called to the Torah in the morning, followed by a festive luncheon. Among the songs is '*Echad mi yodeah*?', which in other Jewish communities is sung after the Passover meal.[66] After *Minchah* services in the afternoon, the traditional 'third meal' is an occasion for another festive wedding banquet, during which *shirot* and Malayalam songs are sung. Like her Hindu counterparts, the bride is dressed in red.[67]

The next Monday is known as *palipuca* or the 'day of going to the synagogue'. The community accompanies the bride and groom to and from the synagogue. Walerstein noted: 'Apparently, going to the synagogue consecrated not only the legal and religious aspect but also the sexual one since the couple did not consummate the marriage until one week after the marriage ceremony. Like in many other communities the sheet was shown as proof of consummation.'[68]

Wedding celebrations conclude on the seventh day after the marriage ceremonies. A final feast is arranged, which is the time for gifts. The *Song of Songs* is chanted, and the seven blessings are repeated for the last time.[69] Weddings in Cochin are not only family celebrations, but major community events—as in many Jewish communities.[70] When a poor couple marries, the community provides sufficiently so that there is 'no distinction between the weddings of the poor and the rich... so that he who has not sufficient resources need not feel ashamed'.[71]

There is a unique thematic orchestration to Jew Town wedding observances: the theme of royalty. In Malayalam and Hebrew songs, in repeated processions accompanied by drummers and musicians, in the very scale, length and lavishness of the celebrations, there are recurring images of royalty.

The royal aspect of a Cochin wedding echoes a second century Kerala wedding:

> The noble parents . . . sent maidens of uncommon beauty, mounted on elephants, throughout the city to summon with courteous words many a guest to a splendid bridal feast. When, on the chosen day, the bride and groom advanced, white parasols shone high in the sky, as if for a royal parade, through streets echoing with the din of conch and drum. With youthful grace they entered together a pavilion of blue silk sown with pearls, its glittering pillars studded with precious gems and adorned with garlands of auspicious flowers.[72]

In Hindu wedding rites today, the bride and groom are treated as royalty, too. The groom rides an elephant or a horse in his procession to the wedding ceremony, accompanied by torch-bearers and musicians. The couple sit upon a 'throne' throughout the *samskara* (ritual), as well as to receive their guests as though in a *darbar* (royal court). These and other images connect the couple with the royalty; more precisely, through Hindu rites the couple ritually become royalty for a time. In their rich wedding traditions, the Cochin Jews emulated their Hindu neighbours, who themselves imitated their royalty.

There is a drawback to the grandeur of Cochin weddings, according to Hillel: 'Their marriages, like those of the Hindus, are attended with considerable expense as to deter many young men from marrying. They double the number of days of matrimonial feasting customary among the Jews.'[73]

Brit Milah

The circumcision rite is one of the most joyous and ancient of all Jewish observances. Long before the Torah was given, Abraham was instructed to circumcise himself and his son, Isaac, as a tangible sign of his covenant with God.[74] Ever since, circumcisions have been a reaffirmation of this covenant by each generation.

A Cochinite, Judah David Ashkenazy, migrated to Bombay around the turn of the century, where he set up the Lebanon Printing Press. The foremost Hebrew-English press at the time, it published liturgical books for both the Cochin and Bombay communities. Ashkenazy was also the *mohel* (circumciser) of Bombay. He merged his two careers—publisher and *mohel*—in publishing an anthology of texts associated with the *milah* ceremony, *Sefer Brit Yitzchak*, in 5669/1909. His book, which includes 'certain portions of the Bible, Talmud, Midrashim, and the Zohar',[75] serves as a guide to many aspects of the Cochin traditions of the *milah*.

As there were no married women of childbearing age in Jew Town, no *milah* was observed during 1986-7. However, Linda Salem Hertzman, daughter of Gamliel and Reema Salem, give birth to Cocha ('Little') Nathan in Toronto on 3 January 1987. Reema had gone to Canada to be with her daughter, and she telephoned to give the news. The event was celebrated *in absentia*.

Many of the customs relating to the *brit milah* are drawn from mystical, Qabbalistc sources because, it is believed, birth and death are too mysterious to be explained by exoteric means.[76] One such rite is the *shalom zachor*, the 'peaceful welcome to the boy-child'.[77] According to tradition, the embryo enjoys a nine month state of sanctity, learning Torah from a guardian angel in the womb. At the moment of birth, the angel taps the child on the lip, leaving a small cleft and causing the child to forget all the angel's teachings.[78] As the child is born into a world of free will, the sanctified state must be terminated, and the *shalom zachor* meal is a sort of consolation to the infant for the loss of this sanctity. Round foods, traditionally identified with mourning and rebirth, are served to comfort the newborn.

Learning of Cocha Nathan's birth, after Havdallah Gamliel organized the *shalom zachor* meal of fruits, boiled eggs, and boiled potatoes. (In Ashkenazi countries, the traditional 'round' foods are lentils and chick peas.) Plenty of toasts were offered. The elder men—Samuel Hallegua, Jacob Cohen and Raymond Salem—lead the community in loudly singing unique Hebrew *milah* songs and pounded their fists on Gamliel's dining table. The *shalom zachor* meal was equally lively as *bris* parties in the West, but the main event was yet to come!

Another important Qabbalisitc circumcision rite is performed the night before the *milah*. It is believed that Satan makes every effort to prevent the *milah* from taking place, and the night before the rite is particularly dangerous. So the father spends the entire night beside the baby's crib, reciting psalms and meditating. This custom is known as the 'night of watching', or *wachnacht* in Yiddish. Ashkenazy wrote that he compiled his *Sefer Brit Yitzchak* as a devotional text to be used for the 'night of watching'.[79]

On the day of the *milah*, the baby boy is carried from the house to the synagogue under a ceremonial canopy—an emblem of royalty in India.[80] The baby is first taken upstairs to the women's section where he is passed from lap to lap. His father then carries him downstairs where the circumcision takes place, after which he is taken back to the women's section and serenaded with Malayalam songs.[81] For the circumcision, the baby is held by the *sandek*, the infant's defending counsel against Satan, on a special *milah* chair. The chair resembles a throne and is 'reserved' for the Prophet Elijah, who is believed to witness all circumcisions. According to Rabbi Abraham Chill.

> In many Sephardi communities . . . this (Chair of Elijah) is brought to the home of the infant. An ornately embroidered cloth is placed upon the chair which is adorned with scented flowers and plants. The Scroll of the Law is placed upon the thus bedecked chair and during the night visitors come to kiss the Scroll and wish the family and child well. The next morning, the chair is returned to the Synagogue to be used in the circumcision ritual.[82]

The *milah* party was held at Uncle Raymond's house on 10 January. All the folks of Jew Town, as well as some people from Ernakulam and friends of the community, attended the huge, festive dinner. The highlight of the party was the *milah* songs. One could not imagine that the honoree of the occasion was some 10,000 miles away!

The birth of a girl is celebrated in a far more subdued fashion. A naming rite is held, either in the synagogue or at home followed by a modest party.[83]

The baby is heartily welcomed into the community by these rituals and by the extensive care he or she receives from all of the women. 'For a month after birth,' Johnson noted, 'the women of the community take turns sleeping in the home of the new mother, getting up at night when the baby cries or when the mother needs any help.'[84]

FIRST HAFTARAH READING AND THE BAR MINYAN

As in most orthodox communities, Jewish education in Cochin begins at the age of three. Every synagogue in Kerala had a Talmud-Torah, a traditional religious school, attached to it, and the standard of Hebrew was high for all—men, women and children. Not only was there never a shortage of Torah readers, a skill which demanded high proficiency in Hebrew, but also correspondence with Jewish communities from Cairo to New York to Shanghai was conducted in Hebrew. The community also had its share of Hebrew poets and essayists.

The community's standard of Hebrew education is evident in the unique observance of a boy's first public reading of the *Haftarah*, the 'additional' reading from the Prophets chanted after the Torah portion itself.[85] In most Jewish communities, a boy first reads from the Torah and the *Haftarah* at his *bar mitzvah* at the age of thirteen. In Cochin, a boy reads his first *Haftarah* between five and eight years of age!

In addition to revealing the high standards of Hebrew education, the first *Haftarah* reading also resonates with south Indian beliefs and customs. Five years represents the completion of a cycle in the Vedas, and in Hindu thought a child crosses the dangers of infancy at that age.[86] Reading his first *Haftarah* at the age of five or six means that infancy and its attendant dangers have been crossed.

It is one of the most elaborate celebrations in a boy's—and his mother's—life! Not only is it an occasion for an extravagant feast, but also for the mother's wardrobe. An elaborate silk *mundu* is embroidered with gold and silver. 'These garments used to take up to a year to embroider', reported Johnson,[87] and are often as not the most elaborate costume in a woman's life, as grand as her bridal *mundu*. Often this *mundu* is used to cover the woman's casket and is subsequently converted into a beautiful *parokhet* to adorn the ark and walls of the synagogue, the site of her son's proud achievement of early years.

Again, resonances with south Indian culture are clear. A woman's status as a *cumankali*, Reynolds noted, 'depends not on the woman's own being as female, but on . . . possession of a husband and of children.'[88] That a woman wears an elaborate, new *mundu* for her son's *bar minyan*, and for her wedding is significant: the action of donning a new *mundu* connects the husband with his children. Such a garment which is 'wound around and covering the body, especially. . . the loins, the loc(us) of female generative power,'[89] signifies the *cumankali*'s *shakti*, which is procreative as well as moral power, and as *tapas* is both ascetical power and the 'heat' (the literal meaning of *tapas*) which 'cooks' the embryo. The use of these *mundus* as *parokhets* before the synagogue's holy of holies, the *aron hakodesh*, and their lavish display on Simchat Torah indicate the spiritual, generative *shakti* of the Jewish women of Cochin.

Sons of the leading families of Cochin read the *Haftarah* for the first time on Simchat Torah, an occasion when the women's *mundus* were most conspicuously displayed. Mandelbaum described this pivotal event in a boy's life in 1939:

> On the festival of *Shemini Azereth*, the six year old son of a leading family reads the portion from the Prophets (*Haftarah*), for the first time. . . . The boy's relatives dress in their finest costumes. The women bring out the dresses which they reserve for weddings and for special celebrations. The boy himself was attired in neatly tailored white jacket and shorts and ascended to the lectern draped in a long prayer shawl. After he had bravely piped through the liturgy, he descended from the balcony and made the round of the synagogue, being blessed by each man. He held out a corner of this prayer shawl, when the adult had touched it he brought the corner to his lips; the one who blessed him kissed the fingertips which had touched the shawl. As he came around to his uncles and his grandfather, he was garlanded and his girl cousins came shyly forward to present him with gifts. Later in the day his parents gave a grand feast for the entire community. The importance of this event in the life of a six year old cannot be overstressed. It is a day when tokens of approbation pour in on him, when he becomes the cynosure of the community, his world. It burnished him, when his character is yet plastic, with moments of personal triumph which leave an ineradicable impression. And the medium of his triumph and the scene of his success is the synagogue. Small wonder, then, that the synagogue holds the loyalty and devotion of the individual throughout his life.[90]

Sarah Cohen's comment that the young boy was also blessed by the women confirmed Mandelbaum's observation: '[A]fter a young boy reads *Haftarah* for the first time, he first receives blessings from the men downstairs in the synagogue, then climbs upstairs to kiss the hands of the women elders and be blessed by them.'[91]

At the age of thirteen, a boy is called to read from the Torah scroll and is proclaimed an adult religiously. This coming of age rite is known as *bar mitzvah* ('son of the commandments') in most of the Jewish world, but in Cochin it is called *bar minyan*, 'son of the prayer quorum'. From that day on, the boy is counted as part of the quorum, and is called upon to recite the blessings over the Torah or read from it. He is subject to the regulations governing Jewish life—to wear a *tallit* and *t'fillin*, to fast on specified days, and in general to participate fully in religious life. However, the *bar minyan* pales in comparison to the first Haftarah reading.

LAY *CHAZZAN* ORDINATION

In many observant communities, a boy's *bar mitzvah* is also the occasion for him to play the role of *shaliach tzibur*—emissary of the community, the one who leads congregational chants. In Cochin, however, this aspect of attaining religious adulthood provided an occasion for another unique ritual: the lay cantor's ordination known by its Malayalam name, *Pattankaran*. *Pattan* means certification, and *karan* denotes a performance; in other words a *pattankaran* certifies one to perform as *chazzan* according to the Cochin rites.

To be eligible for *pattankaran* calls for much study. One must learn how to read all portions of the Torah, the *Haftorot*, the Shingly tunes and prayer services for Shabbat and all festivals and holy days. In short, one must master the entire, elaborate Cochin *minhag*. The lay ordination itself is conferred during Shabbat morning services, when the entire service and Torah readings are performed by the candidate. Special blessings and a unique *kaddish* prayer are chanted in Shingly melody, and a banquet is usually held in honour of the new *chazzan*.

Although the requirements are stringent, most of the men of Cochin had attained the lay ordination. It was very touching to see Keith Hallegua assiduously study with his father, I.C. Hallegua. Every evening father and son sat at their kitchen table, chanting from the prayer books and *Chumash*. Keith had plans to migrate to Israel or North America, and he believed that he should carry as much of Jew Town with him as possible—and what was more Jew Town than its unique rites? Shortly after Keith attained *pattankaran*, his father passed away, but not before he handed down the tradition to the next generation.

Coming of age rites for boys in Cochin, all closely tied to educational achievements, are achieved in three stages: (*a*) the first *Haftarah* reading between five and eight years of age; (*b*) the *bar minyan* at age thirteen; and (*c*) the *pattankaran* ordination, which is not fixed at any age. In all observant communities elsewhere, these three stages are tied to the *bar mitzvah*.

FUNERALS

Death pervades the atmosphere in Jew Town. Places at dinner tables are routinely set for departed family members. Black humour punctuates many conversations. Visions, curses and plagues are recalled. The atmosphere is pervaded not by any individual's death, but the imminent demise of the community is the subtext of many conversations. Fortunately, no funerals took place during 1986-7, but people talked about them—especially Raymond Salem, who described Jew Town funeral rites at length.

Despite divergent views on the body, the soul and the afterlife, there are significant coincidences between brahmin Hindu and Jewish death and bereavement rites and attitudes. However, practices in Cochin bear little evidence of borrowings, strictly adhering to the Middle Eastern Sephardic *minhagim*.

The Cochinim consider it important that immediate family members be present to witness the exit of life from the body. The family is summoned to the deathbed, and women as well as men wear *kippot* (caps). At the moment of death, mirrors are covered and a family member, preferably the eldest son, closes the departed's eyelids. The body is removed to the courtyard where the hands and face are washed and, if necessary, any soilings are also cleaned. It is then dressed in fine, bright clothes like a bridegroom or a bride. The body is then placed on a special charpoy (rope bed) with sawed off legs, and candles are placed around it.[92] The candles are lit because of several verses in Proverbs,[93] to symbolize the teaching that 'the light of the good deeds performed by the deceased during his lifetime will accompany his soul to its heavenly rest'. This practice is found among all Jews except the Yemenites.[94]

When the body is laid out and the candles are lit, the time for the funeral is announced, it usually takes place within ten or twelve hours.[95] Both Jewish and brahmin attitudes reflect a primary sensibility about the polluting nature of a corpse (*tumah* in Hebrew). Priests, whether brahmins or *kohanim*, are especially endangered by this type of pollution.[96] In Jewish law, the corpse is so polluting that the *kohanim* are forbidden to have any contact whatsoever with it; a *kohen* may not even visit the grave of a parent, lest he become polluted by neighbouring graves.

A second *halakhic* principle governing a corpse related to that of honouring the dead, *k'vod hamet*. Although the corpse is *tumah*, nevertheless, it must be respected. These two principles govern Jewish behaviour towards the departed.

Halakha recommends that the body be interred on the very day of death, if possible. Failing that, it should be buried before the onset of Shabbat. This statute is known as *halanat hamet*, the prohibition against postponement of the burial.[97] Similarly, when a brahmin dies, his family ensures that the *samskaras* (rites) are performed without any delay and that the cremation takes place that very day.[98] Lower castes may delay the funeral, but the avoidance of pollution is more imperative for the brahmins, as it is for the *kohanim*.

Just as the brahmin may neither eat nor sleep while a corpse lies uncremated, so also the bereaved Jew is referred to as an *onen* from the moment a close relative dies until the burial. During this period called *aninut*, the Palestinian Talmud teaches: 'One whose dead relative lies before him is exempt from the recital of the Shema, and from prayer, and from *t'filin*, and from all the precepts laid down in the Torah.'[99] In short, normal life is suspended until the body is interred. These prohibitions reflect more than the intense grief during the initial hours or days after the death of a loved one; they are reflective of deep sensibilities about pollution which must be purified through appropriate funeral rituals.

Immediately after the funeral is announced the body is removed to the courtyard where it is again washed, but more thoroughly. The first washing is done by the family and the second by non-family members. There is no formalized *chevrah kadishah* (the Jewish burial society which oversees funeral preparations) as in most Jewish communities, probably because there are knowledgeable and willing neighbours available at all times. When the corpse is washed the second time, the entire body is scoured with soap and its nails are cut. Till about fifty years ago, the head of a male corpse was shaved.[100]

After the body is washed, each of twelve people take a clay pot filled with water and pour the water over the body, and then smash the pot.[101] This spilling of water dates back to ancient times. Since water was a precious commodity in the Middle East, spilling it on the ground was likely to attract the community's attention. Thus, a puddle of water in front of house was a indication that death had just visited.[102]

After the second washing, bits of earth from Jerusalem and Cranganore are placed in the eyes and mouth of the corpse. It is dressed in a white linen shroud called a *takhrikhim*.[103] Because the *kohanim* of the Temple wore white linen when entering the *sanctum sanctorum* on Yom Kippur, it led to the tradition that one should wear white linen when standing before God, as do the departed soul and the Temple priest.[104] After the head is wrapped in white linen, a man is wrapped in his *tallit*, from which one of the four fringes has been removed so that a *kosher* ritual object is not buried. Rose water is sprinkled over the corpse, a Sephardic custom, and the body is placed in a plain, wooden coffin.

A grave is dug at the nearby cemetery and, chanting dirges and Psalm 91,[105] the coffin is carried on a palanquin to the site of the grave. The slow procession pauses seven times, corresponding to the seven appearances of the word 'vanity' in Ecclesiastes. The coffin is lowered into the grave and the lid is removed. It is filled with dirt and mud, the lid is replaced and the grave is filled.[106]

As the mourners leave the cemetery, they pass between two rows of friends in attendance, symbolic of the community's support for the bereaved. At this point, the emphasis shifts from the burial to mourning, from the departed to those who remain. They throw bits of dirt or grass over their shoulders, symbolizing both the tearing of the hearts of the bereaved, as well as a belief in resurrection, since grass grows back when torn.[107] The tossing of the grass, according to Qabbalah, is a token of the permission of the living for the departed to ascend to heaven.[108]

Upon returning home, the seven-day period of intense mourning known as *shiva*, derived from *sheva* or 'seven', begins. After washing hands while declaring, 'Our hands have not shed this blood, neither have our eyes seen it', rather than the usual blessing,[109] 'round' foods such as eggs, which symbolize rebirth, are eaten. Special prayers for the bereaved are appended to the usual grace at the end of each meal.[110] Thus, the same foods which herald birth at the *brit milah* ritual, also mark the funeral meal, the *se'uda havra'ah*, or the meal of comfort.

Three weeds are planted to mark the grave. A year later, the grave is dug out and filled with stones to a height several feet above ground level. The Cochin Jews fashion a much more substantial marker than a tombstone for their dead: the stones are built into the monument which covers the entire grave.[111]

NOTES

1. Chill, *The Minhagim*, p. 275.
2. Reinman, 'Masa'oth Shlomo b'Kogin'.
3. Sapir, 'HaYehudim b'Kogin'.

4. Rabinowitz, 'A Jewish Wedding in South India'.
5. Cowen, *Jews in Remote Corners of the World.*
6. Simon, 'The Songs of the Jews of Cochin and Their Historical Significance'. We eagerly await the publication of Barbara Johnson's recent research on these songs.
7. Caspi, 'Wedding Customs of the Jews of Cochin'.
8. Walerstein, 'The Cochini Jewish Wedding of the Malabar Community in India and Israel: Change in Custom Symbol and Meaning'.
9. Chill, *The Minhagim*, p. 278.
10. Reinman, 'Masa'oth Shlomo b'Kogin', p. 34.
11. Ibid., p. 34.
12. Caspi, 'Wedding Customs of the Jews of Cochin', p. 231.
13. Cowen, *Jews in Remote Corners of the World*, p. 199.
14. Ibid., p. 199.
15. Reinman, 'Masa'oth Shlomo b'Kogin', p. 34.
16. Cowen, *Jews in Remote Corners of the World*, p. 199.
17. Walerstein, 'The Cochini Jewish Wedding', p. 255.
18. So, too, for Kerala's Christians, especially the Knani. Swiderski connected Knani weddings with the 72 royal privileges which were the subject of their copper plate grant. He argued about the Knani, similar to our argument about the Jews, that 'wedding ritual and Knanaya identity are strongly interdependent and the wedding is no less than a symbolic assertion of identity'. Swiderski, *Blood Weddings*, 3, 68.
19. Jacob Cohen and Gamliel Salem, 6 October 1986.
20. Walerstein, 'The Cochini Jewish Wedding', p. 254.
21. Reinman, 'Masa'oth Shlomo b'Kogin', p. 34.
22. Cowen, *Jews in Remote Corners of the World*, p. 199.
23. Reinman, 'Masa'oth Shlomo b'Kogin', p. 34.
24. I.S. Hallegua, personal communication, 28 July 1989.
25. Cowen, *Jews in Remote Corners of the World*, p. 200.
26. Chill, *The Minhagim*, pp. 286-7.
27. Cowen, *Jews in Remote Corners of the World*, p. 199.
28. Danielou, *Shilappadikaram*, p. 117.
29. Rabinowitz, 'A Jewish Wedding in South India', p. 44.
30. Cowen, *Jews in Remote Corners of the World*, p. 200.
31. Walerstein, 'The Cochini Jewish Wedding', p. 256.
32. Cowen, *Jews in Remote Corners of the World*, p. 200.
33. Walerstein, 'A Jewish Wedding in South India', p. 256.
34. Cowen, *Jews in Remote Corners of the World*, pp. 200-1.
35. Reinman, 'Masa'oth Shlomo b'Kogin', p. 34.
36. Rabinowitz, 'A Jewish Wedding in South India', p. 42.
37. Cowen, *Jews in Remote Corners of the World*, p. 201.
38. Jacob Cohen and Gamliel Salem, 6 October 1987.
39. Rabinowitz, 'A Jewish Wedding in South India', p. 41.

40. Cowen, *Jews in Remote Corners of the World*, p. 201.
41. Reynolds, 'The Auspicious Married Woman', p. 44.
42. Walerstein, 'The Cochini Jewish Wedding', p. 256.
43. Reynolds 'The Auspicious Married Woman', p. 36.
44. Ibid., pp. 37-8.
45. Ibid., p. 35.
46. Egnor, 'On the Meaning of Sakti to Women in Tamil Nadu', p. 15.
47. Ibid., p. 17.
48. Reynolds, 'The Auspicious Married Woman', p. 38.
49. Reinman, 'Masa'oth Shlomo b'Kogin', p. 34.
50. Rabinowitz, 'A Jewish Wedding in South India', p. 42.
51. Walerstein, 'The Cochini Jewish Wedding', p. 249.
52. Reinman, 'Masa'oth Shlomo b'Kogin', p. 34.
53. The Cochin wedding liturgies as well as *Milah* and *Havdallah* ceremonies were published in *Sefer Chupat Chatanim*, edited by Roby and published by Judah David Ashkenazy at his Lebanon Printing Works in Bombay in 1917.
54. Chill, *The Minhagim*, pp. 276-7.
55. Reinman, 'Masa'oth Shlomo b'Kogin', p. 34.
56. Rabinowitz, 'A Jewish Wedding in South India', p. 43.
57. Ibid., p. 43.
58. Translated by Rabinowitz, ibid., p. 43.
59. Rabinowitz, 'A Jewish Wedding in South India', p. 44.
60. Ibid.
61. Walerstein, 'The Cochini Jewish Wedding', p. 261.
62. Ibid., p. 259.
63. Reinman, 'Masa'oth Shlomo b'Kogin', p. 35.
64. Walerstein, 'The Cochini Jewish Wedding', p. 261.
65. Simon, 'The Songs of the Jews of Cochin', p. 15.
66. Kasher, *Hagadah Shelanu*, p. 190.
67. Walerstein, 'The Cochini Jewish Wedding', p. 263.
68. Ibid.
69. Cowen, *Jews in Remote Corners of the World*, p. 204.
70. Caspi, 'Wedding Customs of the Jews of Cochin', p. 232.
71. Reinman, 'Masa'oth Shlomo b'Kogin', p. 35.
72. Danielou, *Shilappadikaram*, pp. 4-5.
73. Fischel, *Unknown Jews in Unknown Lands*, p. 113.
74. Gen. 17: 10-12.
75. Ashkenazy, *Sefer Brit Yitzhak*, p. ii.
76. Chill, *The Minhagim*, p. 294.
77. Ibid., pp. 294-5.
78. Ibid., p. 295.
79. Ashkenazy, *Sefer Brit Yitzhak*, p. ii.
80. Anonymous, 'Cochin', p. 137.

81. Johnson, '"Our Community" in Two Worlds', p. 183.
82. *Massa Bavel*, pp. 131, 200; cited by Chill, *The Minhagim*, p. 300.
83. Anonymous, 'Cochin, ' p. 137.
84. Johnson, '"Our Community" in Two Worlds', pp. 181-2.
85. The Jewish Bible consists of three sections: the Torah, the first five books known as the *Chumash* in Hebrew; the Prophets of *Nevi'im* ; and the Writings or *K'tuvim*. Each Saturday morning, a section from the Torah scroll accompanied by an additional reading from one of the remaining two sections, is read. There are also readings on Mondays and Thursdays.
86. Reynolds, 'The Auspicious Married Woman', pp. 39-40.
87. Johnson, '"Our Community" in Two Worlds', p. 175.
88. Reynolds, 'The Auspicious Married Woman', p. 38.
89. Ibid., p. 44.
90. Mandelbaum, 'The Jewish Way of Life in Cochin', pp. 456-7.
91. Johnson, '"Our Community" in Two Worlds', p. 183.
92. Raymond Salem, 2 April 1987.
93. Proverbs 6: 22-3 and 20: 27.
94. Chill, *The Minhagim*, p. 321.
95. Raymond Salem, 2 April 1987.
96. See Dutt, *The Dharma Shastra*, pp. 450ff.
97. Chill, *The Minhagim*, p. 325.
98. Dutt, *The Dharma Shastra*, p. 117. The postponement of a brahmin's cremation and the attendant calamities are the subject of a intriguing novel in Kannada, U.R. Anantha Murthy's *Samskara*, trans. by A.K. Ramanujan, Oxford University Press, 1978.
99. Quoted by Soloveitchik, 'The Halakha of the First Day', p. 77.
100. Raymond Salem, 2 April 1987.
101. Ibid., 2 April 1987.
102. Chill, *The Minhagim*, p. 322.
103. Raymond Salem, 2 April 1987.
104. Chill, *The Minhagim*, p. 323.
105. Pool, *Seder Hatefilot*, p. 458.
106. Raymond Salem, 2 April 1987.
107. Chill, *The Minhagim*, p. 328.
108. Ibid., p. 329.
109. Pool, *Seder Hatefilot*, p. 464.
110. Ibid., p. 467.
111. Raymond Salem, 2 April 1987.

CHAPTER 6

'Jewish Apartheid' and a Jewish Gandhi

The story of the Cochin Jews interweaves legend with history, creating a charming narrative of honour and affection, of triumph and defeat, of hospitality, of long-standing residence in Cranganore and ancient origin in Israel, a double-*yichus*—all of which served them well in setting up their home in venerable India.

However, one aspect of their story is less savoury. The Cochin Jews evolved a pattern of social organization which reflected Indian values. Some of the Cochin Jews joined a liberal rabbi from Johannesburg in contemptuously denouncing this social system as 'Jewish apartheid', after the system of racial oppression in South Africa. The label is an exaggeration no doubt, but it is also certain that in emulating the Indian castes' tendency to proliferate into endogamous subcastes, the Cochin Jews crossed the fine line of judicious accommodation with Indian society. Here, *Halakha* was breached, as the Cochin Jews have been admonished by foreign Jews ever since the issue was first raised in 1520. But if India was the source of this discriminatory social pattern, it was also a resource for its eradication. Emulating his mentor, Mahatma Gandhi, Cochin activist A.B. Salem led a movement to eradicate this discrimination, earning him the moniker, 'the Jewish Gandhi'.

India is a hierarchical society in which numerous castes 'who may differ in their customs and habits, live side by side, agreed on the code which ranks them and separates them'.[1] This is the basis for the well known 'Hindu tolerance'. One strategy for survival in India was for the Jews to organize themselves as a caste. To be accepted as a caste in India, a group must interact with acknowledged castes according to the principles of hierarchy, separation as regards food and marriage, and evidence strict concerns about purity and pollution. This is precisely what the Cochin Jews achieved through their unique observances of Passover. A group must also achieve caste by enacting appropriate symbols of status, as did the Cochin Jews in their display of royalty symbolism in their distinctive Simchat Torah traditions. Yet again, a group must narrate toothers and to itself appropriate status enhancing themes in a historical legend.

Of these four strategies for cultural adaptation in India, three—ritual enactments of purity and royalty and the generation of an appropriate historical legend—posed no *halakhic* difficulties for the Cochin Jews. Only the fourth method, their proliferation into subcastes, led the Cochin Jews to contravene *Halakha* and defy rabbinic admonition and censure. Not only were these subcastes endogamous, but also one of them was denied a role in the life of the synagogue. In this behaviour they resembled some south Indian castes known as 'right' or 'left'. Each subcaste classified as 'right', according to Brenda E.F. Beck, 'had some essential ceremony to perform as part of the ritual at her temple, while no 'left' subcaste was similarly employed.[2]

THE LINGERING SCARS OF DISCRIMINATION

This mirroring of caste behaviour persisted until very recently. This social pattern left deep scars within the community. Feelings ran high, as was evident from a conversation with Raymond Salem.

On a sultry afternoon in Cochin, while he lingered over the lunch table, Raymond discussed politics. His Christian servant, Mary, removed the remnants of the Kerala-style *kosher* curries, as Raymond, then 68, the eldest son of A.B. Salem, pointed to a newspaper story on South Africa that had piqued his interest.

'What do you know about apartheid?' he asked. 'Do you know what role South African Jews play in it?'

Raymond then listened to a tale about an encounter with a Black South African exile who had been lecturing on the college circuit throughout the United States. Upon being introduced to a sympathetic faculty member with an obviously Jewish surname, he said, 'Let me tell you something about the Jews in South Africa.' The professor winced, expecting the usual 'Zionism-equals-racism' diatribe, but the exile continued, 'You know, I've been imprisoned many times there, and I always found Jews imprisoned for their anti-apartheid activities. I don't know what it is about your people, who are so few but form the majority of white South Africans who join our struggle. You should be proud.'

Raymond was shocked. 'It that so? I'd always assumed Jews were instrumental in designing the apartheid system, not in striving against it. Why, here in Jew Town they devised their own system of apartheid against their fellow Jews. I rather assumed they'd done the same over there.'

Raymond narrated stories of 'Jewish apartheid', by which a portion of the Cochin community discriminated against its brethren for centuries. He also talked about his celebrated father who fought for and eventually succeeded in achieving equal rights for his people. But, as Raymond dramatically concluded, his father could not reverse what was to be Cochin's destiny: 'These people are cursed for their actions. It is this curse that explains the death of the Jew Town community.'

JEWS AND CULTURAL ADAPTATION

Cochin's Jews not only carved out a niche for themselves in Kerala's complex caste system, but also manifested caste behaviour by dividing themselves into subcastes, which followed south India's right-left structure. This internal division was purportedly based on those Jews considered to be, or not to be, descended from ancient Israel, the 'right' subcaste. However, according to some community members, it was based on skin colour, the infamous White Jew/Black Jew/Brown Jew pattern of religious and social organization. Jews who were not part of the white subcaste were denied religious equality in the Paradesi Synagogue and were not allowed to marry members of the white faction.

Many Western Jews are shocked to learn of the Cochin community's discrimination against its brethren. There are two interrelated reasons for this uncharacteristic and unegalitarian behaviour. First, it demonstrates what is characteristic of all Jews: an unflagging ability to adapt to various lands and survive. Second, it reflects the Cochinites' high degree of acculturation, replacing the egalitarianism which is foregrounded from the tradition by most Western Jews, with a hierarchy characteristic of Indian Jews and their Hindu context. Indeed, their aloof behaviour was not an isolated case: the Bene Israel Jews also divided themselves into white and black (*gora* and *kala*) subcastes,[3] Dutch Jews were known not to mingle with their Baghdadi brethren in Indonesia and the same was true of German and Eastern European Jews in America.[4] No doubt Judaism is a common bond, but respective regional cultures are also strong identification factors. As multitudes of Jews arrived from such disparate lands as Iraq, Syria, Yemen, Turkey, Spain and Germany, they found in India a group of fellow Jews who were so different from themselves that these barriers seemed insurmountable. These cultural obstacles were only fortified by Kerala's caste system, to which, typically, these foreign Jews adhered. Within a relatively short span, they became Indianized. Although they never faltered in their faith, they conformed to India's societal norms, caste distinctions and, later, colonial rule.

Ironically, the same society that contributed to creating barriers within the Cochin community also helped to destroy them. Salem adopted such non-violent methods of protest as hunger strikes and sit-ins to fight against the discrimination in his synagogue and community, just as the Mahatma had launched a *satyagraha* for access to temples on behalf of the 'untouchables' at Vikam in neighbouring Travancore State in 1924-5.[5]

Within the last three or four decades, all social and religious divisions have disappeared, but then, so has most of the community. Emigration to Israel, which began in 1950 and accelerated during the 1970s, has decimated this once thriving community.

'SUBSTANCE' AS A MODE OF IDENTIFICATION

Jewish law states that a Jew is the child of a Jewish mother or someone who is converted to the faith according to *Halakha*. These definitions of who is a Jew, hereditary or by proper conversion, are *halakhic* universals. As observant Jews, the Cochinites scrupulously followed these rules and regulations.

At the same time, however, they are Indians. They resemble their fellow countrymen by adopting additional traits, influenced by the Hindu caste system, and applying them to their own religious and social conduct. Preservation of their identity depended on it, as did their coveted high caste status in society at large. As a result, definitions of Jewish 'substance', or 'blood', went several steps further. Not only were the Cochinites concerned about a mother's substance, but about the purity of a father's substance as well. The traditional Jewish identification of substance with blood underscores the role of the mother in conferring Jewish identity; yet the Cochinites' concern for the father's purity reflects the south Indian identification of substance with semen rather than blood.[6] Marriage and sexual relations were, therefore, of paramount concern because if the Jewish blood of a couple was considered 'tainted', the partners and offspring of that union were no longer recognized as Jews by the Cochin community.[7]

Conversions to Judaism were also influenced by the Indian caste system. A *halakhic* conversion did not ensure full religious and social rights among one's fellow Jews. Although a convert symbolically began his life anew, he often carried the baggage of his former caste status into his newly adopted community, a pattern found among India's Christians and Muslims as well as Jews.

An emotionally charged issue of substance focused on those Cochinites who were considered to be, or not to be, *meyuchasim*, those 'with a pedigree' of descent from ancient Israel. As is the case in many south Indian right-left subcastes, descent or *yichus* is the determining factor in subcaste ascription.[8] Though small in number, the *meyuchasim* exerted power over the larger group, whom they denounced as having tainted blood. Contested for centuries by both groups were their competing claims of Cranganore ancestry.[9] Seemingly more a historical than a religious issue, actually it was both. Those who claimed that they had Cranganore blood thereby asserted that their ancestors were the original refugees from ancient Israel. Not only did this give them Jewish *yichus*, but also long-standing Indian lineage, both of which earned them prestige among high caste Hindus as well as Jews.

Jewish substance, judged by Cochin Jews to include biological inheritance and ancient Israeli ancestry among other factors, was strictly regulated, and these regulations were not just Jewish in origin, they were also Hindu. For several centuries, Cochin's religious and social policies were dictated by what could only be described as a merging of both traditions. Those who were judged to have impure substance were barred from prayer services in the Paradesi Synagogue as well as from marriage with Cochinites for fear of pollution. It is undeniable that colour also played a role in defining and enforcing Jewish substance, adding fuel to this fiery debate. Colour distinctions were a way of life in India long before the arrival of white European conquerors and immigrants; however, these foreigners exacerbated the situation and used it to their advantage.

By going well beyond *halakhic* practice—at time even *defying* it by opting for Hindu caste behaviour over standard Jewish law—not only did the Cochin community assert its status among non-Jews, but Jews as well. The inevitable friction this caused among its own people led to bitter divisions in an already tiny religious minority. These ongoing splits and disputes, believed to have persisted for at least four centuries, no longer exist. Yet many Jews in India or resettled in Israel, still remember and bear painful scars of this 'Jewish apartheid'.

EARLY DIVISIONS WITHIN THE COCHIN COMMUNITY

It is impossible to pinpoint when divisive problems among the Cochinites first arose and among whom. A popular legend, or one version of it, has it that the first internal dissension dates back to Cranganore, where the Jews were granted an independent principality and their leader, Joseph Rabban, special privileges by the ruling Hindu king. In the fourteenth century, there was a power struggle for the Jewish territory between Joseph Azar, then leader, and his brother Aaron. The rivalry was further complicated by the brother's wives joining the fight; according to another version sides were taken by the two factions of the community, with the Hindu raja then in power supporting Joseph. In the end, there were no winners. The raja expelled Aaron and his supporters and, later, Joseph swam 20 miles to Cochin with his wife on his back.[10]

This legend bears similarities to those narrated by several south Indian 'left' merchant castes. According to Beck,

> [T]hese folktales indicate that a body of stories exists explaining the history of all the higher-ranking communities of the left division (most merchant communities are high caste and 'left' according to Beck) . . . each story mentions an angry king . . . who time and time again tries to destroy a particular left-division group . . . . Their escape is associated with a flood or with the crossing of a swollen river.[11]

The Jews' story differs from that of the Hindus in that the latter typically concludes with marriage to a bride from a family in their new locale and the progeny resulting from the mixed marriage establishing a new descent line. The Jews, for whom intermarriage was anathema, instead resolved this thorny issue by claiming that Joseph carried his Jewish wife across the river. Analogies to the Exodus story are inviting and indicate a coincidence of Jewish and Hindu motifs: a king persecutes a group which flees, crossing a dangerous river (the Reed Sea) and establishing a new home for itself.

Less colourful reasons for the Jews' departure from Cranganore were to escape attacks by warring Muslim and Portuguese powers as well as to improve their economic situation after a massive flood silted up the Cranganore harbour and made sea related trade impossible.

The first documented account of strife dates back to the early sixteenth century, when a letter of inquiry was sent from Cochin to Rabbi David ben Solomon ibn Zimra in Cairo. The Hebrew letter dated around 1520 reads in part:

> . . . (F)rom the island of Cochin . . . there are about nine hundred heads of households. Of these one hundred are Jews by origin and of (Jewish) stock, and they are *meyuhasin*: the rest are rich and devout and charitable. The *meyuhasin* do not intermarry with them and call them slaves, and on this account they have contention and quarrels without end. Among these rich persons are some who are called partial slaves. A group are (descendants of) Jewish traders who came . . . from . . . Turkey . . . , Aden . . . , Germany and . . . Caucasia, and they bought female slaves and begot from them sons and daughters and emancipated them . . . in their land with the status of Jews. Another group did not emancipate them, but . . . after

the master had gone, (the slave) remained with the status of Jew. . . and there is no-one who would object to it. . . . (Another). . . group who had become *gerim* (proselytes) were mingled among them. All sections of these gentiles have intermarried among themselves and have held to the religion of Israel; they have become a large community who observe the Torah and are rich and intimate with royalty and the princes. They are the root of the negotiations between traders and (attested) *meyuhasin* Jews. The (latter) on the contrary are a minority and poor, but they call the others the offspring of slaves out of jealousy and hatred. There is no-one who can prove that they are slaves. But apparently not a single one of them was given a document of emancipation because (people) were not expert at this and they did not know how to explain the matter. Now let the teacher indicate whether it is permissible for the *meyuhasin* to interfere with them, whether they have the rights of slaves or *gerim*—if they are slaves, whether they have a remedy or not, and if it is proper to rebuke those who call them slaves or not. Please write about everything at length because there are no learned people . . . who can deduce one matter from another.[12]

The inquiry provided ibn Zimra with ample background about the Cochin community. Of its 900 Jewish families, 100 were *meyuchasim*, 'Jews by origin'. They refused to intermarry with their coreligionists—a 'rich, devout and charitable group', close to the rulers of Cochin and dominant in the sea trade—whom they called slaves. The self-segregating group indulging in name calling was, by contrast, an impoverished minority which acted seemingly 'out of jealousy and hatred'. Their aloof, superior behaviour, the anonymous petitioner noted, led to ongoing divisive arguments in the community.

The complainants understandably were concerned about their social standing in the community and how it may affect them from a religious standpoint. As the petitioner acknowledged, they were a mix of peoples: offspring of foreign Jewish traders and local slave women, the mothers and children having been freed by their masters; descendants of slaves who were not properly manumitted by their masters but were eventually accepted as freemen and as Jews; and *gerim*, or converts. Over a period of time, they grew into a large, prosperous group which 'held to the religion of Israel'. Despite their professed religious learning and practice, however, they were unfamiliar with the *halakhic* rules concerning liberating slaves. None had in his possession an official document of manumission (*shichrur*) for his ancestors to prove he was a Jewish freeman. Moreover, no one in the community was knowledgeable enough to determine whether intermarriage between the *meyuchasim* and non-*meyuchasim* should be permitted or prohibited according to Jewish law. Clearly, someone well-versed in Jewish matters was needed to act as an arbitrator.

In his response, ibn Zimra recounted that over the last two decades, since the Portuguese takeover in 1498, reports of Cochin had begun to reach Egypt. Included in these reports were numerous requests for books, since the community did not possess any copies of the *Mishnah*, *Talmud* and law codes. This would explain why no one knew how to liberate slaves in a Judaically proper way, or whether marriage was permissible between the *meyuchasim* and non-*meyuchasim*. After deliberating the case, the rabbi decided the two groups could marry, providing that the non-*meyuchasim* first underwent a symbolic conversion—*t'vilah*, ritual immersion before three witnesses, which is ordinarily performed by converts, to remove any stain of doubt regarding their previous manumissions and conversions. From that time forward, he declared, they were considered to be Jews; those who called them slaves were fundamentally wrong.

INCREASED FRICTION BETWEEN THE *MEYUCHASIM* AND NON-*MEYUCHASIM*

It would seem that the good rabbi's decision would settle the matter. But that was not to be. His advice was ignored by the *meyuchasim*, which prompted a similar letter of inquiry a generation later; ironically it was sent to ibn Zimra's student, Rabbi Jacob de Castro, in Alexandria. De Castro studied his teacher's arguments, and in his response reiterated that Jewish law permitted marriage between the two groups, the only prerequisite being *t'vilah* for the larger faction. Again, the *meyuchasim* disregarded this advice and segregated themselves from the others. The exclusionary behaviour continued, with two more attempts in 1882 and 1951 to petition rabbinical authorities, both of whom upheld the original sixteenth century decision, although it was to no avail.

Why did the non-*meyuchasim* care whether or not the *meyuchasim* accepted them? It is, indeed, curious that a large group that seemingly had everything would clamour for acceptance by a self-segregating, impoverished group, a fraction of its size. Obviously, the smaller group possessed something the larger group did not have and wanted. That something was status, unquestioned Jewish status. Attested lineage was what ostensibly kept the *meyuchasim* apart from the others. In Kerala's rigid caste society, those claiming to have Jewish substance, due to fear to pollution refused to mingle with or marry those who could not prove such purity, fit neatly into that hierarchical Hindu system.

There was also the question of the non-*meyuchasim* being called slaves.

Petitioners of the sixteenth century letter to ibn Zimra claimed that the *meyuchasim* called them the 'offspring of slaves out of jealousy and hatred'. Indeed, the larger group had ample reason to envy the others. Although they did not have their much-touted Jewish substance, they had everything else—wealth, mercantile clout and a high place in Hindu royal society. Perhaps, the non- *meyuchasim* feared all that was at risk by being branded slaves—a low caste stigma from which they sought to rid themselves. With one's livelihood and social standing determined by caste, it is possible that their place near the top of Kerala's social and economic hierarchy could be jeopardized. But they had a problem: they could not prove that their ancestors had been emancipated because none of them had a *shichrur*. The remedy to this problem, as prescribed by ibn Zimra and his successors, was ritual immersion; it would pronounce them free men and women—symbolically dissolving, as it were, any doubts of earlier manumissions.

Indeed, their fears foreshadowed inequities that lay in store for them when the long-standing partisanship they had enjoyed from the Hindu royal family was withdrawn and extended to the *meyuchasim*. Almost forty years after the petition to Rabbi ibn Zimra, there was a marked increase in the *meyuchasim*'s business, economic and social status and, simultaneously, a sharp decline in these areas among the non- *meyuchasim*. At that time the Maharaja of Cochin gave the *meyuchasim* a parcel of land, adjoining his palace grounds, on which they built their own synagogue. During the Dutch colonial period, Governor Adriaan Moens observed that the maharaja 'always considered (the non-*meyuchasim*) as somewhat inferior' to the *meyuchasim*.[13] Indeed, whenever internal disputes arose between the rival Jewish factions, invariably the maharaja ruled in favour of the *meyuchasim*. Could it be that the non-*meyuchasim* had fallen out of favour in part because they continued to be denounced—and gradually came to be accepted by the other communities—as low caste slaves?

SEGREGATION BETWEEN THE FOREIGN AND MALABARI JEWS

The *meyuchasim* never considered the non-*meyuchasim* equals. While they did recognize them as Jews, they apparently saw no other commonality to warrant interaction with them. Who were the *meyuchasim*, and why were they so intent on segregating themselves from their own people? When did the divisions between these two factions become so pronounced? A viable explanation was offered by David Mandelbaum, one of the most astute scholars of Cochin Jewry.[14] Mandelbaum believed that the distinctions were introduced by Jewish immigrants from Europe and the Middle East. Those described as *meyuchasim* in the early sixteenth century letter to ibn Zimra may have been recent arrivals who had fled religious persecution in Spain and Portugal. Upon reaching Malabar, these foreign Jews faced a cultural dichotomy: they found a group of fellow Jews who were so utterly different from them—in language, dress and diet—that they could not readily associate with them. These social barriers were further exacerbated by the caste system, which they came to adopt. Desirous of carving a niche for themselves in their newly adopted society, they used whatever assets they had to their advantage. Aside from boasting attested Jewish lineage, the newcomers did have greater Jewish knowledge than their Malabari counterparts who had been somewhat cut off from the rest of Jewish world. More important, the foreign Jews were familiar with European trade practices and were well versed in languages of the Portuguese and other European merchants who came to south India. They were useful to those in power and thereby became powerful themselves.

Not surprisingly, they enjoyed their newly developed power base and were determined to maintain it. Conforming to their surroundings implied that there was no room in their coveted circle for their fellow Jews who did not 'measure up'. They were not alone in their exclusionary behaviour. Indeed, they resembled Kerala's high caste Christians and Muslims, who shunned social or religious interaction with their own 'lesser brethren' to prove their purity and thus maintain their high status in the dominant Hindu society.[15] Similarly, Bombay's Baghdadi Jews affected superior attitudes towards Maharashtra's Bene Israel, in part to identify with the British against the 'natives'.[16]

However, it is not possible to uphold the Jews' claims that they never intermingled with indigenous peoples. Since the reign of King Solomon, Jewish merchants along with other traders from the Middle East, the Far East and Europe had undertaken long, hazardous, yet profitable journeys to India for valuable goods, spices in particular. Some of these Jewish merchants and crews settled in Malabar. On these early expeditions, fraught with physical hardships and marauding pirates, it was unlikely that they would have taken any family members with them. What appears more plausible is that they married or lived with local women. The mates and offspring of these unions, as also many household servants and slaves, embraced Judaism, and along with the original settlers they comprised the Malabari community. This social pattern continued for centuries virtually uninterruptedly, occasionally augmented by small influxes of Jewish traders, a few of whom may have brought their families. Because there were few foreign settlers, there were probably no formal social distinctions between them and the local Malabari Jewish converts.[17] What abruptly changed that dynamic was the mass migration of European Jews, entire families fleeing Spanish and Portuguese persecution in the fifteenth and sixteenth centuries. There is ample documentation to show that these foreign Jews kept to themselves, refused to mingle with their co-religionists who preceded them, and ultimately drove a wedge between themselves and the others which only widened with time.

THE IMPORTANCE OF ANCIENT JEWISH AND INDIAN ANCESTRY

Why and when this polarity arose between the local Malabari Jews and Paradesi, or 'foreign', Jews, as they were called, are at best speculations. For centuries, this segregationist behaviour figured in foreign travellers' accounts of the community. One such report was authored by de Paiva in 1686, who noted that despite the two groups' commonality of worship, there were cavernous fissures between them. The Paradesis kept their distance, religiously and socially, from the Malabari Jews. They condemned intermarriage, did not count a Malabari Jewish man as part of a *minyan* (quorum) for prayers, and would not eat meat ritually slaughtered by the other group. Why? According to de Paiva, 'They allege as a reason they (the Malabari Jews) are slaves of slaves and they they are mixed with Canaanites, converts and Muslims.'[18] Echoing the past, the Paradesis denounced the others as having tainted lineage, a belief they passed on to foreign travellers who usually heard only the Paradesis'—who spoke European languages—side of the story.

Understandably, the Malabari Jews were furious with the Paradesis, whom they accused of spreading slanderous lies about their origin. The Malabari Jews countered that their lineage was actually more impressive than that of the Paradesis. Unlike these newcomers, they claimed that a number of their Jewish ancestors had arrived in Kerala from ancient Israel more than 2,000 years ago. A foreign traveller who was 'inclined to believe correct' the Malabaris' version of their history was Rabbi David D'Beth Hillel. He recorded that they 'believe themselves to be the descendants of the Israelites of the first captivity who were brought to India and did not return with the Israelites who built the Second Temple'.[19] Further, these Israelites who remained in India were the first settlers of Cranganore. The Jewish population of Cranganore increased steadily, periodically absorbing foreign Jewish traders and families as well as converted servants or slaves from Jewish households. Among these early Jewish settlers was the celebrated Joseph Rabban. However, if this were so, then why were the copper plates in the Paradesis' and not the Malabaris' possession? According to some Malabaris, this was because the Paradesis were guilty of absconding with the plates, or that the plates were actually copies of the originals which were lost long ago. There is no way to ascertain which group is the true beneficiary. There are no written accounts or, if there were, they did not survive Portuguese colonial rule, when all Jewish religious and historical books were burnt by the fanatics of the Inquisition. In fact, little is written about the Malabari Jews; foreigners did not even begin to document their views until the nineteenth century.[20] Some Jews like Hillel as well as non-Jews tended to believe the group's origin theory that many of their ancestors were descendants of the Israelites who may have first docked in India after the destruction of the First Temple. Thus, not only could they claim ancient Jewish lineage, but also ancient Indian lineage.

The Paradesis vehemently refuted these claims, and over the course of time developed their own origin theory. They asserted that not only they were the only Jews descended from ancient Israel, but also they were the true descendants of the original Cranganore settlers. During his visit in 1686, de Paiva recorded the community's origin as espoused by the Paradesis. Most of the Paradesis, or 'Spanish Jews', as he called them, actually journeyed from various parts of Europe and the Middle East, first arriving on the Malabar coast in 1511. However, he noted that at the time of his visit, there lived Joseph and Zacharias Zackai and Abira Aaron, who were 'descendants from the first families of Cranganore'.[21] Over the next three centuries, the Paradesis continued to embellish and hone this origin story in a series of chronicles and correspondences, written in both Hebrew and English.[22] With the passage of time, these writings became increasingly vehement about the group's antiquity and assertion to being the true Cranganore settlers, refuting the Malabari Jews' claims to this ancestry.[23] In 1895, a Paradesi resident noted,

> The presence of the copper plates in the possession of the White Jews, the *real meyookasim*, is an insurmountable impediment to the pretensions of the black Jews, and therefore they try their utmost to make them theirs, and it is for the same purpose that they now call themselves by the names of *meyookasim*, Anjuvanam (= Cranganore) Jews . . . and even White Jews . . . ! Even now the family 'Zackai' exists whose forefathers came to Cranganore many centuries ago. There are others among us, not from Cranganore, but their residence in Cochin covers a period of more than 10 generations.[24]

By then the Aaron clan, one of the 'first families of Cranganore' according to de Paiva's report, had died out. However, at least one member of the Zackai household, allegedly of Cranganore origin, was reported to have lived in Cochin as late as 1937.[25] A dwindling Cranganore lineage as well as arranged marriages between members of 'approved' households was enough for the Paradesi 'whites' to hold firm to the belief that they all had Cranganore blood. Writing in 1940, A.I. Simon reflected the views of his group,

> (De Paiva's) list of surnames proves that the descendants of those Pardesi Jews who were in Cochin in 1686 are still here and some of them originate from Cranganore, and they have all bred in and in such a way that Cranganore blood runs in the vein of every Pardesi class of Jews seen here today.[26]

They claimed Joseph Rabban as their own. The Paradesis repeatedly referred to him in their letters and chronicles, eulogized him in their Hebrew and Malayalam folk songs and symbolically likened a bridegroom to him in their wedding rituals. Joseph Rabban was embraced as an ancestral hero. Also held in high esteem was the Hindu royal family, called by the Paradesis their protectors from the time of Sri Ravi Bhaskara Varma's rule in Cranganore to his descendant, the Maharaja of Cochin's reign. Even today, some Paradesi Jews who trace their ancestry to Iraq or Spain, speak proudly of their forefather, Joseph Rabban. Sarah Cohen, of Yemeni origin, was a typical example. Like other Paradesi women, she maintained notebooks of songs, meticulously handwritten in Malayalam, that she and other women sang on special communitywide occasions. After an impromptu performance of a traditional wedding tune, Sarah offered a brief English translation of its meaning. 'On that day,' she explained, 'the bridegroom is like Joseph Rabban; he is like a king.'[27]

Undoubtedly the Cochin Jews were not the only ethnic group in India that could be accused of having selective recall of history. They conformed to their milieu and emulated Kerala's Nambudiri Brahmins, Knani Christians and some upper echelon Muslims who claimed descent from early immigrants.[28] The distinction between the Paradesi and Malabari Jews has parallels within the Muslim community:

> The Muslim communities were usually distinguished by the Portuguese into two groups: the 'Moors of the land' (*mouros da terra*) and the 'Moors from Arabia' (*mouros da Arabia*). The distinction was in fact meant to distinguish the Mappila Muslims from all Middle Eastern Muslims; the latter (were) . . . called *Paradesi* Muslims. . . .[29]

Like the Jews, Christians and Muslims also claimed early Cranganore settlements, along with privileges similar to those of the Jews, granted by the Hindu royal family. Among the Paradesi and Malabari Jewish factions therefore, *yichus* was not just a matter of who had descended from ancient Israel, but from Cranganore as well. Indeed, for centuries the Jews have drawn certain parallels between the destruction of Jerusalem and that of Cranganore as well as their subsequent dispersions from both places; the two homelands have a dual history of tragedy and reverence.[30]

There has been much debate as to which group, the Malabaris or the Paradesis, could lay proper claim to ancient ancestry from both Israel and India. Participating in this debate have been the two groups themselves, and scholars, foreign travellers and colonial officials belonging to various periods who lived in Cochin. One of the most compelling arguments in support of the Paradesis' claim of pure Jewish lineage is that they have families of *kohanim*, or hereditary priests, who obviously descended from ancient Israel. Despite their inherited posts losing much of their importance after the destruction of the Temple, *kohanim* continue to be an integral part of Jewish ritual practice and are needed for certain duties that only they can perform, such as conducting the ceremony of *pidyon haben*, or redemption of the firstborn male.

Unlike the Paradesis, however, the Malabari Jews 'have not among them a single priest (*kohen*)', reported Hillel in 1828.[31] While no one can definitely say if this were always the case, it appears to have been so at least as far back as the eighteenth century. In a letter dated 1768, the distinguished Paradesi leader, Ezekiel Rahabi, wrote that most of the Malabari Jews did not observe the redemption of the firstborn male. As Mandelbaum observed, the 'important rite . . . requires the participation of a *kohen*, a Jew of the traditional priestly descent. There were none among the Malabar Jews and apparently men so qualified among the . . . (Paradesi) Jews were either not acceptable to the others or else would not accept their invitation.'[32] Instead, the Malabaris waited until a foreign *kohen* visited Cochin; because these visits were sporadic, there were times when the ritual was performed for a number of males, many of whom were young men. Mandelbaum concluded, 'the absence of priestly descent tends to confirm the possibility that the . . . (Malabari) Jews were originally converts, for converted natives could naturally not occupy hereditary offices.'[33]

However, basing a group's ancient Israeli ancestry on whether it has—or does not have—*kohanim* among its population could be misleading. Although it can be confirmed that the Paradesis have ancient Jewish lineage because they were known to have *kohanim*, by the same token it cannot be proved that the Malabari Jews do not have such lineage because they do not have *kohanim*, as documented over the last three centuries.

Consider the story of Yaakob and Daniel Cohen. In the early nineteenth century, the Paradesis urged a foreigner, a *kohen*, to remain in Cochin when they feared that their own *kohanim* were dying out. The Baghdadi visitor, one Yaakob David Cohen, apparently got more than he had bargained for when he arrived on the Malabar coast for commercial purposes—he was married to a Paradesi woman also of priestly descent and remained in India. However, the man was already married and had a family in Baghdad. Within a few years his son Daniel arrived in Cochin in search of him. With yet another *kohen* in their midst, the Paradesis pressed the son to remain in Cochin with his father. Apparently, they were persuasive because that was exactly that Daniel did and, in turn, also married a Paradesi woman. After studying the genealogies of many Paradesi families, Mandelbaum observed 'their farsightedness was justified, because the descendants of Jacob (Yaakob) David Cohen and his wife Rachel have all died out, while the family of Daniel and his wife Esther Moses Sarphati now provide the lay priests of the synagogue.'[34] No doubt, the Paradesis' farsightedness was to be applauded. However, based on this information, it is not far-fetched to speculate that had they not convinced Cohen senior and junior to remain in Cochin, they would have been without any *kohanim* of their own. Nor is it difficult to conjecture that perhaps the Malabaris had had families of *kohanim* that became extinct and, unlike the Paradesis, they were unable to 'import' new blood. There is simply no conclusive proof, at least on the basis of priestly descent, to deny a group's claim to ancestry from ancient Israel.

FOREIGNERS' IMPRESSIONS OF THE PARADESIS' AND MALABARIS' ORIGINS

Indeed, it is just as frustrating to try to prove a group's ancient Indian ancestry or, for that matter, to determine who first settled in Cranganore. Any early records that may have existed were destroyed by the Portuguese when they burned and sacked Jew Town in 1662. Later, the Paradesis chronicled their people's history, which was disseminated to numerous colonial officials and foreign travellers. As noted, most foreigners heard only the Paradesis' version of Cochin history. Yet there were others like Hillel who not only heard but also believed the Malabaris' version. Rev. J. Henry Lord, an English missionary, upheld the Malabaris' claim to be 'the lineal descendants of the earliest Jewish settlers'.[35] Although he noted that such a view would 'bring him into conflict with many modern writers', Lord listed fourteen reasons to support their claim.[36] One 'modern writer'

Plate 17: Sattu Koder sanctifies the wine at the family Seder.
(Photo by Ellen S. Goldberg, 1987.)

Plate 18: Emulating their Hindu and Muslim neighbours, Cochin's Jews leave their shoes at the door of their house of worship. (Photo by Ellen S. Goldberg, 1987.)

Plate 19: Jacob Cohen reads from the Torah scroll on Shabbat.
(Photo by Ellen S. Goldberg, 1987.)

Plate 20: Women pray upstairs, in the *ezrat nashim* (women's section). (Photo by Ellen S. Goldberg, 1987.)

Plate 21: Elias Hai Elias of Ernakulam holds a traditional bridegroom's vest. (Photo by Ellen S. Goldberg, 1987.)

Plate 22: Bride Glennis Simon in the Cochin Synagogue.
(Photo courtesy of Esther 'Pearlie' Simon.)

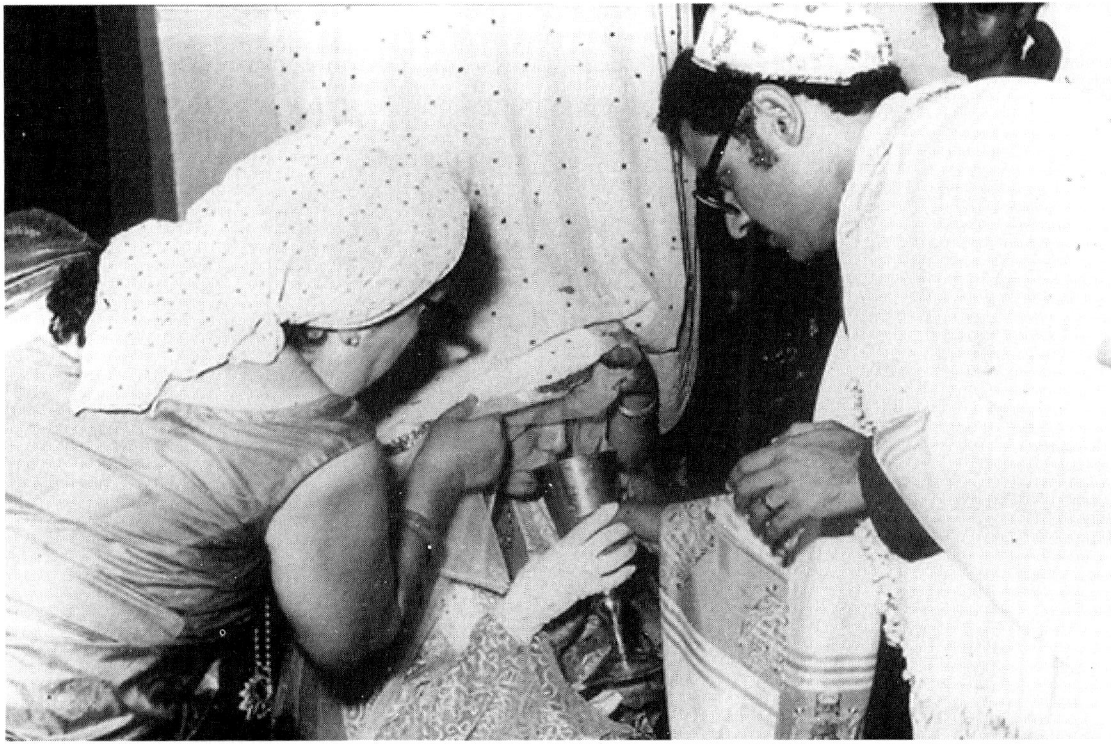

Plate 23: Sarah Cohen lifts the Cochin veil from Glennis Simon as she drinks from the Synagogue's gold wine cup, offered by bridegroom Leslie Salem. (Photo courtesy of Esther 'Pearlie' Simon.)

Plate 24: Cochin women safeguard their *ketubot* (wedding contracts) in silver holders, like this one displayed by Malkah 'Queenie' Hallegua. (Photo by Ellen S. Goldberg, 1987.)

Plate 25: A *milah* (circumcision) celebration in the Salem household. Baby Nathan Hertzman was in Toronto, but celebrations were held in Cochin nevertheless. (Photo by Ellen S. Goldberg, 1987.)

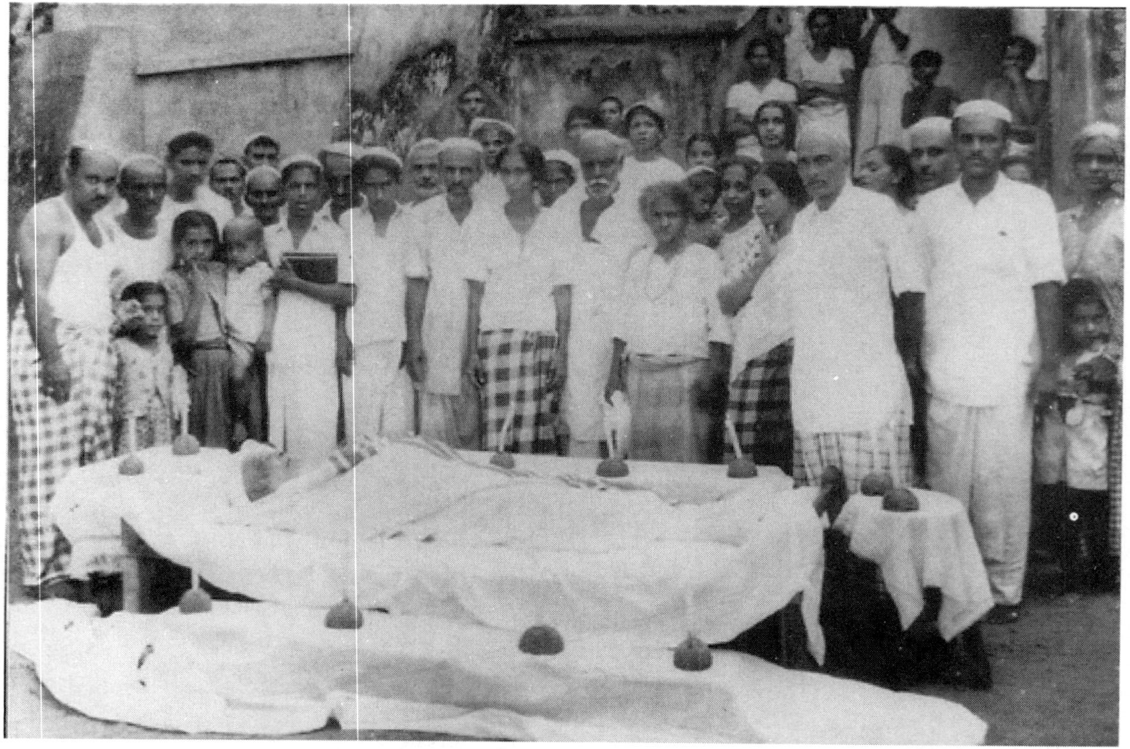

Plate 26: A funeral in the rural village of Chendamangalam. (Photo courtesy of P.A. Aron.)

Plate 27: Avraham Barak Salem. (Photo courtesy of Prem Doss S. Yehudi.)

Plate 28: Avraham Barak Salem (r.) meets with President Yitzhak Ben-Zvi in Jerusalem in 1953. Salem was sent to Israel on a mission to facilitate the emigration of the Malabari Jews. (Photo courtesy of Raymond Salem.)

Plate 29: Avraham Barak Salem in the Cochin Synagogue in 1964 on Simhat Torah. Ephraim Roby is in the background. (Photo courtesy of Raymond Salem.)

Plate 30: The wedding that caused a minor revolution. Balfour Salem and Seema 'Baby' Koder were married in Bombay in 1950. (Photo courtesy of Raymond Salem.)

Plate 31:Torah scrolls from Cochin in the Ark at the Cochini style Synagogue near Beersheva in Israel. (Photo by Ellen S. Goldberg, 1987.)

who dismissed most of Lord's argument as 'irrelevant or factually inaccurate' is Mandelbaum; yet he conceded that 'two do bear some weight'.[37] One was that the smaller Cochin group was called, as was its synagogue until very recently, *Paradesi*, which certainly suggests that it was not the first group to settle in India. Another argument was that the Kochangadi Synagogue, built in 1344 and the oldest synagogue in Cochin, was used solely by the Malabari Jews, indicating that at the very least the Malabaris preceded the Paradesis in Cochin. In addition to these two arguments, Mandelbaum accepted that a third argument of Lord's is also worthy of consideration. The Malabari Jews in Cochin and Ernakulam built two synagogues respectively, both of which were called Kadavumbagham, or 'Riverside', and Thekumbagham, or 'Southside'. Lord argued that the names referred to the positions of two earlier synagogues in Cranganore, names only the Malabaris continued to use, which was 'another indication that the . . . (Malabari) Jews were at Cranganore, and that the . . . (Paradesi) Jews were not.'[38]

Claudius Buchanan, a missionary who stayed in Cochin from November 1806 to February 1807, and again visited in January 1808, divided the Jews into two classes: the 'Jerusalem or White Jews' and the 'Ancient or Black Jews'.[39] Of the latter he wrote, 'It is only necessary to look at the countenance of the Black Jews to be satisfied that their ancestors must have arrived in India many ages before the White Jews.'[40] However, he assigned the epithet 'Jerusalem Jews' to the Paradesis, implying that regarding the matter of 'pure' Jewish lineage, they and not the Malabaris were the ones with *yichus*. He further described the Malabaris thus:

> Their Hindoo complexion, and their very imperfect resemblance to the European Jews, indicate that they have been detached from the parent stock in Judea many ages before the Jews in the West; and that there have been intermarriages with families not Israelitish. I had heard that those tribes, which had passed the Indus, have assimilated so much to the customs and habits of the countries in which they live, that they may be sometimes seen by a traveller, without being recognized as Jews. In the interior towns of Malabar, I was not always able to distinguish the Jew from the Hindoo. . . . The white Jews look upon the Black Jews as an inferior race, and as not of a *pure* caste; which plainly demonstrates that they do not spring from a common stock in India.[41]

It is, indeed, curious that almost twenty years later, Hillel reported that the Malabaris were 'of somewhat darker complexion than the white (Paradesi) Jews, yet they are not of the colour of the natives of the country or of persons descended from Indian slaves'.[42]

COLOUR AS A DETERMINANT OF JEWISH 'SUBSTANCE'

No one can deny that skin colour played some role in determining whether one had Jewish 'substance', or blood.

It was the Portuguese who in the late fifteenth century first introduced the term *casta*—meaning breed, race or lineage—to describe the complex social stratification they found in India.[43] During their rule, the colonists developed numerous racial distinctions among themselves and others. For example, at the top of their racial hierarchy were *brancos*, or 'pure' whites: those Portuguese who were born in their homeland and not in India.[44] A notch below that coveted group were Portuguese who had been born in India; despite both their parents having been born in Portugal, they were not considered *brancos*. This multi-tiered social stratification, which dictated every area of public policy, was elaborate and extended to all Portuguese subjects, colonists and indigenous peoples.

When de Paiva arrived in Cochin to conduct a census of the community, he indicated before each Paradesi household whether or not it was *branco* by inserting a 'B' before the family name. However his interpretation of what constituted *branco* differed from the earlier Portuguese definition. Three families named Aleva, which were second generation Cochinites from Aleppo, Syria, were not *branco*. Yet the *chazzan* (cantor), whose great-grandfather came from Aleppo, was *branco*, as were the Zackai and Aaron families, described by de Paiva to be descendants from ancient Cranganore. 'It is reasonable to assume', explained Segal, 'that the term *branco* is here applied to persons whose families had not yet acquired an Indian strain.'[45] But, Segal was quick to point out that all the families de Paiva listed in his census, *branco* or not, evidently were members of the so-called 'white' Jews' synagogue, despite the fact that some were not considered to be 'white'.

Obviously 'whiteness', like beauty, lies in the eye of the beholder. De Paiva himself observed that the Paradesis' 'colour is brown, which is certainly due to the climate, seeing that they are wholly separate from the Malabaris in rank, and consider it a great disgrace to marry them'.[46] If this were the case, then how were these non-*branco* Jews, with 'an Indian strain', allowed to mix, religiously and socially, with Paradesis while the other Jews were inexplicably excluded?

The onslaught of foreign colonization and domination led to a profound change in Indian Jewry. Rather than defining Jewishness solely by religion, as they always had, they adopted new classifications which sometimes were erratic, subjective and based on such factors as one's skin colour or economic situation. It has been reported that some converts who were fair-skinned foreigners and high caste Indians were automatically accepted into the 'white Jews' synagogue, whereas some Jewish émigrés from Yemen 'allegedly were not accepted as "white" Jews because of their darker skin color-complexion being in some cases more important than "substance"'.[47]

Two sets of distinctions were made about the Cochin community; while these systems often overlapped, they were not identical. One was the indigenous distinction between the *meyuchasim*, those with attested Jewish lineage, and the non-*meyuchasim*, converts to Judaism who were, or were descendants of, *meshuchrarim* (manumitted slaves) or *gerim* (proselytes). These divisions, drawn along religious lines, were based on whether one had long-term Jewish lineage or had converted to the faith.

The second distinction, established by European conquerors and immigrants, was no longer defined by whether or not one had ancestry from ancient Israel but, rather, by the colour of one's skin. From the perspective of the Paradesis and most European visitors and scholars, in general the 'white' Jews were the *meyuchasim* whereas any non-'white' or 'black' Jews were defined as *meshuchrarim*. However, as mentioned, there were alleged instances where fair-skinned European converts were accepted as 'white' Jews despite the obvious fact that they did not have Jewish lineage. Similarly, some Yemeni Jews who had proper lineage were considered 'blacks' and were not accepted into the 'white' synagogue. Our view of Cochin Jewish social stratification becomes confused by conflating these two distinct systems of discourse. Keeping them separate, on the other hand, presents a clearer picture, even if Cochin Jews today often blend them.

Although it was the Portuguese who introduced these colour-based distinctions, manifestations of this practice continued among the Cochin community long after the Portuguese had left Malabar's shores. During the reign of the Dutch, the most benign of colonial rules, the Paradesis promulgated a law that their congregation did not recognize as equals children born from unions between 'white' men and any non-'white' women. A 1757 entry in the Paradesi record book stipulated:

> If an Israelite or Ger (convert) marries a woman from the daughters of the Black Jews (Malabaris) or the daughters of the Meshuchrarim, the sons who are born to them go after the mother; but the man, the Israelite or Ger, he stands in the congregation of our community and he has no blemish.[48]

Put another way, a child born to a woman from the Malabari or *meshuchrar* faction and a man from the 'white' congregation—be he a Jew of lineage or an 'acceptable' convert—inherited the mother's 'impure' substance; however, the man's substance, even if he was a convert, had 'no blemish' and remained pure. This particular example illustrates that not only were the Paradesi Jews influenced by foreigners who came to their shores, but also by the neighbouring Indian communities. The idea of a Jewess from a low status group passing on 'impure' substance goes against Jewish law. However, the concept fits neatly into the Hindu scheme of things. This type of arrangement is described by Manu as *anuloma*, the Sanskrit term for hypergamy. Among the Nambudiris, for example, men take as lovers women from the lower Nayar caste—or, to be exact, Nayar women select Nambudiri men. Any offspring of that union inherit the mother's Nayar lineage. Although there are 'allowable sexual relations between (these) high-status men and low-status women, (it) did not lead to acceptance of the children into the father's group, nor to any sort of social or ritual equality'.[49]

Indeed, the Paradesi Jews walked a tightrope, trying to please both high caste Hindus—in particular the Maharaja of Cochin, upon whom they could depend for support in times of trouble—and various colonial powers, which often determined their livelihood. As a result, the 'white' Jews were known to bend their own religious rules when it proved advantageous.

BRITISH COLONIAL INFLUENCE

Although the British did not directly rule Cochin, which was technically under the Maharaja's jurisdiction, they exercised a considerable degree of control over every facet of the princely state, including its people. True, they were not like the Portuguese who unleashed discriminatory, even racist, policies; the British government was far more discreet, first refining these policies, then institutionalizing them. In the guise of egalitarianism, British Protestant missionaries set up English medium schools and promptly set about to convert 'heathens', especially the economically and socially disadvantaged. The Jews of Cochin were no exception. Children from both the Paradesi 'white' and non-'white' factions attended mission schools. Although school teachers and administrators hoped to win over Jews to Christianity, especially the *meshuchrarim* who faced discrimination from their own people, they had few takers. The children of the Malabari Jews, at least during the nineteenth century, never even set foot in the Christian schools, receiving a solely Jewish education from their own teachers.

Indeed, the Jews kept close vigil to ensure that they did not lose their brethren to missionaries, one of whom was transferred because he was so unsuccessful, and another was actually chased out of town for harbouring a family that expressed an interest in conversion. Whether or not it was perceived consciously by the Cochin Jews, most missionaries 'shared with administrators and British entrepreneurs a colonial mentality which limited their reform efforts to breaking down caste distinctions among Indians, whom they had no intention of treating as social equals to themselves'.[50]

British government officials and commercial powers introduced sweeping reform in Kerala's economy. Whereas the Dutch had dominated trade but largely left the governance of other matters in the hands of Indians, the British took charge of everything with money-making potential. Kerala's rich, fertile lands, which had been the inherited property of high caste communities, could be purchased by anyone with money, regardless of religion or caste. Understandably, a good number of low caste Hindus followed the formula for upward mobility: conversion to Christianity, English language education and employment in the newly-created bureaucracy, which earned them places in an equally novel middle class. Breaking with centuries-old tradition, class rather than caste emerged as an increasingly important factor in determining one's status. By the mid-nineteenth century, the British had made slavery illegal. Although on the surface it seemed a humanitarian act, it actually enabled new landowners, especially colonial entrepreneurs, to hire suddenly available cheap labour. As a result, the British 'introduced commercialized agriculture, plantation technology, and eventually joint stock companies to dominate the process of production as well as the export trade'.[51]

Directly affecting the Paradesi Jews was the lucrative international trade business, in which they had always played a major role. They had enjoyed special privileges under the Dutch, and acquired much wealth as agents for the Dutch East India Company. However, British India changed all that. The Jews were no longer the favourites; instead, they were forced to compete with powerful merchants from their own country as well as foreign entrepreneurs. Moreover, following the rapid development by the British of the northern port cities of Bombay and Calcutta, trade was no longer concentrated in Malabar. A change in colonial rule was accompanied by a drastic change in their fortunes, as they lost their privileges and key means of livelihood.

Indeed, the Paradesi Jews' economic decline within a relatively short time was dramatic. In the autumn years of Dutch colonial rule, Moens described the 'white' Jews as 'among the wealthiest and most distinguished merchants'.[52] By contrast, Moens noted that the 'black' Jews lived more modestly, earning their living from agriculture, cattle rearing and as small traders of food items such as butter and poultry.

Almost fifty years later, Hillel described a profound reversal of fortunes. He noted that during the time of the Dutch, the 'white' Jews

> were great and wealthy merchants, but they have since that time sunk weak and are even in a miserable state, living chiefly by the sale of trinkets and furnitures purchased in more fortunate days. They are too proud to work for their livelihood, but spend their time chiefly in making visits . . . But some families still retain their landed property in value from about two thousand to ten thousand rupees.[53]

> Many of the 'black' Jews, on the other hand, are in easy circumstances, and scarcely a poor man is to be found among them. Yasoni, a ship builder, is reputed to be very rich and is in every way a respectable man. . . . Most of them are engaged in mechanical employments. There are no agriculturists among them. Even their garden grounds are cultivated by Hindus.[54]

It had been a long time coming, but the Malabari Jews, most of whom according to officials' and travellers' reports had been at the bottom of the Cochin community's economic ladder for nearly 300 years, were back on the top again. The fortunes of the Paradesi Jews, many of whom had depended upon the good graces of colonial rule and then found themselves out of favour, plummeted and within a half a century, these 'merchant princes' as they were called were reduced to pawning their effects.

British rule was a period of tremendous economic and social upheaval for everyone. Among the Cochin Jews, the worlds of the Paradesi 'whites' and the Malabari 'blacks' had been turned topsy-turvy. No doubt, the 180 degree change in the two groups' economic fortunes was a sore point for the Paradesis, most of whom had dominated business as well as social and religious life of their community since shortly after their arrival in Malabar. This trying period may have exacerbated the already testy feelings the 'white' Jews had for their non-'white' coreligionists, for 'this was a time of increasing hostility between Paradesis and Malabaris, and a serious split within the Paradesi congregation itself'.[55]

During this time in particular, many social issues came to a head in the Cochin community. The Paradesi 'whites', at a low ebb and perhaps to boost their bruised egos, wrote prolifically of their group's history, which often reached grandiose proportions. They portrayed their old rivals, the Malabaris, in anything but a complimentary light—labelling them the offspring of slaves and denying they had *yichus* from either ancient Israel or Cranganore. Not surprisingly, the Malabaris vehemently countered these charges, which they asserted were false, slanderous and hurtful to their people. Ironically, the situation resembled events that had transpired between the two groups' ancestors three centuries ago, when a large, prosperous faction tried to right what they considered a terrible wrong—being branded by a small, impoverished clique of foreign Jews as slaves. Appeals to eminent rabbis abroad had not resolved this issue centuries ago. During this phase of economic hardship for the Paradesis, it only seemed to grow worse as they lashed out at the more prosperous Malabaris with poison pens. For their part, the Malabaris were determined to rid themselves of the hateful 'slave' label that had been attached to them for so long. Around this time we first find documentation by foreigners, such as Hillel and Lord, who not only heard but also supported the views espoused by the Malabari Jews pertaining to their history. As they had done repeatedly, the Malabaris were

asserting their legitimate Jewish descent and also refuting implications of low caste origin within the Indian social system. Indeed, the descendants of their own slaves and converts (called non-*meyuchasim* or *orumaker*) had been given a separate status in the Malabari congregations, paralleling the separation of converts in Christian churches.[56]

THE *MESHUCHRARIM*'S FIGHT FOR RELIGIOUS EQUALITY

The group that seemed most determined to shake off its second class status among Cochin Jewry was the so-called *meshuchrarim*. Although *meshuchrarim* means 'the manumitted ones', a reference to slaves freed by their Jewish masters and converted to Judaism, in fact, the Hebrew word was used loosely by the Paradesi 'whites' to describe any of their fellow synagogue congregants they judged to be non-'white'. This subgroup not only included manumitted slaves, but also their descendants, *yal' dei bayit*, who were the offspring of 'white' men and native servant women, as well as a number of Jews 'of lineage' and converts. This derogatory—and for many factually inaccurate—label stuck, and continued to be used by the 'whites' long after slavery was abolished by the British in the mid-nineteenth century. Unlike the Malabaris, who had seven synagogues to accommodate their people in the 'Jew Town' section of Mattancheri and neighbouring towns and villages, the *meshuchrarim* did not have their own house of worship. Instead, they prayed at the Paradesi Synagogue, in the face of tremendous opposition. Indeed, they resembled the Malabari *orumaker* Jews who were subordinate to the high status *meyuchasim* in every facet of life, including religion. Not only were the Paradesi *meshuchrarim* denied ritual equality—they could not chant certain liturgical hymns, be called to the Torah to recite prayers or read a portion of the Scripture, bury their dead in coffins or, for that matter, in the Paradesi cemetery—they were also prohibited from marrying any members of the 'white' faction. All these prohibitions went against Jewish law. Moreover, they had to suffer the indignity of not being allowed to sit on benches inside the synagogue; they were forced to stand or sit on the floor of the synagogue ante-room, from where they could hear the religious services conducted by the 'whites'. Rabinowitz lamented:

> That . . . the Jews of Cochin could deny full Jewish rights not only to emancipated slaves but even to their descendants, is but one more example, of which we have so many in South Africa, that irrational prejudices take precedence over law and logic and ethics.[57]

Although Jewish apartheid was a long, dark chapter in Cochin history, its comparison to South Africa is certainly an overstatement. Yet, one cannot help but draw certain parallels. The 'whites' dictated every aspect of life in Cochin, even though at one point they constituted less that one-third of the Paradesi congregation, the balance being non-'white'.[58] Whenever 'white' ruled powers were challenged, the maharaja or colonial officials intervened on behalf of the 'whites'.[59]

With the *meshuchrarim* suffering such injustices, we may logically ask why they did not protest the action of the 'whites'. They did. Repeated efforts were made to change discriminatory ritual practices in the Paradesi Synagogue, but to no avail. In fact, a number of foreign Jews who had heard about or witnessed these practices also argued the *meshuchrarim*'s case, but the status quo remained unchanged. By about 1840, many *meshuchrarim* found their lowly status intolerable. Those who had actively protested the religious inequalities were thrown out of the Paradesi Synagogue, whereupon they requested to build a synagogue of their own in Jew Town. When permission was denied them in 1842, the *meshuchrarim* settled for conducting prayer services in a Jew Town home. This, unfortunately, did not settle matters. After a particularly ugly open quarrel between the 'white' and *meshuchrar* factions on Purim, the 'whites' complained to the Diwan, who directed a subordinate to ensure that no prayer services be conducted by the 'group with impurity in the house appropriated for that purpose, and told (them) that they should walk submissively to the 'white' Jews'.[60]

AVO'S STRUGGLE AND LEGACY

This 'group with impurity' was led by a man named Avraham, known as Avo. There is some debate as to Avo's parentage. One version has it that Avo was the son of slaves owned by the prominent landowner Shlomo Hallegua. Yet another version asserts that Avo was a *yeled bayit* ('child of the house')—allegedly the son of Shlomo Hallegua and a woman named Hannah. Not much is known about Hannah's background. According to some reports, she was either a native born slave or the descendant of a poor foreign Jewish family. Whatever her origin was, she was not accepted by the 'whites', who branded her a *meshuchrar*. Because of that, the story went, the couple was barred from getting married in the Paradesi Synagogue, so Hallegua arranged a Jewish wedding for himself and his bride at his private estate, Vettacka. The result of that union was a son, Avo, who grew up in the Hallegua household and lived there for years with his mother. During this time, according to a document of manumission, Hannah was freed—appropriately on Passover eve—in 1826, with a stipulation that any sons she bore would be counted in the *minyan*.[61] After Avo was emancipated, it was reported, Hallegua—and in the other version, Avo's *meshuchrar* father—'lavished much money on his son to teach him Torah and wisdom'.[62] Eventually, Hallegua bowed to social pressure and married a Paradesi 'white' woman, with whom he had another son. When Hallegua died, Avo managed Vettacka singlehandedly, since the other son was still a child. Things proceeded smoothly until his alleged half-brother grew up.

> Then he had intended to manage himself all the matters and trades, and to keep the son of the liberated mother (Hannah) away from the house of his inheritance. And the son of the liberated mother was proud to say: 'Am I not your elder brother, for thus my mother told me that your father was my father—and why cannot I also inherit the possessions of the house of our father?'[63]

The Paradesi community became embroiled in the family matter—the 'whites' supporting the younger brother and the *meshuchrarim* siding with the elder brother. Ultimately, the matter was brought before the maharaja, who ruled in favour of the 'white' brother. Not only was Avo denied any inheritance from his later father's estate, but he was also ousted from the only home he had ever known. Later he became embroiled in the biggest fight of his life with the Paradesi 'whites'—not over inheritance rights, but religious rights.

Avo went on to become a leader of the *meshuchrarim*, who agitated for ritual equality in the Paradesi Synagogue. After the Diwan denied Avo's faction permission to build their own synagogue in Jew Town and directed them to 'walk submissively to the "white" Jews', they decided to break off entirely from the congregation. The group shifted to the British territory of Fort Cochin, where they founded their own makeshift synagogue in a large private house. Avo served as a *sofer* (religious scribe) and *shochet* (ritual slaughterer) for the new community. For a number of years they did well, enjoying religious freedom and social acceptance from their non-Jewish neighbours. According to a foreign traveller's account of 1860, many members of the Fort Cochin community were fairly prosperous, even employing gentile servants. One British official noted that the women wore gold jewellery, something he claimed they would not have been allowed to do publicly in Jew Town. By contrast, the Paradesi 'whites' were much lower down on the economic ladder. They were described by another British official as 'miserably poor', with few engaged in any 'regular or lucrative profession'.[64]

However the Fort Cochin community's seemingly idyllic life met with a tragic end: a cholera epidemic wiped out most of them in a matter of days. The few who survived either moved north to work in the new cities of Bombay and Calcutta or returned to Jew Town where they had to pay a fine to the Paradesi Synagogue to be accepted back. What is contradictory and puzzling is the reaction of the Paradesi 'whites' to the departure of the *meshuchrarim*, as well as their ultimate fate. Rather than being pleased that they had finally left, the 'whites' viewed the act as a form of blasphemous rebellion. Reinman wrote about the episode. Although he sympathized with the *meshuchrarim*'s quest for religious equality, he nevertheless believed that the breakaway faction was in the wrong for abandoning the congregation and had to pay the ultimate price for its unseemly act.

> God punished the sin of the *meshuchrarim* who were disloyal and withdrew from the synagogue of the White Jews and desecrated its holiness . . . almost all of the *meshuchrarim* died with the plague and epidemic . . . and many who remained became mad and got out of hand. The remainder of the refugees turned to the White Jews, and paid a fine to the synagogue to accept them, as before. The *meshuchrar* Avvo who wrote the Sefer Torah died naked and for want of everything, and his only son went out of his mind. From this case, we are able to observe the sanctity of the house of prayer of Jews, even if justice was with the *meshuchrarim*.[65]

Despite—or perhaps because of—their having survived such a terrible human tragedy, the few *meshuchrarim* who returned to Jew Town refused to let their spirits die. They continued to fight for their religious rights in the Paradesi Synagogue, where nothing had changed since they left. In 1882, they petitioned the Diwan to allow them to worship in a private house in Jew Town. They even enlisted the help of David Sassoon, the Bombay business magnate, who wrote a letter on their behalf to the British Resident. Again, their appeal was rejected.

During this period, word had spread about the discriminatory religious practices of the 'whites' toward the *meshuchrarim*—not only in Cochin, but also in Calcutta and Bombay where a number of them had resettled and subsequently worshipped in Baghdadi synagogues which followed customs similar to the Paradesis—that rabbinical emissaries from Jerusalem came to India to rectify the situation. It was a case of *dejà vu.* As two of his predecessors had advised the Cochin community three centuries earlier, the Chief Rabbi of Jerusalem, Rabbi Phanizel, ruled in 1882 that the *meshuchrarim* should enjoy full religious privileges, provided they underwent *t'vilah*. As their ancestors had done in the past, the Paradesi 'whites' refused to follow the ruling—despite an emissary actually visiting Cochin to argue the case. The *meshuchrarim* were back to square one.

A.B. SALEM, THE 'JEWISH GANDHI'

However, the next generation brought about dramatic changes in the *meshuchrarim*'s status. Most of these changes were embodied in one man who, fittingly, was the grandson and namesake of Avo: Abraham Barak Salem. Born into a poor family in 1882, A.B. was the first university graduate among the *meshuchrarim*. He held a degree in law, but he always seemed more interested in arguing cases for the masses on street corners than in a courtroom. Indeed, so frequent were his public addresses on a hillock in nearby Ernakulam that the spot was dubbed 'Salem *Kunnu*', or 'Salem Hill'. He was a champion of the underdog, striving to improve the lot of the low caste, low paid workers, such as boatmen and rickshaw drivers, by actively working to organize labour unions. Outgoing and charismatic, Salem became involved in politics, co-founding and serving for many years on the Cochin Legislative Assembly. In 1929, as a delegate of the Native Princely States of Cochin and Travancore, he participated in the Congress party's session in the city of Lahore, where Mohandas K. Gandhi launched a struggle for Indian independence from the British.

Salem had the opportunity to meet many prominent Congress leaders all over India, but the one man who made a lasting impression on him was Gandhi. At one time he called 'Moses and Aaron, the Gandhi and Nehru of ancient Egypt', describing both men as tireless 'champions of the cause of the down-trodden'.[66] Impressed by the Mahatma's teachings of non-violent protest, Salem decided to adopt some of his mentor's tactics to further the cause of his own people within the Paradesi community.

In particular, he was impressed by the Mahatma's campaign on behalf of the untouchables' right to use certain roads around the Hindu temple at Vykom in neighbouring Travancore State,[67] which itself drew inspiration from Narayana Guru, a turn-of-the-century, Ezhava (low caste) activist who campaigned against brahmin orthodoxy and religious inequality in Kerala.[68] Emulating the Mahatma, Salem organized various forms of *satyagraha* within the synagogue. Salem, like Gandhi, considered discrimination in the religious sphere the 'most pernicious'[69] of all imposed disabilities. At one time he threatened a fast until death, although his most frequent protest was refusing to sit on the floor of the synagogue's ante-room. Instead, along with his three sons he sat on the steps leading upstairs to the *bimah* where the Torah was read, effectively blocking the way for those who were called to recite the blessings over the Torah who had to climb over them to do so.

Salem never gave up the fight. For decades, he continued to protest the 'white' status quo, which prohibited the *meshuchrarim* from sitting on the synagogue benches, being called to the Torah to recite blessings or read a portion of the Scriptures (They were allowed to read publicly from the Torah only after the third *aliyah* blessing on Simchat Torah and could not be honoured by being called by name), or be buried in the Paradesi cemetery. Frustrated by the reluctance of the 'whites' to change, Salem periodically held full prayer services at his home or attended them at the homes of other non-'whites' who also could not bear the humiliation they were forced to endure in the synagogue. However, Salem's stamina, as well as his lawyer's oratory skills to convincingly argue his group's case to any 'whites' who were willing to listen, finally paid off. Indeed, a number of young Paradesi 'whites' supported Salem and protested their conservative elders' actions. When the young men threatened not to carry the heavy Torah scrolls for the Simchat Torah processions unless something was done to improve the situation, some changes were introduced. A compromise was worked out that was acceptable to both sides: two benches were set up at the back of the synagogue for the *meshuchrarim*. In addition, Mandelbaum reported during his visit to Cochin in 1937, 'the *meshuchrarim* ... may read from the Law on week days, though not on the Sabbath. These allowances still did not satisfy the grandson of the original rebel.'[70] However, in 1942 the latter-day rebel recorded excitedly in his journal:

For the first time in the History of the Paradeshi Synagogue I got the chance, by stressing on the Law of the religious services regarding the reading of Torah, the privilege of reading the Maphtir of this Sabbath and Rosh Hodesh. May God be Praised. . . . May the innovation become the order of the day![71]

By the late 1940s, the group could bury their dead in a separate area in the Paradesi cemetery. In the synagogue, the men could be called to the Torah to read on the Sabbath as well as to recite blessings, although only the fifth of seven *aliyot*. Synagogue rituals were far from being equal—non-'whites' were still barred from holding weddings or circumcisions, which were conducted in private home—yet it was a significant beginning.

BABY AND BALFOUR: THE FIRST PARADESI 'INTERMARRIAGE'

There was no turning back. In 1950, a wedding took place that shocked the sensibilities of the Paradesi conservatives. As fate would have it, one of the parties involved in the controversial marriage was a Salem: Balfour, the middle son of A.B. and Ruth, fell in love with and married a woman from the 'white' faction, Seema 'Baby' Koder. Barred from marrying in the Paradesi Synagogue, the young couple were married in a Baghdadi synagogue in Bombay with the bridegroom's father and older brother, Raymond, as the only family members in attendance. Indeed, even many Cochinim who had resettled in Bombay refused to attend the ceremony. As for the Cochinim at home, most were so outraged by the couple's action that when Rabinowitz visited the community well after the wedding took place, he was consulted as to whether the marriage was actually legal. He held to the original ruling made four centuries ago—marriages between members of these two groups were indeed legal according to Jewish law. The reaction of Baby's parents reflected the sentiments of most members of the Paradesi community: shock and dismay. They refused to answer their daughter's letters from Madras, where she and her husband had settled after Balfour accepted a job as an engineer in the All India Radio. As Yom Kippur neared, they broke their silence and invited Baby home for the holiday. Surely, no one could have foreseen what lay in store.

Before Baby Salem arrived in Cochin, the more conservative faction among the Paradesi 'whites' passed a resolution barring her from the synagogue premises. While they obviously could not stop the marriage, a *fait accompli*, they could express their outrage at this controversial union in a tangible manner, by denying them access to the synagogue. According to them, Baby was no longer a member of the 'white' community—she had forfeited that status when she married Balfour and, like him, was now one of the *meshuchrarim*. Therefore, it was reasoned, she was no longer entitled to her former place upstairs in the 'white' women's section. It was a desperate attempt to stop the inevitable move toward social and religious equality, which Baby and Balfour's marriage represented.

When Baby arrived in Cochin for Yom Kippur, her parents and in-laws advised her to stay away from the synagogue during the services. The congregation, she was told, had even arranged a contingency plan if she did show up: they would move the services to nearby Sassoon Hall, in protest, leaving her alone in the synagogue. Some of the synagogue's Torah scrolls already had been taken to Sassoon Hall in the event of a mass exodus. Baby heeded her family's advice and stayed at home for Yom Kippur. It was a moment, she recalled many years later, when she felt very much alone.[72]

Like her father-in-law, Baby was a fighter. Rather than remain alone while the Sabbath services were being held the next morning, she braved the congregation and walked into the synagogue to take her old seat upstairs in the women's section. The reaction was both swift and hostile. Most of the women as well as the men left the synagogue. One man went upstairs to advise Baby to leave, but he was left speechless by the arguments of the brave young woman. She stayed until she had finished her prayers and then left. From that time onwards, Baby attended services in the Paradesi Synagogue, but no longer in the seat she had always occupied—instead, she sat alone on a bench downstairs in the synagogue's ante-room. Having forcefully made her point that day, she said, was enough.[73]

It is important to note that not everyone in the Paradesi community was against Baby and Balfour. Following their stay in other parts of India because of Balfour's job relocations, the couple decided to settle down in Cochin. Although they were ostracized by some families, a number of people, especially their contemporaries, supported them and made it a point to invite them to their homes. In fact, some 'whites' who refused to attend a social event when they learnt that Baby and Balfour had been invited, were themselves blacklisted for a prolonged period from future Paradesi functions.

GRADUAL CHANGES

In 1957, Balfour's younger brother, Gamliel, also married a Paradesi 'white' woman, Reema Roby. Although Baby and Balfour had broken much ground for the younger couple, they, too, were married in a Baghdadi synagogue in Bombay. Following her marriage to Gamliel, Reema could attend services at the Paradesi Synagogue, but she never went upstairs to her usual seat in the 'white' women's section. 'I'm not a fighter', smiled

Reema Salem, by way of explanation.[74] Like her sister-in-law, from that time onwards she always sat downstairs on a bench in the synagogue's ante-room. Reema made light of her situation, and did not seem particularly perturbed by it. A religious, well liked woman, she joked that she actually preferred being downstairs where she could hear the services, rather than upstairs with the rest of the women who at times were prone to gossip instead of prayer.

Of course, humour often is a way to mask unhappiness. Not surprisingly, there was still bitterness among some non-'white' community members who were subjected to what Raymond called 'Jewish apartheid'. The entire Salem family—whether they were born or married into the clan—were often forced to fight. Gamliel recalled that when he was young, religious discrimination was enforced primarily by members of his parents' generation rather than his own. Disgusted by some of the elder hardliners' behaviour, he boycotted synagogue services for twenty-five years following the completion of his *bar mitzvah* or *bar minyan*. Although he had long since returned to the synagogue, Gamliel admitted that he was not religious. He only attended services on major holidays or, because of the dwindling number of Jews in Cochin, when he was needed for the *minyan*. Gamliel's two sisters, Esther Salem Rao and Malkah Salem Antony, had married 'outside the community'—Esther to a Hindu, Malkah to a Christian—partly because they, too, were fed up with the hurtful attitudes of the Paradesi 'whites'.

The community tended to leave their prejudices at the synagogue. Although the Paradesi 'whites' severely restricted the religious life of the *meshuchrarim*, the two groups interacted socially. In fact, a number of close, lifelong friendships developed between individuals who, under other circumstances, were each other's nemesis. They ate at each other's homes, shared confidences, helped each other in times of illness and financial crisis, enjoyed summer vacations together; in short, they were the best of friends. Yet when it came to synagogue matters, there was an unbridgeable chasm between them. To a Westerner, it seems strange that 'Jewish apartheid' would exist in a religious setting, where people ideally should be on equal terms. When told that any number of American synagogues count blacks as well as whites as full-fledged members, Gamliel, who had spent his university years in the United States, aptly observed: 'I bet it was completely equal in the synagogue, but completely unequal socially—the opposite of Cochin.'[75] It was not possible to argue with him; and it was no less strange or hypocritical to experience the converse.

THE NEXT GENERATION: FINAL BARRIERS ARE TORN DOWN

As for the offspring of these 'mixed' marriages, some ritual barriers were still enforced by conservative, mainly affluent, hardliners. When Baby and Balfour's son Leslie was born, they were clearly told that they could not have the baby circumcised in the synagogue but in Sassoon Hall. The couple was outraged by the decision, insisting that the *brit milah* ceremony be held in a proper house of worship. However, the conservatives refused to yield and Baby and Balfour opted for a Malabari synagogue in Ernakulam. Many Paradesis were appalled that the couple went to the rival community to have the baby circumcised, and only a few attended the ceremony. The vast majority remained behind at Sassoon Hall, and behaved as if nothing out of the ordinary had happened. They held a feast to celebrate the occasion, with the obvious absence of the parents and the child. A few weeks later, however, when the *pidyon haben* (redemption of the firstborn son) ceremony was held in Jew Town, most Paradesis were in attendance. Reema and Gamliel's son, Kenneth, born in 1962, shared the same fate as his cousin. The parents were not granted use of the synagogue for their child's *brit milah*, so they held the ceremony in Sassoon Hall. According to Gamliel, shortly after that any remaining distinctions ended. Like other Paradesi boys between the ages of five and seven, Kenneth read his first Haftarah in the synagogue, and at the age of thirteen celebrated his *bar minyan* with the entire community. Today, all men share the same rights and privileges. The term *meshuchrar* is no longer used or applied in any way, and discrimination against others in the Paradesi congregation belongs to the past.

Each Salem couple also had a daughter, both of whom experienced no problems whatsoever. Linda and Cynthia Salem sat upstairs with their female friends and relatives—except, of course, their mothers who remained downstairs. As Baby recollected in Israel, there was no reason for her daughter Cynthia to join her downstairs since 'she had done nothing wrong, and her rightful place is upstairs' with the other women.[76] No one contested the seating arrangement, reflecting a new sign of the times. Jewish behavioural practice had become more important than Jewish 'substance'. Indeed, the four Salem cousins asserted that they grew up experiencing no discrimination from the Paradesi community members, upon whom they looked with real affection. That affection, in turn, was warmly reciprocated—whether in Cochin or Israel.

Perhaps the most tangible example of equality came in 1978, when Baby and Balfour's son Leslie married Glennis Simon, from a prominent 'white' family, in the Paradesi Synagogue. Not only were there no protests, but also the community came out *en masse* joyously to celebrate the occasion. No doubt, it was an event A.B. Salem, who died in 1967, would have loved to see. The tireless struggle of the 'Jewish Gandhi' had largely contributed to make that a reality. By the time of his death at the age of 85, Salem could take consolation in the fact that the *meshuchrarim* finally enjoyed all the synagogue privileges denied to them for centuries.

Relations with the Malabari Jews improved as the numbers in both communities dwindled. Ever since the Malabari synagogues closed down, the two groups prayed together in the Cochin Synagogue for holidays, and they celebrated one another's weddings or *brit milahs*. Casual visits were not uncommon, but intermarriages between the Paradesis and Malabaris remained unknown.

CONCLUSION

The twentieth century saw profound status changes in the Cochin community, reflecting the vast social, political and economic metamorphoses occurring throughout Kerala and India. On the state and national levels, the powerful status quo—British colonialism and a rigid caste system—were challenged and at least the former ultimately was brought to its knees by a new kind of 'army' that employed Gandhian, non-violent methods as its weaponry.

The impact of education cannot be overestimated. Not only did it alter many people's vision of their world theoretically, but also in a very real, concrete way. Western-style education was increasingly accessible to the masses as never before. Individuals from poorer families, such as A.B. Salem, were for the first time able to obtain university degrees, which opened doors to professional employment and vastly improved their economic conditions. No longer so tied to caste, they were part of India's new emerging middle class with greater economic and social clout. Young Paradesis, from all types of backgrounds, got a taste of this independence and found it a heady experience. The changing, volatile world around them, coupled with the relatively progressive Westernized viewpoints espoused in the universities, had expanded and irrevocable altered their universe. Many of them no longer patiently accepted the restrictive social mores dictated by their elders or, more specifically, the economic elite. It was no coincidence that the young Paradesi 'white' men who threatened not to carry the heavy Torah scrolls for Simchat Torah unless the *meshuchrarim* were granted synagogue rights were the first generation to attend universities on a large scale.

Nevertheless, as influenced as Cochinites were by modern Westernized thought, they were—and still are—very much Indian in their identity. As noted, they carved out a niche for themselves in Kerala's caste system. Typical of an Indian caste, the Jews proliferated into endogamous subcastes, each with its prescribed, exclusionary practices.[77] Indeed, the concept of Jewish 'substance' or 'blood' was defined not only by Judaice law, but also by certain high caste Hindu dictates. Certain community members who were judged to have impure substance were initially barred from prayer services in the Paradesi Synagogue for fear of polluting the house of worship—very much a Hindu phenomenon. Substance was also determined by one's ancestry, both from ancient Israel and India, whether or not one was a convert, and even by the colour of one's skin. Indeed, the Cochinites went well beyond *halakhic* practice, at times even *defying* it by opting for Hindu caste behaviour over standard Jewish law. In so doing, they asserted their identity among non-Jews as well as their own people.

The concept of Jewish substance, based loosely and subjectively on these complex definitions, has given way to shared behavioural practice as the paramount concern. No longer is one's pedigree more important than whether one is observant of Jewish law. This eventual breakdown of differences among the Paradesis has resulted in distinct subcastes, the 'whites' and the so-called *meshuchrarim*, consolidating into a single group.

Due to various factors—be they political, economic, social or demographic—such that a caste's position becomes weaker, subcastes sometimes reaggregate into more viable units.[78] The Cochin Jews are a model case. As Raymond Salem aptly put it, the 'whites' finally acceded to the demands articulated by the oppressed *meshuchrarim* because 'their wings have been cut'.[79]

But for all changes, some Cochinites who were lumped in the *meshuchrar* category still harboured pent-up pain and bitterness from the discrimination they faced. One elder of Jew Town was convinced that the irrational, hurtful behaviour of the 'whites' led to a curse on the entire Cochin community. As 'proof', he pointed to the fact that there were a number of unmarried people, those who married were either childless or had small families, some households have a history of mental illness and, in more recent times, immigration to Israel led to Jew Town's demise. A devout Jew who often quoted the Bible forcefully when making a point in conversation, he said that there was 'no other explanation'—both for the terrible injustices to which innocent people were subjected for centuries as well as the recent decimation of a once-illustrious community. 'These people are cursed for what they did', he asserted. 'It is this curse that explains the death of this Jew Town community.'[80]

Let the reader decide.

NOTES

1. Dumont, *Homo Hierarchicus*, p. 191.
2. Beck, *Peasant Society in Konku*, p. xiv.
3. On Bene Israel caste formations, see Roland, *Jews in British India*, p. 4, cf. Isenberg, *India's Bene Israel*, pp. 98-111.
4. Mandelbaum, 'The Jewish Way of Life in Cochin', p. 447.
5. Gandhi, *Non-Violent Resistance*, pp. 177-203.
6. Daniel, *Fluid Signs*, pp. 179-81.
7. Johnson, '"Our Community" in Two Worlds', pp. 109-10.
8. Beck, *Peasant Society in Konku*, p. xvi.
9. Johnson, '"Our Community" in Two Worlds', p. 136.
10. Segal, 'White and Black Jews at Cochin', p. 229.
11. Beck, *Peasant Society in Konku*, p. 39.
12. Segal, 'White and Black Jews at Cochin', pp. 230-1. From a French translation of the original Hebrew by Marx, 'Contributions a l'Histoire des Juifs de Cochin', pp. 293-6.
13. Segal, 'White and Black Jews at Cochin', pp. 238-9.
14. Mandelbaum, 'Social Stratification among the Jews of Cochin in India and in Israel', p. 173.
15. Mandelbaum, 'Social Stratification among the Jews of Cochin', p. 200.
16. Roland, *Jews in British India*, pp. 65-9.
17. Mandelbaum, 'The Jewish Way of Life in Cochin', p. 446.
18. Mandelbaum, 'Social Stratification among the Jews of Cochin', p. 177.
19. Fischel, *Unknown Jews in Unknown Lands*, p. 114.
20. Johnson, '"Our Community" in Two Worlds', p. 136.
21. Fischel, 'The Jewish Way of Life in Cochin', p. 443.
22. See Rahabi, 'Letter of 1768'; Hallegua, 'Letter of 1895'; Kohut, 'Correspondence between the Jews of Malabar and New York'; Roby, *Divrei Y'mei HaYehudim b'Cogin*.
23. Johnson, '"Our Community" in Two Worlds', p. 135.
24. Hallegua, 'Letter of 1895', pp. 16, 23.
25. I.S. Hallegua, personal communication, 1987.
26. Cited by Johnson, '"Our Community" in Two Worlds', pp. 136-7.
27. Sarah Cohen, 1 January 1987.
28. Mandelbaum, 'Social Stratification among the Jews of Cochin', p. 200.
29. Subrahmanyam, *The Political Economy of Commerce*, p. 117.
30. Stritzower, *Exotic Jewish Communities*, pp. 93-4.
31. Fischel, *Unknown Jews in Unknown Lands*, p. 114.

32. Mandelbaum, 'Social Stratification among the Jews of Cochin', pp. 179-80.
33. Mandelbaum, 'The Jewish Way of Life in Cochin', p. 450.
34. Ibid., pp. 436-7.
35. Lord, *The Jews of India and the Far East*, p. 77.
36. Ibid.
37. Mandelbaum, 'The Jewish Way of Life in Cochin', p. 445.
38. Lord, *The Jews of India and the Far East*, p. 87.
39. Buchanan, *The Works of the Revered Claudius Buchanan, LL. D., Comprising this Christian Researches in Asia: with Notices of the Translation of the Scriptures into the Oriented Languages*, p. 251.
40. Ibid.
41. Buchanan, *The Works of the Revered Claudius Buchanan*, . . . pp. 255-6.
42. Fischel, *Unknown Jews in Unknown Lands*, p. 114.
43. Anonymous, 'Caste', p. 3.
44. Similarly, 'Fair skin is a way of Knanaya proclaim that they are not of Kerala but come from another place where skins are fairer, such as the Near East . . . . The Knanaya also believe that their Near Eastern origin is evident in their peculiar assemblage of facial features'. Swiderski, *Blood Weddings*, p. 122.
45. Segal, 'White and Black Jews at Cochin', pp. 236-7.
46. Ibid., p. 237.
47. Johnson, '"Our Community" in Two Worlds', p. 117.
48. Sarphati, *Piqas* (Record Book) of the Paradesi Synagogue, pp. 82-3; cited by Johnson, '"Our Community" in Two Worlds', pp. 120-1.
49. Johnson, '"Our Community" in Two Worlds', p. 65. While this practice apparently reflects the Malayali *anuloma* marriage pattern, the reverse *pratiloma* pattern seems not have been adopted.
50. Johnson, '"Our Community" in Two Worlds', p. 66.
51. Ibid., p. 54.
52. Moens, *Memorandum on the Administration of the Coast of Malabar*, p. 198.
53. Fischel, *Unknown Jews in Unknown Lands*, p. 113.
54. Fischel, *Unknown Jews in Unknown Lands*, p. 114.
55. Johnson, '" Our Community" in Two Worlds', p. 58.
56. Ibid., p. 59.
57. Rabinowitz, *Far East Mission*, pp. 112-13.
58. Sarphati, *Piqas*, p. 83; cited by Johnson, "Our Community" in Two Worlds', pp. 120-1.
59. When similar cases were brought by Bene Israel before the British court in Rangoon the matter was decided in the aggrieved plaintiffs' favour. Joan Roland, personal communication, 1991.
60. Johnson, " Our Community" in Two Worlds', p. 61.
61. Rabinowitz, *Far East Mission*, p. 112.
62. Reinman, 'Masa'oth Shlomo b'Kogin', p. 20.

63. Sapir, 'HaYehudim b'Kogin', p. 29.
64. Johnson, '"Our Community" in Two Worlds', p. 62.
65. Reinman, 'Masa'oth Shlomo b'Kogin', p. 37.
66. Salem, *Eternal Light or Jewtown Synagogue*, p. 41.
67. Gandhi, *Non-Violent Resistance*, pp. 177-203.
68. Menon, 'The Namboodiris: Traumatic Decline', p. 92.
69. Gandhi, *Non-Violent Resistance*, p. 185.
70. Mandelbaum, 'The Jewish Way of Life in Cochin', p. 449.
71. Quoted by Johnson, '"Our Community" in Two Worlds', pp. 85-6.
72. Baby Salem, June 1987.
73. Ibid.
74. Reema Salem, April 1987.
75. Gamliel Salem, April 1987.
76. Baby Salem, June 1987.
77. Dumont, *Homo Hierarchicus*, p. 34.
78. It seems that when a caste fails to maintain a 'critical mass' in any given location, its subcastes tend to reaggregate into a larger unit. Such was the case for the Jews in Cochin, but the same phenomenon can be observed among smaller immigrant Indian communities in America. See Katz, 'Tampa Bay's Asian-Origin Religious Communities'.
79. Raymond Salem, 15 April 1987.
80. Ibid., 28 October 1986 and 16 April 1987.

CHAPTER 7

Some Speculations about Caste, Jewish Survival and Hindu Tolerance

The first thing the Cochin Jews want an outsider to know about themselves is the respect, affection and privilege they have enjoyed during their 2,000 years in India. 'The word antisemitism', said Sattu Koder with pride, 'just doesn't exist in our Indian dictionary'.[1] Indeed, the word 'tolerance' does not describe India's attitude toward its Jewish population. Approaching this subject from a Jewish point of view, the uniqueness of a Jewish community so beloved by its neighbours demands an explanation.

To view the matter very broadly, Jews have lived in three general types of environments: hostile, friendly-but-assimilating and friendly-and-not-assimilating.

Living in a hostile culture has been the most common experience of the Jews, a series of experiences which has shaped their consciousness. The paradigm of a hostile culture has been European Christendom, and one need not catalogue such viciousness—it is well known. Muslim countries, while markedly less hostile than Christian ones, have—with rare and notable exceptions—kept Jews in the inferior and despised position of a *dhimmi*, a 'protected' minority. In such cultures, Jewish solidarity was ensured by the host's hostility. This type of experience has been the rule, and it has shaped scholarly and popular notions about Jewish identity being essentially defensive in nature.

The second type of host culture constitutes those nations which welcomed Jews and treated them kindly, but which offered them assimilation into their culture. During periods of liberalism, some European nations have treated Jews in this way, but the paradigm is China. Jews lived for nearly 1,000 years in several communities in the Chinese Middle Kingdom, experiencing neither persecution nor discrimination.[2] Many Jews attained high positions at the court of the Mandarin Emperor in Beijing. But it is here that the key to the demise of Chinese Jewry lies.

As is well known, China was the first civilization to evolve a meritocracy. Access to high positions was possible by competitive civil service examinations, and Jews pursued this course avidly. These examinations were based on Confucian classical texts, and success demanded a high degree of proficiency and acculturation. Perhaps it was too much to expect of a Jew to master both Jewish and Confucian learning, and since it was the latter which ensured success, the former was sacrificed.

The Jews of China were simply assimilated out of communal existence. While there remain of few Chinese with vague recollections of their Jewish ancestry and even a handful who have recently made efforts to return, the last Chinese Jewish community became effectively extinct more than 100 years ago.

Some are of the opinion that the Jewish experience in America most closely resembles that of China. Despite periodic anti-Semitic episodes, and a constant anti-Semitism from the far right, for the most part America has been hospitable to Jews. However, success for the American Jew has been as America defines it. It requires mastery on two fronts: first, of a highly specialized and complex technical body of Jewish knowledge; and second, of the norms of behaviour and interaction dictated by a Christian world. As in the case of China, it is too much to expect the Jew to master his or her own culture's learning and mores and those of a secular culture as well. Then again, perhaps by replacing the 'melting pot' with the 'cultural mosaic' model, American culture is becoming more acculturationist and less assimilationist. Many American Jews hope so, indicating the vice-presidential candidacy of Senator Joseph Lieberman, an observant Jew, as a watershed event.

The third type of host culture is, like China and America, hospitable, but this type is not assimilationist. This is India, were assimilation is not an option. As has been argued earlier, there is no overarching, pan-Indian Hindu religion or culture into which to assimilate. Rather, India is a complex system of localized and caste-bound cultures which interact through the principle of hierarchy—at least this has been the case in traditional India; as a modern nation, India poses new issues of secular cultural hegemony, as the contemporary rise of 'traditionalist' political parties amply demonstrates. Hindu 'tolerance' (a term which does not do justice to the actual experience of Jews in India) is the antithesis of the modern meanings of the term. It does not posit either a universal culture, a universal religion or a universal human nature to which all must conform. Rather, its hierarchical nature creates the societal space for human diversity in its extreme.[3]

The Jews' judicious borrowing from Hindu symbol and ritual complexes, the process which resulted in the elaborate and exotic *minhagim* of Cochin, enable them to establish and celebrate a fully integrated Indian-Jewish identity. These borrowings or 'shared features' between local Hinduism and Cochin Judaism

> involved much more than superficial borrowings or 'accretions' from local . . . religions. The sharing of such all-pervading themes and principles of worship transcended divisions of community or confessional attachment, and it provided a powerful focus for . . . (Kerala's Christians, Muslims and Jews) who began to form into cohesive caste groups contending over tokens of ritual 'honor' and precedence.[4]

Living among Hindus who respected them, Indian Jews foregrounded threads of tolerance from Jewish tradition. The polemical insistence upon superiority proclaimed by some Jews who endured persecution from Christians and Muslims was more or less unknown in India.[5]

The view that other religions are complete paths in themselves was the assumption of most Indian Jews. Assuming the basic moral principles of the seven Noahide commandments symbolized by the rainbow,[6] when a gentile practises religion sincerely, he or she 'fulfills the purpose of . . . creation and receives a share of the World to Come (*olam ha-ba*), the blessed spiritual world of the righteous.'[7]

Living among Hindus, Jews discovered a virtually identical spirit in the *Atri Samhita*, a Hindu sacred text on society and kingship. According to it, not only should one adhere to one's own religion, but a king's duties also included encouraging his subjects to avoid 'lusting' after others' faiths: 'The king who punishes them who, renouncing their own religion (*dharma*), follow another's, becomes glorified in the celestial region. By following his own religion even a Shudra (low-caste Hindu) enjoys the celestial region. Another's religion should be renounced like the most beautiful wife of another person.'[8] Based on field observations as well as such texts, Dumont succinctly observed:

> People have often noted what has been called the tolerance of Indians, or Hindus. It is easy to see what this feature corresponds to in social life. Many castes, who may differ in their customs and habits, live side by side, agreed on the code which ranks them and separates them. *They will assign a rank, where we in the West would approve or exclude*. It may be supposed that the more loosely society is integrated, the greater is the permitted variation, but what happens here is more radical. In the hierarchical scheme a group's acknowledged differentness whereby it is contrasted with other groups becomes the very principle whereby it is integrated into society.[9]

NOTES

1. Sattu Koder, March 1984.
2. See Pollak, *Mandarins, Jews, and Missionaries.*
3. Recently, there has been a trend among some South Asianists to debunk or 'deconstruct' certain Hindu self-perceptions, especially their cherished claim that Indian culture is especially tolerant. Wilhelm Halbfass argued that India is 'inclusive' rather than 'tolerant', defining inclusivism as 'a subordinating identification of the other, the foreign, with parts or preliminary stages of one's own sphere' (Halbfass, *India and Europe*, p. 411) a view generally wedded to a non-dualist metaphysic and 'typically, even exclusively Indian' (Halbfass, *India and Europe*, p. 415). However, when Christian thinkers attempt to 'include' other religions 'as preliminary stages, unfulfilled promises, implicit steps towards the fullness of Christian revelation', Halbfass claimed this 'is clearly different from its Indian counterpart by virtue of its historical or "kerygmatic" orientation', although he does not say why or how this difference might be significant. In what appears to be a circular argument, he claimed that genuine tolerance 'is inseparable from modern European secularism, from the separation of church and state . . . from the ideas of personal freedom and human rights' (Halbfass, *India and Europe*, p. 410). In other words, Halbfass argued that tolerance could only be conceived as it pertains to an individual who possesses freedoms and rights, and that only Europeans have conceived of an individual in that way. Having defined matters so neatly, Halbfass concluded that the tolerance claimed by modern Hindus, Swami Vivekananda in particular, is really inclusivism and not tolerance.

   Of course, the European secular version of tolerance which 'whishes to destroy (the concrete, the particular, the individual) . . . and leave nothing . . . but . . . the abstract and universal subject of rights of man and the rights of the citizen' (Sartre, *Anti-Semite and Jew*, p. 57) is not identical to classical Indian tolerance, which embraces the concrete person as a member of a particular community. It is as a member of a community that one is integrated within classical Indian society, and one is so integrated on the basis of hierarchy and exchanges.

   Halbfass was quite correct in his textual argument that the neo-Vedantin's concept of tolerance could not be supported on the basis of the texts of classical Advaita Vedanta, the eighth century philosophy of Adi Shankaracharya, whom the neo-Vedantins claim to follow (Halbfass, *Tradition and Reflection*, pp. 55-9). However, Shankaracharya was writing from a specifically brahmin point of view which was under serious challenge from Buddhists at the time, one which elevated his own community at the expense of its rivals. One should not assume that Shankaracharya was speaking for all of India, or that he could.

   The experience of the Cochin Jews has nothing to do with the modern, urban forms of Hinduism which Halbfass criticized. The Cochinites lived for millennia in the traditional Hindu society of Kerala, and we would argue that a minority itself is the best arbiter of a society's claim of toleration of them. It seems pointless to debate whether or not Indian civilization is inherently tolerant on philological or philosophical grounds, or how Indian tolerance based on Emperor Ashoka Maurya's third century BCE multireligious model compares with modern European secularism, or whether classical Indian Vedanta is compatible with modern Hinduism's reading of it, or whether Mughal Emperor Akbar was 'inclusive' or not, or whether Indian tolerance was borne of the marketplace rather than high-minded ethical ideals (Narayanan, *Cultural Symbiosis in Kerala*, p. 5). Rather, our attention has been directed towards describing and analysing the mechanisms by which Indian Jews became so well integrated into their milieu. Discussions about whether or not Hindu civilization is tolerant ought include the claims of India's 'foreign' minority religious communities—Jews, Christians, Muslims and Zoroastrians—and all their narratives emphasize the hospitality of their Hindu hosts.

4. Bayly, *Saints, Goddesses and Kings*, p. 455.
5. See, for example, Judah Halevy, *The Kuzari*, p. 52, who disparaged Hinduism as a religion of 'idols, talismans, and witchcraft . . . (with) only . . . a few books . . . written to mislead the weak-minded.'
6. Gen. 9: 1-17.
7. Clorfene and Rogalsky, *The Path of the Righteous Gentile*, p. 4.
8. *Atri Samhita* I: 17-18; tr. Dutta, *The Dharma Shastra*, pp. 287-8. The idea that one should follow one's own religious traditions is not confined to the brahmanical version of Hinduism embodied in the *Atri Samhita*; it finds expression in virtually all sects, including Bhagavata Hinduism. This sect, popular among Kerala's Nayar maharajas, is not caste-oriented. Its central text, the *Bhagavata Purana*, poetically admonished against individual religious innovation during this degenerate age of *Kaliyuga*:

   Like a bee, a wise man takes the essence from everything. Expedients (religious teachings or techniques) for the accomplishment of the welfare of men in this world as well as in the next, have been discovered and employed by sages who have realized the truth. Anyone belonging to the later periods, who properly and with faith adopts the measures demonstrated by the ancients, easily accomplishes his objectives. Even if a learned person, disregarding those expedients adopted and tested successfully by the ancients, tries to accomplish those objectives in his own (independent) ways, his objectives are never realized, despite his frequent efforts and experiments. (*Bhagavata Purana* IV.18.2-5)
9. Dumont, *Homo Hierarchicus*, p. 191. Emphasis added.

CHAPTER 8

Why Did They Leave India?

It is our sincere ambition,
To be freed from foreign domination.
Palestine is our inspiration,
To build our home, a Jewish nation.
Chorus:
For God is always on our side,
He is our sincere guide,
Then why should we fear,
When we have Him near,
In days of sorrow and darkness.

We have passed through darker situation,
And won for us thrilling admiration.
Jerusalem is our destination.
The home and hope of our salvation. (*Repeat Chorus*)

Now we make an open declaration
To every anti-Jewish nation,
All their baseless, ruthless persecution
Will never bring our ruination. (*Repeat Chorus*)[1]

Growing up in Cochin, Cecil Koder knew of no wars, no persecution, no fear as a Jew living among millions of Hindus, Muslims and Christians. At the time he penned these lines in the 1930s, Koder could not have known—nor could anyone have imagined—the terrible fate that awaited his European brethren. The poem was likely inspired by religious fervour and Zionist teachings, both of which point to what was then known as Palestine as the Jews' true 'home and hope'. Noble as those sentiments are, not everyone in 'Little Jerusalem', as Jew Town is fondly called, shared Koder's sentiments. In an ironic twist of fate, they saw Zionist idealism, and not 'ruthless persecution', bring about the 'ruination' of their proud diaspora community.

The dismantling of Cochin's Jewish community began in the nineteenth century under British rule. Lured by social and economic prospects in such rapidly industrializing cities as Bombay, Calcutta and Rangoon, a number of families moved north where they assimilated into other Indian Jewish settlements. While their migration did not significantly deplete the community's population, it did drain off some of its vitality.

Much more devastating to Cochin Jewry's numbers was the creation of the state of Israel in 1948. Emigration to Israel, which began with a few families in 1948 and accelerated during the early to mid-1950s, took its toll. Of the 1,935 Cochin Jews reported in 1941, only about 100 remained twenty years later.[2] A second mass exodus in the 1970s and early 1980s was so great that it left behind a profound void. Today, Cochin's Jewish population—which includes the communities of Cochin, Ernakulam and Parur (there are no Jews in Mala and Chendamangalam)—is reduced to less than 50 people. Of that small number, most are 60 years or older. The time is not too far when there will be no Jews left at all.

The signs are everywhere. For the first time in its long history, Cochin's Paradesi Synagogue was unable to get a *minyan* one Sabbath in July 1987. In North Parur, only one Jewish family remained, but its elderly matriarch, Esther Simon, tenaciously kept the synagogue's *ner tamid* (eternal light) burning. The two synagogues in Ernakulam had long been abandoned as places of worship; although the buildings were in the hands of local Jews, one housed a horticulture business and the other a poultry farm.

The obvious question is: Why did the Jews leave Cochin? Why did they abandon a land where they were accepted and allowed to live happily for centuries? Much like the individuals who departed, the answers are numerous and complex.

As has been suggested, the Biblical prophecy to return to Eretz Yisrael to help build a Jewish homeland was the motivation for many to leave. Indeed, Zionist groups began to mushroom in villages and cities all over India, including Cochin, around the turn of the century. Many Cochin Jews had an undaunted commitment to make *aliyah* (immigrate) to the Promised Land. Declared a group of Malabaris in the 1950s: 'When we heard of the establishment of the State of Israel, we decided to go up and rebuild the land of our forefathers. Many have already gone, and others are waiting for their turn.'[3]

Not so lofty, but no less compelling a reason for emigration, was better economic prospects. Two general groups fell into this category: the poor who had little to lose, and the once-wealthy who had lost much of what they possessed. Among the latter group were those who had made their fortunes through import trade ventures, only to see their businesses fold when the national government, soon after independence in 1947, proscribed the import of luxury goods. It was also during this period that the government took over the regional ferry service, which had been a privately-run Jewish concern. Beginning in 1957, vast tracts of land owned by Jewish families were seized and redistributed among the general population by Kerala's Communist government. This was followed in 1979 by the nationalization of the Jewish-run electric company. Fortunes fell, generations-old family businesses disappeared, and with their key means of livelihood gone, Jews who owned or were employed by these companies also sought new economic opportunities.

Others left India because of the changing political climate. There were no pogroms to threaten them like the systematic tyranny that plagued European Jews at times of political upheaval. Nor did they face sectarian violence, a common occurrence among religious and ethnic groups seemingly everywhere today. It was more a case of the Cochin Jews becoming invisible, losing certain privileges after being swallowed up in a sea of humanity—a disenfranchisement many minorities felt when India became a majority-rule nation.

Another segment sought the excitement of a new life. In India, Jews, like their countrymen, had the security—and monotony—of carrying on the traditions and livelihoods of their elders. Israel was an unknown world where they could start anew, which particularly appealed to a number of pioneering young people.

On a more mundane but no less ardent level were the myriad personal reasons Jews had to leave. The respectability of emigrating to Israel masked what could actually be an escape from family squabbles, a business fallen on hard times, or the lack of eligible marriage partners.

Finally, there was the mysterious curse, mentioned by a number of Cochin's elders, which they believed was responsible for the modern-day exodus. With no experience of persecution or ill-will, they argued, what other fathomable excuse could there be for the Jews' departure from a land they loved? As Raymond Salem noted solemnly, it could only be a terrible destiny, unshakable and irreversible, that 'explains' the death of Jew Town, divine retribution for the sin of discrimination.

Our discussion will focus on the religious aspects of the migration of the Jews from Cochin to Israel; the economic and political aspects are discussed in the companion volume, *A Jewish King at Shingly*.

JOINING THE INGATHERING OF THE EXILES

The Zionist movement created by you has put your coreligionists throughout India into great excitement... (e)specially after your interview with the Sultan of Turkey.... [Y]ou can draw (an) enormous sum from India in aid of your movement if you inform the Jews of India (of) your aim. Therefore it will be of great importance if you authorize the leading Jews of India . . . to collect money for your valuable aim and (at) the same time to authorize me to collect from the 7 congregations of Cochin, Ernakulam, Paroor, Shenomangalam and Mala of Malabar Coaste. Wishing you Godspeed and every Success.[4]

So wrote N. E. Roby, a leading member of Cochin's Paradesi community, to Theodor Herzl in Vienna, on 15 October 1901. Excited by Herzl's meeting on 17 May 1901 with Ottoman Sultan Abdul Hamid II in Constantinople, Roby seemed eager to help spread the Zionist movement to the Asian diaspora. His pledge of financial support to Herzl was accompanied by a list of Jewish leaders in Cochin, Bombay, Calcutta and Rangoon whom he thought should be contacted to raise funds towards that end. In addition to his direct communication with Herzl, Roby sent another letter the same day to Herzl's Zionist newspaper, *Die Welt*.

The Zionist idea has made its victorious entrance also into Cochin. We have already many enthusiastic friends in the Jews Town in Cochin, in Bombay, in Calcutta, in Rangoon, in Mala, on the Malabar Coast, in Ernakulum, in Shenomangalam, etc. I hope in a very short time to be able to submit to you . . . a report about the formal establishment of Zionist branches in the above mentioned and other cities as well as about the consolidation of these branches into Sub-Federation of the 'English Zionist Federation'. . . .[5]

In fact, a Zionist chapter had been established in Rangoon by 1901, according to a letter in *Die Welt* of 1 February 1901. Mayer A. Sofaer of Rangoon declared: 'I am happy to be able to inform you that a Zionist group has been formed here with a considerable number of members.'[6] Two years later, in 1903, Cochin followed suit.

Fischel noted the significance of Roby's reference to 'congregations (on) the Malabar Coaste' in his letter to Herzl.[7] By doing so, Roby included the congregations of the Malabari 'black' Jews with the Paradesi 'white' Jews. Despite the two factions' ongoing, centuries-long dispute, they were unambiguously united in their love for Zion.[8]

The Malabaris and Paradesis of Cochin were in many ways separate communities, with segregated synagogues, residential areas, even cemeteries. Although they chose to remain apart from one another, they had much in common: they shared a religion, Kerala's culture and the Malayalam language.

That commonality extended to the Cochin Jews' love for and loyalty to the Promised Land. Their prayers and songs reflect that love, as they extolled the virtues of their blessed Zion.

We want to return to the place where King David dwelled,
Where we lived long ago.
We are generations in exile,
We are certain we'll return to Zion within this generation.
The land will be like a lily,
Jerusalem like the Garden of Eden, gold and milk.
Grant us the permission and strength to return there.[9]

Many Cochin songs reflect the Jews' longing to end generations of exile by retuning to Zion. These songs were traditionally rendered on special communitywide occasions, such as weddings or festivals, but sometimes on an impromptu basis for no reason others than the sheer love of the Promised Land. And it is to that land that they indeed returned 'within this generation'.

The Cochin Jews' love for Israel was mythic. By the late 1940s and early 1950s, the Malabaris, for example

> . . . saw in the State of Israel the fulfillment of their messianic dreams and were actively preparing to join in the historic movement of the Ingathering of the Exiles. 'I think they are making a mistake,' (said) the unromantic and severely practical (Trade Commissioner to the Government of Israel for India and the Far East F.W.) Pollack, '. . . a mistake from every point of view. But after visiting them and talking to them, I have had no option but to report to the Government of Israel that there is no power in the world which will stop them. They are possessed with a messianic fervour of the most exalted order.'[10]

Of concern to Pollack and other Israeli officials who met them was the Cochin Jews' unrealistic expectations of Israel. The idea of fulfilling the biblical prophecy to return to the Promised Land, was thrilling to a people who had structured a large part of their lives around the synagogue. They imagined Israel as their vehicle for even more scrupulous Jewish practice, a place where they could engage in endless hours of study and prayer. Moreover, as Gilbert Kushner emphasized,

> they thought all the people (there) would be meticulous in their observances; all men would wear head-coverings at all times; none would travel or make fires on the Sabbath; all would spend their time in the synagogue. . . (In other words,) in the Holy Land they would live as authentic Jews amidst other Jews on Holy Soil.[11]

However, even before they left India, they discovered that their idealistic perception of Israel-or, at least, of Israelis—was far removed from reality. 'When the Israeli officials came to Cochin without hats, smoking on the Sabbath, the Cochini were amazed. . . . This was to be only the first of many surprises and disappointments. . . .'[12] Nevertheless, they remained steadfast in their devotion and loyalty to Eretz Yisrael. While travelling throughout Asia on a fund-raising mission for Israel in 1951, Rabinowitz briefly visited Cochin, where he gave two addresses. The reception, particularly from the Malabaris who packed the courtyard of Ernakulam's Thekumbagham Synagogue, was overwhelming. 'The response to my appeal literally brought tears to my hardened eyes.... They gave of their last annas (small coins) and made a magnificent response', he recalled.[13] Of the Paradesis, 'the attendance was disappointing, but the response of those present (was) most gratifying.'[14]

For the Cochin Jews, Zionism was an expression of their fervent religiosity. This was not unusual for the Sephardim, who embraced the messianic message with particular zeal.

> The concept of the 'return' of the Jews from exile to the biblical homeland in Zion—the promised land—was an integral part of Jewish life everywhere, but nowhere was it more fervently held or more inextricably interwoven with daily life and long-range hope than among the Sephardim. They were intense in their religious observances. . . . They spoke their prayers with understanding and expectation of eventual fulfillment. Their implorations for deliverance from the austerity of exile in foreign lands, and the promised ingathering of the Jews back in the Holy Land was, for many of them, not mere cant recited by rote, but a sincere profession of anticipation and desire.[15]

The Muslim world in which most Sephardim lived had not yet been transformed by the forces of modernization and secularization which had swept Europe during the nineteenth century. Reflecting their host cultures, Sephardic Jews remained within a sacralized demi-monde of meanings from which most of their Ashkenazi brethren had been willingly or unwillingly removed. Sephardic communities were tightly-knit, and secularization barely permeated their mythic universe. Yet they never divorced themselves from the non-Jewish world, even when they were subjected to discrimination or persecution.

> In a very real sense the Sephardic world was never outside of the political arena. Even in the aftermath of Spanish exile, at the darkest period of their history, Sephardic leadership sought remedies for the Jewish condition in the political arena through alliance with the Ottoman Turks against their Christian persecutors, and in efforts to restore at least a measure of Jewish self-rule in Eretz Israel. These efforts failed, but the fact that they were made reflects the kind of practical messianism that the characteristic of the Jewish people and for a long time was given particular emphasis in the Sephardic world.[16]

That practical Messianism expressed by the Sephardim was a political movement firmly steeped in religious conviction.

By contrast, most Ashkenazi Zionist leaders were cosmopolitan, university educated 'modern thinkers' who moved in Europe's pluralistic, *secularized* society. The Israel they envisioned was one fashioned in their own image. Its ethos was to be socialist and humanistic rather than messianic and religious. For them, Zionism was a political response to the very pragmatic problem of anti-Semitism. The movement attracted adherents in direct proportion to the level of discrimination on the continent. Of course, not all Ashkenazim tended to agree with this rationalist, areligious approach to Zionism. For some pious Ashkenazi Jews, Eretz Yisrael was the embodiment of religious fulfillment. This did not mean, however, that the Sephardim easily blended into Ashkenazi Orthodox versions of Zionism. The Sephardim in general often considered some Orthodox Ashkenazim to be 'fanatics'—not because of their fastidious observance of *Halakha*, but because of their tendency to isolate themselves from the world, including less observant Jews as well as gentiles.

Sephardim are noted for and pride themselves on being less fanatic than Ashkenazim in virtually all matters, especially religion. Sephardim are often bewildered by the Ashkenazic pursuit of *humrot* (difficult *halakhic* refinements), because they have traditionally sought to balance the requirements of the observance with those of living in order to achieve a form of religious expression that takes into consideration the whole human being, to encourage and cultivate the range of human attributes. . . . It is difficult for Sephardim to understand the isolationist trend that is dominant among so many Ashkenazim who have not broken away from their heritage, who see the salvation of Judaism only in separating it from those who do not meet the current religious standards, which seems to be always moving to the right. Sephardim see no hope or virtue in isolation; to them, the result is a warping of Jews and a distortion of Judasim.[17]

Zionism is deeply rooted in the Jewish soul, although it is expressed in a dazzling array of metaphors. It is not simply a European invention, as popular wisdom holds. Centuries before Herzl gave shape to a European consensus, the Sepahrdim had contributed to the discussion with their bodies. Some walked to the Promised Land from as far away as Yemen. Others resided in the holy cities of Hebron and Tsfat for long periods. While Sephardic Zionism differs in expression from that of the Ashkenazim, its basic metaphors, rooted in the Torah and *siddur* (prayer book), inspired them to act by leaving their homes of millennia.

What is special about Sephardic Zionism is its unquestioned merging of religious and political aspirations. Having never undergone secularization on one hand or embraced otherworldly pietism on the other . . . the Sephardic world was earlier attuned to seeking political solutions to the Jewish condition, at the same time never divorcing such solutions from a deep religious commitment. . . . Sephardim consider this synthesis of religious and political impulses integral to their Jewishness. . . . If there is any contrast between Ashkenazic and Spehardic Zionism, it is that the former was a Zionism that demanded internal revolution as much as a transformation of the Jewish condition, while the latter was a Zionism of redemption that sought continuity with tradition and did not require revoltion.[18]

That commingling of religious and political aspirations was precisely how Naphtali Koder viewed his and other Cochinites' determination to make *aliyah*. 'You know, Judaism is a political religion', he said. 'To stay in Cochin after the creation of the State of Israel would be to live an anachronism.'[19]

But the world of the Cochin Jews was, in some important ways, distinct from those of the Ashkenazim and Sephardim. The modernized secular society of their European Ashkenazi brethren was alien to them. In the West, pluralism involved a competition between exclusivistic religious worldviews, which resulted in the desacralizaiton of society. In India, pluralism was built upon the bedrock of a multifaceted and hierarchical tolerance in which sacred communities coexisted without losing their sacredness. 'Religious feelings in India are very strong for Jews—for *everyone*,' emphasized Balfour Salem during a return visit to Cochin.[20] Therefore, pluralism in India never challenged the Jews' unfaltering faith, an outgrowth of which was their Zionism. Indeed, the essential nature of their religious world had remained largely unchanged since their arrival on the Malabar coast centuries ago. Even

a few accretions of Hindu custom, several modifications in harmony with changes in Jewish practices elsewhere, (and) some original innovations, have not altered the essential nature of Jewish society (in Cochin). It has been successfully armored against the bombardment of alien influence because the synagogue complex has knit the community together so tightly that outside interests and customs could not penetrate. The synagogue provided for every communal need; there was no necessity for other social mechanisms.[21]

India's caste system, while criticized by foreigners and many modernized Indians as repressive, served as a buffer to prevent assimilation and homogeneity in society, thus never providing the Jews with the option to discard their Jewishness—not that they ever wanted or needed to. In that way, the Cochin Jews differed not only from the Ashkenazim, but also from their fellow Sephardim. They never had to separate themselves from the mainstream, nor view Israel as their only hope for survival as a people. The Cochin Jews had the luxury of being a tightly-knit religious enclave, praying for the return of their people to Israel, all the while living as a full-fledged, integrated community in Indian society. 'It's the call of the Land for these Oriental Jews', P.M. Jussay, a Christian friend of the community, explained of their departure from India: 'You have to be a devout Sephardi Jew to feel the call of Zion in your bones.'[22]

A SIGN OF THE POLITICAL TIMES

Someone who felt the call of Zion was Gloria Koder, who left Cochin in 1972 and settled in Haifa with her husband and two sons. She conceded that it was difficult to pinpoint the reasons for her decision to leave. 'It's easy to understand why Jews left their homes in Europe, where there was persecution', she said. 'They had clear reasons to go, whereas we've had a good life in India. Still, I have no regrets about moving to Israel'; I've always been a Zionist.' Raised in such an observant community as Cochin, Koder asserted, 'You can't ignore prayers you say over and over again to return to the Land.'[23] For her, a return to Eretz Yisrael was the most natural thing in the world.

Along those same lines, there were practical considerations. Koder added that she wanted to raise her sons as observant Jews. However, she faced a problem that was common among all diaspora Jews: schools and employers scheduling classes and workdays that coincided with Jewish holidays. In India, perhaps the most tolerant of countries in the diaspora, Jews usually took for granted that they would be exempt from secular endeavours that fell on their Sabbath, festivals and holy days. An example of this tolerance was a fifty-year-old memorandum from the state's Education Department to the Jewish Youth Organization in Chendamangalam which officially declared:

> . . . the following days as . . . holidays for Jewish pupils and teachers in the Departmental Calendar. 1. First day of Passover (Pesach) 2. Seventh day of Passover 3. Feast of Weeks (Shavu'oth) 4. First day of New Year (Rosh Hashanah) 5. Second day of New Year 6. Day of Atonement (Yom Kippur) 7. First day of Tabernacle (Sukot) 8. Seventh day of Tabernacle (Sukkot). The Director of Public Instruction . . . (has) also been informed that the Jewish pupils and teachers may be granted special leave on all Saturdays which are working days.[24]

However, the Jews' shrinking numbers in what was already a microscopic minority meant that they had to contend with schools and employers not always being so lenient. A.B. Salem petitioned the state's Director of Public Instruction in 1952 on behalf of three Jewish students who were scheduled to take university examinations that fell on a Jewish holiday—Rosh Hashanah. As Salem noted, tongue in cheek, it was history repeating itself. 'This question of Sabbath and Examination has been agitated and relief given always from 1899 to this day. I had the honour of moving the University to exempt me from the ordinary sabbath day in 1899 for my Intermediate and again for my B.A. examination avoiding Saturdays & Holydays.'[25]

The problems faced by Jews at schools were more acute in the workplace. As for those who already had jobs, there was the issue of having to take 'casual leave' when Jewish holidays fell on working days. Although they were allotted a generous number of paid personal days, Jews argued that they had lost something important: recognition by the government, which previously had declared Jewish observance official paid holidays. Now they had to give excuses to their employers for taking off time from work.

In Erstwhile Cochin State all Jewish Holydays were recognized by Government, and these days were Gazetted as Holydays, special to the Jews. Now-a-days, Jews are compelled to take Casual Leave if they wish to get a holiday on their Holydays. This is a great grievance and an injustice. Almost all the holidays in India are based on the various religions of the Country: Bakrid, Ramzan etc. for Mohammedans, Easter, Christmas, New Year etc. for Christians, and the other Holidays are also religious days of Hindus. Why should a small minority, who wish to keep the observances of their ancestors, be denied these privileges. . . .[26]

As the number of Jews diminished, so did certain privileges, such as refraining from work on Shabbat. A fact of modern life was that 'Jews in Kerala, who were in service with government or in the private sector had to work on the Jewish Sabbath . . . Saturday (also) became a working days for schools and colleges.'[27]

To the religious Cochin Jews, violating their Sabbath was devastating. This wresting with God and society became all the more painful during the twilight years of the community, when every man was desperately needed to form a *minyan* for Shabbat prayers; often the determining factor was whether or not some foreign Jewish tourists happened upon the synagogue at the right time. During recent years, when they were desperate, they even waived the prohibition to drive or ride in a car on Shabbat, and sent a chauffeur-driven car for a man who lived in Fort Cochin, beyond walking distance of the synagogue.

It was the same every Saturday morning. Long retired from their jobs, a handful of elderly men congregated on the synagogue steps as the sun's hot rays peered over the buildings, torching Synagogue Lane to signal the start of a new day. Though eager to conduct prayer services, the men first had to round up that critical number so as to began the rituals. While the *shamash*, or synagogue caretaker, went in search of some stragglers, the others waited. More than once, they spotted a young man, one of their own, emerge freshly groomed and dressed from his home, only to turn in the opposite direction and head off toward the ferry which took him to work on the mainland. It was a bitter reality, one that everyone including the young man, resented. 'I don't like going to work on Shabbat, but what can I do?' asked Keith Hallegua, a travel agent who was obliged to work half-day every Saturday. 'I have no choice; I don't want to lose my job.'[28]

The encroachment of secular society upon the Cochin Jews' world manifested itself in a number of ways. Though they proudly continued to observe their holy days and festivals throughout the 1980s, they seemed to be more defensive or secretive of their beliefs. As their numbers diminished, they were increasingly reluctant to practice ritual customs in the presence of non-Jews for fear that the latter would 'mock our ways'. Sarah and Jacob Cohen, who had invited gentile friends for dinner, rushed through their Saturday evening prayers in order to finish before their guests arrived. On another occasion Lily Koder was incensed when, at the conclusion of a Rosh Hashanah festival dinner, some gentile guests whispered to each other through part of the after-meal prayers. 'These people have no respect for our traditions; they are mocking our ways', she said.[29] This reaction, which was a far cry from the characteristically warm, hospitable interactions Cochin Jews had always enjoyed with Muslims, Hindus and Christians, was no doubt a defensive response to the Jews' threatened way of life, brought on, in part, by the changed political climate.

Recently, even the hard-earned *minyanim* were but a memory. Congregational prayers were possible only when a Jewish tour group arrived, or on major holydays when Jews from Ernakulam came.

OTHER REASONS FOR THE COCHIN JEWS' DEPARTURE

Of course, there was no one reason why the Jews left Cochin. Typically, it was a combination of factors which made them seek new lives in a completely different environment. Indeed, for a number of young people, simply the idea of breaking the chain of tradition was appealing.

Although the Jews of Cochin carried with them a number of Indian customs to Israel, 'a major consequence of life in Israel was the distribution of nuclear families into separate houses.'[30] The usual custom of a newly-married couple moving in with the bridegroom's family was no longer so iron-clad, as living conditions in Israel were primarily dictated by economics and convenience. Depending upon the circumstances, a couple could live with the bride's family or, what became increasingly more common, move into a private dwelling of their own.

Among a group of 203 Malabari Jews placed by the government in a *moshav* (cooperative agricultural settlement) near Jerusalem, Kushner reported in 1961-2 that

> numbers of sons and their families were now living apart from their parents. Indeed, several men had to travel for hours to visit their fathers and brothers living in distant *moshavim* (plural of *moshav*). Each family was assigned its own land, furniture, and equipment. Meals were prepared and eaten in the family's own home. And, of course, each man's income was separately recorded and turned over to him.[31]

Ironically, the Cochin Jews' exposure to a cooperative setting emphasized the individual over the group, as they understood it. The modernized Western notion of the nuclear family had replaced the extended family, the *sine qua non* of the Indian social structure. Back in Cochin, their daily lives were marked by the close interaction of a large, multi-generational clan, which provided continuity, security, companionship, as well as sharing daily chores and economic burdens, through an elaborate, multi-tiered system. Indeed, some of the new emigrés found the system in Israel to be alienating and more demanding physically. Yet a number of young couples enjoyed the additional living space and privacy separate housing afforded, not to mention being liberated from the dictates of their elders.

Miriam 'Koko' Ashkenazi belonged to the latter camp, as she packed a few clothes and a lifetime of mementos into two large suitcases, to join her daughter Doreen and her family in Israel. Doreen, who worked for the American Consulate in Jerusalem, finally convinced her mother to spend her remaining years with loved ones rather than living alone in her Fort Cochin residence. In preparation for her arduous trip, which included a two-day train ride to Bombay where she had to board a plane for Israel via Cairo, Koko carefully weeded through her possessions, taking only the most precious. She either gave away or sold most of her saris because in Israel she planned to wear only Western clothes. While she packed, many Jew Town friends dropped by carrying small parcels of foodstuffs, clothes and letters for her to take to their families in Israel.

A few days before her departure, Koko made special arrangements to attend Saturday morning Shabbat services at the Paradesi Synagogue. She had planned to spend the previous night at the home of friends in Jew Town because she lived too far away to walk to the synagogue. 'Who knows if

I'll ever see this place again?' she said of the Paradesi Synagogue. 'I have to go for one more Shabbat.'[32]

Koko's departure on 1 April 1987, fell a week before '*massa* day', the Sunday preceding Pesach when the community prepared its unleavened bread for the festival. Her absence was the topic of much discussion among those who planned and participated in the day-long activity, which became increasingly difficult with every helper who left for Israel. 'One less person to make *massa* this year', said one *massa* day organizer, to which another added, 'We keep losing hands to make the *massa*'. Knowing full well how her lifelong friends felt about her leaving Cochin, Koko, a rather reserved woman, was physically and emotionally distant as her departure drew near. 'How cool she is about leaving', remarked Queenie Hallegua. 'Well, she's going to be with her children', responded Queenie's sister-in-law, Esther Simon. 'Here, she's not leaving anybody—except a community.'[33]

It seemed conspicuous that no farewell party was planned for Koko by her Jew Town friends. 'No one does that anymore', said Raymond Salem. 'Once upon a time, for the littlest reason, people would sing and dance. Now, who is there to sing? Who is there to dance? There's nobody left.' Instead, he explained, Koko would be given a big party by Jew Town friends and family, who would receive her at the airport in Israel.[34]

LACK OF MARRIAGE PARTNERS

For the Paradesis in particular, one of the most pressing factors for emigration was the lack of eligible marriage partners. By 1984, when their numbers had dwindled to less than three dozen people, community members cited that as the second most important reason for emigration.[35] At that time, 'more than fifty per cent of the households (were) unitary. These people were living with other members of their family. After the departures of their relatives to Israel, they (lived) as single members.'[36] Though some of the people in that group were widowed, divorced or separated, most had never been married. And the prospects for marriage hardly looked promising when the median age of the community at that time was 56.[37]

The high proportion of unmarried men and women became even more obvious two years later in 1986; among the generation that came of age in the 1940s were the unwedded Lily Koder, Shalom Cohen and Jackie Cohen, who lived with their siblings, and the single households of I.S. 'Hallen' Hallegua, Raymond Salem, and Isaac Ashkenazy. Of concern to community members was a new generation of unmarried 'youngsters' in their 20s: Leonore Simon, Keith Hallegua, Fiona Hallegua, David Hallegua, Kenneth Salem and Brian Hallegua, whose two sisters, Seema (18 years) and Ya'el (15 years), would soon face the same dilemma. 'So what are you going to do? Go off to Israel?' Jacob Cohen asked Kenneth Salem, who planned to leave the community on 4 July 1987. 'What else is there for me here?' responded the young man. 'You should meet a woman in Israel and bring her back here to live', Cohen thundered. 'That's what everyone should have done if they couldn't find someone (in Cochin) to marry; they should have brought them back here and built up the community. Now that the root is dead, the leaf can no longer blossom.'[38]

The lack of marriage partners was not a new problem taking the Paradesis. During his visit to Jew Town more than sixty years ago, Mandelbaum noted that

> the number of unmarried adults over the age of twenty-five is unusually high. [Of the 125 'white' Jews,] there are eleven bachelors and twelve spinsters, 18.4 per cent of the group. Mental eccentricity and illness are among the contributory causes to this high proportion of unmarried adults, but perhaps the most vital reason is that in so small a group it is difficult to find a spouse one's own age or generation. Men of forty are married to girls half their age, and a young man in his early twenties may have a wife nearing forty.[39]

Mandelbaum's mention of 'mental eccentricity and illness', which, according to him, accounted for 13.6 per cent of the population then, was attributed to the fact that

> the white Jews are a highly inbred community, although infiltrations of Jewish blood from other countries have occurred. There are two women among them at present who are of Bagdadi stock, and one of the leading families was founded by an immigrant from Bagdad. But these additions have been comparatively few over a span of four hundred years, and the community exhibits the weaknesses that are popularly supposed to attend inbreeding.[40]

To make matters worse, there was a markedly low birth rate among the Paradesis, who were unable to make up for the steady decline in their population.

Compounding this problem was the 'white' Jews' refusal to marry members from the 'black' and the so-called *meshuchrar* communities. The 'white' enforcement of this discriminatory custom, which amounted to a breach of Jewish law, ironically proved to be the nail in their coffin. The minuscule pool of prospective mates led to a number of Paradesis either remaining single, finding acceptable Jewish spouses elsewhere (usually members of the Baghdadi community in Bombay), or marrying 'outside the community', as it was euphemistically called. Marrying non-Jews to a certain degree was inevitable, as an increasing number of young Paradesi men and women left Jew Town to pursue university education and professions elsewhere. However, according to Gamliel Salem, his two sisters Esther Salem Rao and Malkah Salem Antony, both of whom were physicians, may have wedded 'outside the community' because they were disgusted with their own community's repressive attitudes pertaining to skin colour.[41]

These social restrictions began to crumble in the 1950s, when two 'intermarriages' took place between members of the previously endogamous 'white' and '*meshuchrar*' factions: the first in 1950, between Seema 'Baby' Koder, a 'white' Paradesi, and Balfour Salem, the son of maverick A.B. Salem; and the second between Reema Roby and Gamliel Salem, Balfour's younger brother, seven years later. Both weddings were held in a Baghdadi synagogue in Bombay. It was not until 1978, when a third 'intermarriage' took place—between Glennis Simon and Leslie Salem, Balfour's son—that there was unqualified acceptance of the union, which took place in the Paradesi Synagogue. But by then, it was too late. The fates of many individuals had been cast, not to mention the fate of the community itself.

Julian Koder had every reason to stay in Cochin, but was among the first 'white' Paradesis to make *aliyah* with his wife and two daughters. Despite his surname, Koder did not belong to the affluent mercantile branch of the family. As a young man, however, he had acquired some wealth. He was a self-made man, a physician and a dentist by training, who ran a successful medical practice that boasted seventeen staff members. His wife Sarah ('Doll' to everyone) oversaw their large home with four servants in Fort Cochin. Yet, Koder made *aliyah* in 1962, becoming 'the one who met all the (Israel-bound) Cochinites at the airport'.[42]

Simply put, Koder left Cochin because he was concerned that his daughters Elizabeth and Florence would not find suitable partners. Indeed, Koder knew how difficult it was for the Paradesis to find prospective mates. He had journeyed hundreds of miles north to Bombay to marry the former Sarah 'Doll' Cohen from a Baghdadi family, returning to Cochin after the wedding with his bride. Like every Jewish father, he looked forward to bringing his daughters some day to the *chuppah* (wedding canopy). One day, it suddenly downed on him: 'During one festival (in Jew Town), I saw eighteen girls and three boys standing on the steps of the synagogue', he recalled. 'I made up my mind then and there to make *aliyah*.'[43]

The Koders settled in the town of Binyamina, situated between Haifa and Tel Aviv, where they lived in a comfortable, spacious home adorned with many distinctive furnishings from their native India. Doctor Julian, as he was known by Cochinites in India and Israel, maintained a small, well-equipped dental office in a separate building behind his house, just a few feet beyond his wife's fragrant rose garden. Eight Paradesi households subsequently settled in apartments near the Koders in Binyamina. Although a large part of the Jew Town community in Israel was scattered all over the country, many of them met at Binyamina on a regular basis for holy day observances and life cycle rituals. 'People come (from all over Israel) for festivals and functions', said Koder. 'Today, there is more of a Jew Town here than the actual Jew Town.'[44]

Of course, with their emigration to Israel, the problem of Cochin men and women finding suitable marriage partners has been solved. However, in its place has spawned a new and even greater challenge for the Cochin community, one that is common to all immigrant groups that leave the Old Country for a New World: how to preserve their unique cultural identity in a modernized society that threatens to engulf them. Though primarily the older Cochinites—those who made *aliyah* as adults—were scrupulous about preserving many of their unique, centuries-old traditions, their children and grandchildren, who either were very young when they came to Israel or were *sabras* (native born Israelis), had assimilated rapidly into Israeli society. Gone are the days when marriages were arranged by elders or blossomed within the limited confines of the community. Now, it is more often the case that Cochin men and women meet their future spouses while serving in the Israeli army.

Within a relatively short span of time, the Cochinites became acculturated and prospered in Israel—so much so, that they earned the praise of other Israelis, according to Eliahu Bezalel, a native of Chendamangalam who, with his Cochin born wife Batzion and their four children, ran a profitable horticulture business on a *moshav* near the southern city of Ashkelon. 'Cochini women are sought after as brides by many Ashkenazim', said Bezalel during a rare visit to Jew Town thirty-two years after making *aliyah*.

> Probably within thirty to forty years, there won't be any Cochin Jews. We are mixing so well and so quickly into Israeli society that soon all differences will be gone through intermarriage (with Jews from other ethnic backgrounds). That is why my wife and I have taught our children to say they're Cochini first, and Israeli second.[45]

The tide, however, is sweeping Cochinites toward an inevitable and ironic destiny. Not only are they facing extinction as a cohesive group in India, but in Israel as well. Indeed, Bezalel sent news that his son, Barak, was to marry an Israeli woman whose parents were from Bulgaria, and his daughter, Bina, to a Canadian.[46]

With 600 people, Moshav Nevatim on the outskirts of Beer Sheva is the fourth largest cooperative agricultural settlement in Israel. *Moshavniks* include Malabaris who migrated in the 1950s from Cochin, Ernakulam, Parur, Chendamangalam and Mala—a far cry from the barren landscape to which they were transported on the edge of the Negev Desert. But through hard work they transformed their government-allotted fields into what many call 'the Israeli miracle'. Their lush, green farmlands can be easily spotted from the roadside, standing in marked contrast to the inhospitable rocky terrain a few feet away. Since its inception almost forty years ago, the *moshav* has prospered from growing flowers and oranges and raising poultry. A good number of new, large, handsome homes in the collective reflected that success—again, a far cry from what these families called home only a generation ago.

Almost as dramatic were the differences between young and old *moshavniks*. A number of old men and women still wore *mundus*, as they had when they lived in India. At home and even in public, they spoke their native Malayalam, preferring it to Hebrew. By contrast, the younger people wore typical Israeli clothes: youths preferred tee shirts, shorts and tennis shoes, men wore button-down shirts, trousers and shoes, and women favoured Western-style sleeveless dresses or blouses and skirts with sandals. Their first language was Hebrew, and a few had learned English in school; even fewer knew Malayalam. One young man in his early 20s, when asked where his family came from, simply answered, 'India'. Pressed to explain where in India, he looked puzzled and shrugged. This *sabra* was no different than an American born Jews whose grandparents came from Russia. A second generation American may know a word or two of Yiddish, but would almost surely draw a blank when asked to name *bubbe* (grandmother) and *zayde*'s (grandfather's) *shtetl* (village) in the Old Country.

THE CURSE

As rational as all these factors are for the demise of Cochin's Jewish community, there is also the less tangible, more mysterious 'reason': Jew Town's curse. 'The curse' was mentioned in private discussions by a few of Cochin's elders, who believed that it was responsible for the modern-day exodus. With no experience of persecution or ill-will, they asserted, what other fathomable excuse could there be for the Jews' departure from a land they loved?

Mention of ghosts, eerie dreams, Kabbalists, vows and unexplained phenomena, all a synergy of Kabbalah and Hindu folk mysticism, was made in a number of conversations; these topics were raised quite naturally, without any apology, embarrassment, or self-consciousness. The storytellers were invariably the elders; the young who heard these tales were clearly entertained by them, although they often listened with indulgent smiles, as if to say, 'I don't believe this superstitious nonsense.' But even the most even-tempered rationalist cannot help but wonder, when listening to a particularly haunting tale in a cavernous house hundreds of years old, whether there is not a certain other-worldly presence that still pervades Jew Town.

Though the setting of quite a few stories was peoples' homes, most of them took place in, or had as their central theme, the Paradesi Synagogue. This is hardly surprising, in view of what the synagogue meant to each and every member of the community. As Mandelbaum aptly observed, 'The community is knit together around the synagogue and closely integrated by it. The synagogue complex is not only the matrix of the communal life, not only a temple for the development of the personal life, is the way of life for the Jews of Cochin.'[47]

Indeed, it is as if the synagogue has its own *neshamah* (soul), a force or a magnet that draws physical, mental and spiritual energy from its congregants just as it also sustains them. Tales, legends and anecdotes tended to personify the synagogue, almost transforming it into a living, sentient being. Little wonder, considering the centuries of fervent prayers offered by countless devout and often mystical Jews, the many weddings and *brit milot*, the countless fasts and vows, the holy days and festivals. The *neshamah* of the synagogue has been a blessing to the community, a source of strength and inspiration, the very cement which bonds the diverse personalities of Jew Town into a tightly-knit, intensely supportive community. The *neshamah* is the essence, the very identity of its people. The question is: who is left to identify with the synagogue?

Those who had no intention of leaving Cochin—all of whom were in their 60s, 70s or 80s—expressed their anger, sadness and resignation about the fate of their synagogue when none of them would be left to care for it. Plans already were under way for the Paradesi Synagogue to be turned over to the Archaeological Survey of India, an arm of the national government, which would oversee the building as a museum. Not only were the community members disgusted that their beloved house of worship would be transformed into a tourist attraction, but they also added that government workers would not take adequate care of the synagogue and that its contents would probably be vandalized. The synagogue and the community—perceived as a singular entity—had been terribly wronged by 'traitors' who did not respect them enough to stay, some elders charged. Though the spirit of the synagogue had up until now been benevolent, they said that God would wreak vengeance on behalf of the house of worship. The fact that it would no longer be a holy place, but a secular monument that ultimately would go to seed, was in itself a grave consequence of their actions, they added. 'People abandoned this place, and (the future fate of the synagogue) will be God's punishment on the community,' said one man. More than that, however, 'God is going to bring his wrath to Earth. He is going to look down and punish those traitors who deserted the community.'[48]

Another elderly man in Jew Town claimed that he had 'already seen' the type of retribution that would befall those who did not respect a consecrated site. That site was the Thekumbagham Synagogue, once the house of worship for one of Cochin's Malabari congregations. The building was located within the 'white' Paradesis' residential area, toward the middle of Synagogue Lane. Constructed in 1489, it was the oldest synagogue in use until the mid-1950s, when all its congregants migrated to Israel and it permanently closed its doors. With the edifice no longer in use, nearby residents suggested tearing it down.

However, the story went, people were skittish about razing the building, afraid of stirring up and angering the ancient spirits that were believed to inhabit the structure. Finally, two of the former congregants returned from Israel and oversaw the demolition of the synagogue around 1964. The men disposed of the timber and valuable building materials, then sold the parcel of land to the Paradesi Synagogue. Their business finished, one man returned to Israel where he committed suicide by hanging himself. The other man, while walking on the streets of Bombay, died of a sudden heart attack. Elias Koder purchased the vacant lot on which, four years later, he built a grand house which he named *Hatiqvah*, 'The Hope', for himself and his family. Within a period of four years after building the house, the tale continues, Koder's wife, Essie, developed breast cancer and died while undergoing surgery, his daughter Gloria, son Samuel and their families emigrated to Israel, and the senior Koder found himself alone on the 'doomed' site. And that, the storyteller concluded, was the curse of the Thekumbagham Synagogue. 'You can believe it or not', he challenged.

'Some people think of it as nonsense. But look at Elias. Now, he's a lonely old man (living) in that big house. What else can you call it but a curse?'[49]

Not surprisingly, it is in this context, when talking of the community's death, that 'the curse' often comes up in conversation. One elderly man listed one problem after another with which Jew Town had been plagued: its so-called 'Jewish apartheid', disproportionate number of unmarried individuals, low birth rate, high incidence of mental illness, financial disasters, political fallout, not to mention that the Paradesis left a land for which they professed nothing but love and loyalty. A religious man, he argued that these community ills, all of which were manifestations of 'the curse', may have been caused by people not observing the teachings of the Bible. God's Chosen People committed sins, such as discriminating against one another, as well as not fulfilling certain commandments, such as the one to be fruitful and multiply, he explained solemnly. As if to underscore his talk of death were the loud tickings of heirloom clocks, several of which filled the rooms of his large ancestral home, now devoid of relatives who had departed for Israel.

NOTES

1. Poem written by Cecil Koder and sung by Cochinites to the tune of the *Hatiqvah.*
2. Reissner, 'Indian-Jewish Statistics', p. 25; cf. Kushner, *Immigrants from India in Israel*, p. 23.
3. Stritzower, *Exotic Jewish Communities*, p. 124.
4. Fischel, 'The Contribution of the Cochin Jews to South India and Jewish Civilization', p. 59.
5. Ibid., p. 60.
6. Ibid.
7. Ibid., p. 61. Actually, at the time there were eight congregations: one each in Mala, Parur and Chendamangalam, two in Ernakulam, and three in Cochin, including the Paradesi Synagogue.
8. If we take Roby's enthusiasm as typical of Cochin Jews, they apparently did not exhibit the ambivalence which characterized the Bene Israel's response to Zionism. See Roland, *Jews in British India*, pp. 146-70.
9. Walerstein, 'The Cochini Jewish Wedding of the Malabar Community in India and Israel', p. 254.
10. Rabinowitz, *Far East Mission*, pp. 89-90.
11. Kushner, *Immigrants from India in Israel*, pp. 22-3.
12. Ibid., p. 23.
13. Rabinowitz, *Far East Mission*, p. 139.

14. Ibid.
15. Peters, *From Time Immemorial*, p. 88.
16. Elazar, *The Other Jews*, p. 197.
17. Ibid., pp. 36-7.
18. Ibid., pp. 197-8.
19. Naphtali Koder, 23 June 1987.
20. Balfour Salem, March 1984.
21. Mandelbaum, 'The Jewish Way of Life in Cochin', pp. 458-60.
22. P.M. Jussay, 19 March 1987.
23. Gloria Koder, March 1984.
24. Quoted by Elias and Isaac, *Jews in India with Who is Who 1963*, p. 16.
25. Ibid., p. 12.
26. Ibid., p. 26.
27. Hallegua, 'The Cochin Jewish Community—Its Twilight Years', p. 21.
28. Keith Hallegua, April 1987.
29. Lily Koder, October 1986.
30. Kushner, *Immigrants from India in Israel*, p. 76.
31. Ibid.
32. Miriam Ashkenazy, 25 March 1987.
33. Queenie Hallegua and Esther Simon, 30 March 1987.
34. Raymond Salem, 30 March 1987.
35. Hallegua, 'The Jewish Community of Cochin—Its Twilight Years', p. 66.
36. Ibid., p. 56.
37. Ibid., p. 57.
38. Jacob Cohen, 23 March 1987.
39. Mandelbaum, 'The Jewish Way of Life in Cochin', p. 451.
40. Ibid., pp. 450-1.
41. Gamliel Salem, 14 January 1987.
42. Julian Koder, 24 June 1987.
43. Ibid.
44. Ibid.
45. Eliahu Bezalel, 15 May 1987.
46. Ibid., personal communication, 20 August 1989.
47. Mandelbaum, 'The Jewish Way of Life in Cochin', p. 442.
48. Jacob Cohen, 25 March 1987.
49. Raymond Salem, 28 October 1986 and 16 April 1987.

CHAPTER 9

Rebirth in Israel

> Who is there beside thee, O Creator.
> Merciful and gracious One, shorten our exile.
> May there be heard in the cities of Judah
> And in Jerusalem, dear and desirable,
> May there come to the Voice of the Herald of Zion.[1]

The religious attitudes of the Cochin Jews echo their centuries-old hymns. They are a devout people, a community whose fervent prayers to end exile and return to Zion are interwoven in their daily lives. As Sephardim of the Asian diaspora, Zionism for them is an expression of their religiosity, a 'Jewish messianism in the process of realizing itself through this-worldly means'.[2] Though they lived in a pluralistic society, India afforded them and other sacred communities free expression of their traditions. The Cochin Jews could remain a closely-knit, religious enclave, praying for the 'Herald of Zion', while continuing to live as a respected, fully integrated community in India. However, content as they were in this unusually hospitable land, they envisioned Israel as an environment where they could be even more religious among others who were also meticulous in their observance. This idealistic misconception was just one factor that contributed to the Cochin Jews' initial difficulty in adjusting to life in Israel.

Upon making *aliyah* to Eretz Yisrael, Cochinites encountered an Ashkenazi-dominated country whose Zionism was primarily expressed as socialist and humanistic—an ethos far different than their own, which was messianic and religious. 'It is a State for Jews, but it is not a Jewish State', asserted Jacob Cohen, who clearly did not approve of Israel's secularization. To 'prove' Israelis' lack of faith, Cohen launched into a story of Israel's 1967 Six-Day War when the tiny country defeated powerful Arab forces with amazing swiftness. Commenting on Israel's stunning victory, Cohen said, 'God himself performed a miracle. But they (Israelis) think they did it themselves. How dense can they be? Clearly, that was God at work.'[3]

Ironically, most Cochinites believed that they could be more observant in India than in Israel. Those remaining in India reiterated this, despite the fact that their dwindling numbers precluded daily prayers in the synagogue several years ago and, more recently, most Shabbat services as well. Jacob Cohen, rather outspoken on a number of issues, made no effort to conceal his views that he thought Israelis were irreligious. 'Israelis don't believe in God', he claimed. They don't go to synagogue. They laugh at people who go to synagogue on Shabbat.' Cohen conceded that, during a visit to Israel several years ago, he found one group to be devout: the Hasidim. 'Because of their righteousness', he said, 'Israel still stands; otherwise, it would be Sodom and Gomorrah. It's not that I ask other Jews to be Orthodox. I don't. I simply ask them to be Jewish.'[4] These sentiments were echoed by Sattu Koder. Of Israel, he argued, 'What kind of Jewish culture are you developing if you don't fast on [Yom] Kippur, if you don't keep Shabbat, if you don't believe in God? At least in some places in the Diaspora, like here in Cochin, we fast on Kippur and we keep Shabbat. Real Orthodox Judaism continues.'[5]

In Israel Cochinites admitted that their religious observance was not what it used to be. 'There's no question that we were more active religiously in Cochin than [we are] in Israel', said Samuel 'Sammy' Koder who, with his wife Seema 'Simi' and three children, lived in Binyamina. Koder sent his son to a *yeshiva*, a religious school, and made sure that the youngster learnt the unique Cochin *shirot* (songs) so that he would be proud of his origin.[6] A sense of religious continuity was perceptible when Cochinites from all over Israel gathered in Binyamina for festivals and special occasions. Julian Koder fondly described these large gathering, but added, 'In Cochin, we always used to pray, "Next year in Jerusalem." Now that we are in Jerusalem, God is with us, and we no longer pray. There was more religion in Cochin than here.'[7]

Most Cochinites, like Balfour Salem, believed that it was futile to linger in a dying community, no matter how religious. An observant Jew, Salem confessed that he was disappointed by the secularization in Israel. He would have preferred to remain in Cochin for religious reasons, hastily adding that if enough people stayed there to make Jewish life possible. Not an enthusiastic participant in the migration, he claimed that he had no choice. 'Don't you see the fate of this town?' he asked sadly during a visit to Jew Town, where his two brothers continued to live. 'There's hardly anyone left.'[8]

'Either you stay in a dying community and die off, or you undertake the change,' said Naphtali Koder. 'I don't want to belong to history, I want to belong to the Jewish world.'[9] The Jewish world is unequivocally Israel, where Koder spoke of his *aliyah* and adopted country with the enthusiasm of a new immigrant.

The Cochin Jews soon discovered that it was not simply philosophical differences that explained why Israelis did not observe religious and life cycle rituals as fully as they once did. The fast pace of Israeli life did not afford the abundant leisure they had enjoyed in Jew Town to devote to their festivals and special occasions. As elaborated earlier, the Cochin community spent inordinately lengthy periods preparing for and observing religious and life cycle rituals. Wedding celebrations could continue for weeks. Passover preparations could extend up to three months. People had abundant leisure. A persons's activities completely revolved around the Jewish calendar, preparing for and observing festivals and holy days. Earning a living in India had been relatively easy; most people did not have to worry about jobs fitting into their time-consuming religious schedules because they derived incomes from various Jewish-run enterprises, subsistence peddling, or family inheritances, and those in need received monthly stipends from their synagogue.

In Israel, on the other hand, leisure was a rare commodity. Both men and women typically worked long hours. 'Life (in Jew Town) was a picnic from morning to evening,' recalled Naptali Koder. 'Here, it is difficult. We leave the house at 6 a.m., and don't return till after 5 p.m.'[10] In addition to earning a livelihood, other practical considerations, such as child care and housework—done without the help of an extended family or servants, like it was in India—left little time for religious observance.

For Cochinites who were motivated to make *aliyah* for religious purposes, the preclusion or limitation of ritual observance was, at times, resented. Recalled Kushner during his 1961-2 field research of a Malabari *moshav* near Jerusalem:

> At the nocturnal feasts which were part of holiday observances the young men would fidget about and complain that they had to rise early to work the next day. In general, the early-to-bed, early-to-rise hours of the agriculturalist interfered with late evening prayers and feasts. This was negatively regarded by the villagers, all of whom agreed that they never realized they would be less strict in their ritual observance in Israel than in India. Their emotionally inspired immigration to Israel had been undertaken in a spirit of religious fervor. Instead they observed what they believed was dissolution of their religious life.[11]

In 1987, Mordecai Mordecai, a resident of Moshav Nevatim near Beer Sheva, boasted that the agricultural settlement's Cochin-style Synagogue held daily prayer services in addition to those on Shabbat. However, most of the men who attended weekday services were elderly retirees because other *moshavniks* laboured all day in the fields. Everyone attended Synagogue on Shabbat, when they could rest all day.[12]

What irony that the Cochin Jews felt that they could not be as religious in Israel as they would have liked to be. On the surface, leading an observant Jewish life in Israel would appear to be easier, or at least more convenient, than in India. Public life in Israel follows the Jewish calendar, with virtually all businesses closed on the Sabbath. Kosher foods are readily available in markets and restaurants. Even modern household conveniences for the Sabbath, such as automatic timers for electric lights, and low voltage electric plates that can be switched on during Shabbat to warm meals and beverages, are used to make *halakhic* observance simpler. As she packed her bags to leave Cochin for Israel, Miriam 'Koko' Ashkenazi imagined what her first Passover in Eretz Yisrael would be like: 'Just think, when I'm in Israel I can buy everything I need in shops. I can go out to eat at people's homes and it's all going to be kosher. It's all going to be so easy!'[13] While these conveniences and labour saving devices inarguably make life easier for people, they still cannot make up for the lack of free time that people in modernized societies, including Israelis, long for. That non-structured time, which was abundant in Cochin, enabled community members to spend lengthy periods preparing for and observing calendric and life cycle events as they had for centuries.

Leisure time allows for something else that is important to Indian sensibilities: socializing. We cannot overestimate the importance of socializing for this closely-knit community. Daily visits are paid to convey news, gossip, share recipes, minister to various physical and emotional needs, solicit or give advice, provide companionship—or for no apparent reason at all. No one needs an invitation, and there is no special ceremony or fanfare. People in Jew Town felt completely at ease to walk through each other's unlocked front doors, flop into the nearest sofa or easy chair, and make themselves at home. Cochinites in Israel waxed nostalgic about the close bonds of friendship that thrived throughout Jew Town, but could not be recaptured in the same way in their newly-adopted country. 'You can't compare the life we had there with what is here (in Israel)', said Samuel Koder. 'The closeness of the community can't be found anywhere else in the world.'[14] One main factor that precludes this community solidarity is the 'lack of leisure time for socializing because of the heavy work schedule and fast pace of Israeli life. More subtle factors might include the influence of an Israeli (especially Ashkenazi) emphasis on individualism and the nuclear family at the expense of Indian . . . values which stress the extended family and the wider ethnic community.'[15] Even those who remained in

Cochin realized what they would have to give up if they emigrated to Israel, Europe or North America. 'If I could stay in India, I would,' said David Hallegua in 1987, who now practices medicine in the United States. 'I don't want to leave (Cochin). It's wonderful living here. People have time for each other. In the west, I understand you're too busy for each other. Things are impersonal. I would miss the closeness (we have) here.'[16]

Israel's ongoing crises—with its hostile neighbours and between its secular and religious citizens—is a harsh reality all potential *olim* (immigrants) face. Though Cochinites received news about Israel from family and friends who lived there, they also got a daily dose of news and editorials from the Indian media, which reflected the government's often negative stance toward the Jewish State and Zionism—especially prior to the shift in diplomatic attitude in 1992. That regular barrage of one-sided reporting had an impact on a number of Cochin Jews who admitted that they were afraid to emigrate to Israel, because of 'tensions' in the country. 'As a Jew, Israel is my country', said Ya'el Hallegua, 15 (in 1987). 'But I'm not so keen to go—there's too much tension there. I'd prefer England or Australia to Israel because there are no tensions.'[17] Echoing those sentiments was her cousin, Fiona Hallegua, 28, who followed her brother David to America in 1989. 'Frankly, I'm afraid of the trouble there', she said of Israel. She elaborated on those feelings by recounting a trip she made a few years ago, where she said that she was frightened on a number of occasions. While visiting relatives in Binyamina, she described how a truck ran over a metal object in the street, producing a loud noise that made everyone start with fear. On another occasion, when she and her family sat down to dinner, a number of helicopters flew overhead and everyone jumped up from the table and ran outside to see what was happening. I couldn't stand to live like that', she said. 'It's too frightening. I don't want that kind of trouble. Everywhere in the world has trouble, but I just couldn't stand to live that way—scared all the time.'[18]

Many Jews, including a good number of men and women from Cochin, excelled in the Indian army. Indeed, one of Ya'el and Fiona Hallegua's first cousins, Glennis Simon Salem, whose father was a career colonel, was in military service. But no one in Cochin had first-hand experience of wars, persecution or fear of being a Jew. Communal violence plagued other parts in India, but rarely Cochin; armed struggle was an intangible, alien concept relegated to newspaper headlines. Thus, the idea of living in a land fraught with such difficulties was a frightening prospect, despite its religious significance. 'In Israel, you get acclimatized very fast', said Naphtali Koder who, along with his two sons, served in the Israeli army. 'War seasons you quickly—so India seems very far away to me.'[19]

Despite initial difficulties, Cochinites reported that they were happy with their decision to emigrate to Israel. Most of them had adjusted to full-time jobs, cramped apartments, a new language, political and economic tensions, and the distinctly different lifestyle of a modernized Israel. Easing the transition for the newly arrived immigrants were numerous family members and friends who welcomed them at Ben-Gurion Airport and made their arrival seem more of a homecoming. There was a thriving Cochinite network in Israel even though most of them were scattered all over the country. The generations-old community bond remained strong and was manifest every time Cochinites gathered for important occasions: festivals, *brit milot*, *bar mitzvahs*, weddings, or funerals.[20] Socializing, once a vital ingredient of life in Jew Town, continued, though inevitably to a lesser degree, by way of telephone calls and planned or impromptu visits to each other's home by car. Visits were usually marked by discussions of Jew Town and a dazzling array of Kerala-style food. Invariably, every apartment carried a colour photograph of the Paradesi Synagogue, hung in a prominent place. Naphtali Koder, who had a large painting of the synagogue in his living room, said of the *aliyah*, 'It had to be done. (Our community) couldn't have survived. It was a miracle that we lasted four-hundred years. I realized that had I stayed, my children would have had to confront the same problems we did. I think we did justice to history; we didn't run from it.'[21] Their future, Cochinites acknowledged, was no longer in India, it was in Israel.

Nevertheless, Balfour Salem, who emigrated to Israel in 1982, harboured deep affection for his birthplace. 'My ties with Israel are religious', he said, 'but I am first and foremost an Indian. I shall love my India always.'[22]

Indeed, there were those in Cochin who vacillated about their own role in the modern-day exodus. For the elders, in particular, the choice was painfully difficult. They recognized that Israel represented the future; on the other hand, memories of a good life in Cochin were not forgotten so easily. 'Israel is the land of our people', explained Isaac Ashkenazy, 'but India is my home. For me, Cochin is *Gan Eden*, Paradise.'[23]

With her eldest daughter and grandchildren in Israel, Esther 'Pearlie' Simon often longed to see them. Although she made two lengthy trips to see her family, she was reluctant to make the move permanent. 'I suppose it's only right that our people should go to Israel. But, you see, I'm an Indian. This is my home, my roots are here, so why should I go? I'm comfortable here, my friends are here. But, most importantly, I'm an Indian.'[24]

'These people had a wonderful life', commented a Jewish Agency official during a visit to Cochin in 1987, 'but now it is over. What can the young people do? This is a model community and I would not like to break it—but it is finished.'[25]

D.B. 'Bapusait' Khona, an old friend of the Paradesi elders, was ambivalent about witnessing the demise of the Jewish community. While he understood the Jews' desire to live in Israel, he stressed that their Indian roots could not be ignored. 'India will continue to survive; it will exist with or without the Jews', he said. 'But it's a real loss to the Jewish community, being without India. A big part of their identity will have gone. And that's a real pity.'[26]

However, the Jews' religious identity was precisely why they must make *aliyah*, according to V.K. Hamza, a Muslim whose close friendship with Jacob Cohen went back fifty years when they were in law school together. 'Israel was once a people without a country. Now they have a country, just like Muslims now have Pakistan. This present generation must go and settle down in Israel. That is the place for them. For the older people, the Malayali way of life has gotten into their blood, and they can no longer change. But the younger ones can and must change with their circumstances.'[27]

Contrasting opinions between older and younger generations were apparent. Teenager Ya'el Hallegua saw the opportunity to leave Cochin as an adventure. 'Everyone's going', she said, 'so I might as well go, too. It's sad to leave your home, especially your friends. It'll be strange. Still, it'll be exciting going to a new place.'[28] Her aunt, Esther 'Pearlie' Simon, was not so enthused. 'At the end of your life, it's hard to start over. But I suppose it's a novelty. Anyway, the important thing is to never look back.'[29]

Jacob Cohen was determined to remain in Jew Town, adding defiantly that even if he was the last person left in the community. His stubborn determination caused a disturbance at a Passover service in the Synagogue in 1987 when, following the congregation's traditional recitation of '*L'shanah haba'ah b'Yerushalayim*' ('Next year in Jerusalem'), he responded in a loud voice, 'I will not say 'Amen' to that', adding, under his breath, '*L'shanah haba'ah b*' Cochin!'[30]

Prem Doss Yehudi, a Jew in Trivandrum who spent Jewish holidays with his friends in Jew Town, sympathized with Cohen. Nevertheless, as an observant Jew, he felt compelled to make *aliyah* as soon as he could (although he was still in India in 2001). 'According to the Torah, every Jew should live in the Promised Land. Therefore, it's a good thing what happened to this community. From a sociological or cultural point of view, it may be sad, but we must have a higher standpoint, and Torah is the higher standpoint. That's why we can say what has happened to this community is a good thing.'[31]

Most Cochin Jews in Israel or still in India agreed with Prem Doss Yehudi's assessment. Whether or not their motivation for making *aliyah* was religious, they believed that they were ultimately fulfilling the dream to return to the Promised Land. Yet none would deny their love for Cochin. Clearly, everyone was sad over the demise of Jew Town, a special place filled with cherished memories. They took their leave of Synagogue Lane with more than a little ambivalence. Many left behind family, all said goodbye to dear friends. No less painful was bidding farewell to their beloved Paradesi Synagogue, a place that had been the focal point of their lives.

It is irresistible to feel sentimental, even sad, about the Jews leaving Cochin. There is always a romance about the past, a nostalgia for what can no longer be. In the abstract, the demise of the Jewish community of Cochin is a loss for both world Jewry and Indian civilization. Certainly, it is painful for the last Jews of Cochin. But encountering the resettled Cochinites in Israel, their optimism and vibrancy is obvious. In their minds, at least, they have made the right choice. All we can do is remember what they left behind.

NOTES

1. Translated by Rabinowitz, *Far East Mission*, p. 136.
2. Hertzberg, *The Zionist Idea*, p. 17.
3. Jacob Cohen, 30 December 1986.
4. Ibid., 23 March 1987.
5. Sattu Koder, 25 October 1986.
6. Samuel Koder, 24 June 1987.
7. Julian Koder, 24 June 1987.
8. Balfour Salem, March 1984.
9. Naphtali Koder, 23 June 1987.
10. Ibid.
11. Kushner, *Immigrants from India in Israel*, p. 77.
12. Mordecai Mordecai, July 1987.
13. Miriam Ashkenazy, 25 March 1987.
14. Samuel Koder, 24 June 1987.
15. Johnson, '"Our Community" in Two Worlds', p. 306.
16. David Hallegua, 15 May 1987.
17. Ya'el Hallegua, 15 May 1987.

18. Ibid.
19. Naphtali Koder, 23 June 1987.
20. See Johnson, 'For Any Good Occasion We Call Them'.
21. Naphtali Koder, 23 June 1987.
22. Balfour Salem, March 1984.
23. Isaac Ashkenazy, 15 April 1987.
24. Esther Simon, 19 March 1987.
25. Edwin Shuker, 1 April 1987.
26. D.B. Khona, 1 April 1987.
27. V.K. Hamza, 1 April 1987.
28. Ya'el Hallegua, 15 May 1987.
29. Esther Simon 15 May 1987.
30. Jacob Cohen, 14 April 1987.
31. Prem Doss Yehudi, 30 December 1986.

Bibliography

Anonymous, 'Wedding in four-century old synagogue after eight years', *The Hindu* (19 June 1986).

———, 'Caste', in *The Encyclopedia of Asian History: A Selection of Sample Articles*, ed. Ainslee Enbree, New York: Charles Scribner's Sons, 1987.

Ashkenazy, Judah David, *Sefer Brit Yitzhak*, Bombay: Lebanon Printing Press, 1917-18.

Bar-Giora, Naphtali, 'Sources—Materials for the History of the Relations between the White Jews and the Black Jews of Cochin', *Sefunoth* 1 (1957): 242-78 (in Hebrew).

———, 'Toldoth Beth-Hakeneseth b'Kogin', in *MiKotsin l'Eretz Yisroel*, ed. Shalva Well, Jerusalem: Kumu Brinah, 1984, pp. 40-59 (in Hebrew).

Bayly, Susan, *Saints, Goddesses and Kings: Muslims and Christians in South India Society, 1700-1900*, Cambridge: Cambridge University Press, 1989.

Beck, Brenda E.F., *Peasant Society in Konku: A Study in Right and Left Subcastes in South India*, Vancouver: University of British Columbia Press, 1972.

———, *The Three Twins: The Telling of a South Indian Folk Epic*, Bloomington: Indiana University Press, 1982.

Beck, Brenda E.F., Peter J. Claus, Praphulladatta Goswami and Jawaharlal Handoo, eds., *Folktales of India*, Chicago and London: University of Chicago Press, 1987.

Berman, Rabbi Jacob, *Popular Halakha: A Guide to Jewish Living*, 2 vols., Jerusalem: World Zionist Organization, 1976 and 1982.

Brafman, Opra, 'Field Work in India among he Jewish Communities: December 1982-February 1983', *Muze'on Yisra'el*, vol. 4 (Spring 1985), pp. 93-8.

Buchanan, Claudius, *The Works of the Reverend Claudius Buchanan, LL.D, comprising his Christian Researches in Asia; with Notices of the Translation of the Scriptures into the Oriental Languages*, Boston: Samuel T. Armstrong, 1812.

Caspi, Mishael Maswari, 'Wedding Customs of the Jews of Cochin According to the Book of Poems and the Songs of Praise', in *Jewish Tradition in the Diaspora: Studies in Memory of Walter J. Fischel*, ed. Mishael Maswari Caspi, Berkeley: Judah L. Magnes Museum, 1981, pp. 231-8.

Chill, Rabbi Abraham, *The Minhagim: The Customs and Ceremonies of Judaism, Their Origins and Rationale*, New York: Sepher-Hermon Press, 1979.

Clorfene, Chaim and Yakov Rogalsky, *The Path of the Righteous Gentile: An Introduction to the Seven Laws of the Children of Noah*, Southfield: Targum Press, 1987.

Cohen, Rabbi Jacob, *The Royal Table: An Outline of the Dietary Laws of Israel*, Jerusalem and New York: Feldheim, 1970.

Cohen, Yaakob Daniel, ed., *Seder Minchah Simchat Torah*, Cochin: Y.D. Cohen, 5637/1877.

Cowen, Ida G., *Jews in Remote Corners of the World*, Englewood Cliffs: Prentice-Hall, 1971.

Daniel, E. Valentine, *Fluid Signs: Being a Person the Tamil Way*, Berkeley: University of California Press, 1984.

Daniélou, Alain, tr., *Shilappadikaram* (*The Ankle Bracelet*), *By Prince Ilango Adigal*, New York: New Directions, 1965.

DeCosta, A., 'The "White" and "Black" Jews of Malabar', *India Church Quarterly Review* (April 1895), pp. 106-25.

Dehija, Vidya, *Antal and Her Path of Love: Poems of a Woman Saint from South India*, Albany: State University of New York Press, 1990.

dePaiva, Mosseh Pereyra, *Notisias dos Judeos de Cochim Mandadas por Mosseh Pereyra de Paiva*, Lisbon: Moses Bensabet Amzalak, 1923 (in Portuguese).

Dirks, Nicholas B., *The Hollow Crown: Ethnohistory of an Indian Kingdom*, Cambridge: Cambridge University Press, 1987.

Dobrinsky, Herbert C., *A Treasury of Sephardic Laws and Customs: The Ritual Practices of Syrian, Moroccan, Judeo-Spanish and Spanish and Portuguese Jews of North America*, Hoboken : KTAV Publishing House; New York: Yeshiva University Press, 1986.

Dumont, Louis, *Homo Hierarchicus: The Caste System and Its Implications*, Chicago and London: University of Chicago Press, 1980.

Dutt, Manmatha Nath, *The Dharma Shastra*, or *The Hindu Law Codes*, Varanasi: Chaukhamba Amarbharati Prakashan, Chaukhamba Amarabharati Studies, vol. V, 1977.

Edeni, Eliahu, *Seder Azharot l'Rabbi Eliahu haEdeni biMinhag Kogin*, Amsterdam: Proops, 1688.

Edgerton, Franklin, *Buddhist Hybrid Sanskrit Dictionary*, Delhi: Motilal Banarsidass, 1977; New Haven: American Oriental Society, 1953.

Egnor, Margaret, 'On the Meaning of Sakti to Women in Tamil Nadu', in *The Powers of Tamil Women*, ed. Susan S. Wadley, New York: Maxwell School of Citizenship and Public Affairs, Foreign and Comparative Studies/South Asia Series, no. 6, 1980, pp. 1-34.

Elazar, Daniel Judah, *The Other Jews: The Sephardim Today*, New York: Basic Books, 1989.

Eliade, Mircea, ed., *The Encyclopedia of Religion*, New York: Macmillan, 1987.

Elias, E. and E. Isaac, eds., *Jews in India with Who is Who 1963*, Ernakulam: Indo-Israel Friendship Publications, 1964.

———, *Jews in India '64 with Who Is Who*, Ernakulam: Indo-Israel Publications, 1965.

Elijah, Samuel H., 'Cochin, India Synagogue', *Philatelic Judaica Journal* 17, 4 (December 1968), pp. 539-46.

Eliya, Ben Eliahu, *Cochin Jewish Records from State Archives*, Haifa: Eliahu Publishers, n.d.

———, *The Synagogues of India*, Kiryat Motzkin: Eliahu Publishers, 1978.

———, *Indian Jewry '84*, Haifa: Ben Eliahu, 1984.

Embree, Ainslee T., ed., *The Encyclopedia of Asian History: A Selection of Sample Articles*, New York: Charles Scribner's Sons, 1987.

Encyclopedia Britannica, 'Asceticism', by 'F.C.C.', in *The Encyclopedia Britannica*, 11th edn., Cambridge and New York: Cambridge University Press, 1910, vol. II, pp. 717-20.

Encyclopedia Judaica, Jerusalem: Keter Publishing House, 1971.

Eschmann, Anncharlott, Hermann Kulke and Gaya Charan Tripathi, eds., *The Cult of Jagannath and the Regional Tradition of Orissa*, New Delhi: Manohar, 1978, rpt. 2005.

Ezekiel, Joseph and Joseph Jacobs, 'Cochin', *The Jewish Encyclopedia*, 1907, vol. IV, pp. 135-8.

Fischel, Walter J., 'David D'Beth Hillel: An Unknown Jewish Traveller to the Middle East and India in the 19th century', *Oriens* 10, 2 (1957), pp. 240-7.

———, *Ha-Yehudim b'Hoddu*, Jerusalem: Ben Zvi Institute, 1960.

———, 'Cochin and Some Prominent Jewish Personalities', in *The Joshua Block Memorial Volume: Studies in Booklore and History*, ed. A. Berger et al., New York Public Library, 1960, pp. 151-64.

———, 'Cochin in Jewish History: Prolegomena to a History of the Jews in India', *Proceedings of the American Academy for Jewish Research* 30 (1962), pp. 37-59.

———, 'Early Zionism in India', *Herzl Year Book* 4, ed. Raphael Patai, New York: Herzl Press, 1962, pp. 309-28.

———, 'A Hitherto Unknown Jewish Traveller to India: The Travels of Rabbi David D'Beth Hillel to India (1828-1832)', in *The Time of Harvest: Essays in Honor of Abba Hillel Silver on the Occasion of his 70th Birthday*, ed. Daniel Jeremy Silver, New York: Macmillan, 1963, pp. 170-85.

———, 'From Cochin (India) to New York', in *Harry Austrynn Wolfson Jubilee Volume*, Jerusalem: American Academy for Jewish Research, 1965.

———, 'The Exploration of Jewish Antiquities of Cochin on the Malabar Coast', *Journal of the American Oriental Society* 87 (1967), pp. 230-48.

———, 'The Rotenburg Family in Dutch Cochin of the Eighteenth Century', *Studia Rosenthaliana* 1 (1967), pp. 32-44.

———, *Jews in the Economic and Political Life of Mediaeval Islam*, London: Royal Asiatic Society, 1968.

———, 'The Literary Creativity of the Jews of Cochin on the Malabar Coast', *Jewish Book Annual* 28 (1970-1), pp. 25-31.

———, 'The Contribution of the Cochin Jews to South Indian and Jewish Civilization', in *Commemoration Volume*, ed. S.S. Koder, 1971, pp. 15-63.

———, *Unknown Jews in Unknown Lands: The Travels of Rabbi David D'Beth Hillel (1824-1832)*, New York: KTAV, 1973.

———, 'The Present State of Research on the History of the Jews in India from the 16th Century On', in *Jewish Tradition in the Diaspora: Studies in Memory of Walter J. Fischel*, ed. Mishael Maswari Caspi, Berkeley: Judah L. Magnes Museum (1981), pp. 23-33.

———, 'Cochin', *Encyclopedia Judaica*, 3, Jerusalem, Keter, 1971, pp. 621-8.

Fischel, Walter J., Paul Gottlieb and Avigdor Herzog, 'India', *Encyclopedia Judaica*, 1971, vol. 8, pp. 349-60.

Fredman, Ruth Gerber, *The Passover Seder*, New York: New American Library, 1981.

Gandhi, Indira, 'Great Heritage', *Commemoration Volume: Cochin Synagogue Quatercentenary Celebrations*, ed. S.S. Koder et al., Cochin: The Kerala History Association and the Cochin Synagogue Quatercentenary Celebration Committee, 1971, pp. 5-8.

Gandhi, M.K., *Non-Violent Resistance (Satyagraha)*, ed. Bharatan Kumarappa, New York: Schocken Books, 1961 (1951).

Ganzfried, Rabbi Solomon, *Kitzur Shulchan 'Arukh: Code of Jewish Law*, trans. by Hyman E. Goldin, New York: Hebrew Publishing Co., 1961.

Gourgey, Percy S., 'Zionism in India', *The Jewish Chronicle Supplement* (London, 30 August 1957).

———, 'Gandhi and the Jews', in *Jews in India with Who is Who 1963*, ed. E. Elias and E. Isaac, Ernakulam: Indo-Israel Publications, 1964: 46-8.

———, 'Indian Jews and the Indian Freedom Struggle', *Indo-British Review* 15, 1 (1988), pp. 85-90.

Greenbaum, Aaron, 'The Cochin Jewish Community: Impressions from a Mission to India, 1966', *Midrashia: A Journal Devoted to Halacha, Jewish Thought & Education*, Spring 1970, pp. 82-94.

Halbfass, Wilhelm, *India and Europe: An Essay in Understanding*, Albany: State University of New York Press, 1988.

———, *Tradition and Reflection: Explorations in Indian Thought*, Albany: State University of New York Press, 1991.

Halevy, Judah, *The Kuzari (Kitab al Khazari): An Argument for the Faith of Israel*, Introduction by Henry Slonimsky, translated from the Arabic by Hartwig Hirschfield, New York: Schocken Books, 1964.

Hall, T.C., 'Asceticism (Introduction)', in *Encyclopedia of Religion and Ethics*, ed. James Hastings, New York: Charles Scribner's Sons, 1958, vol. II, pp. 63-9.

Hallegua, Fiona, 'The Jewish Community of Cochin—Its Twilight Years', M.A. thesis, University of Kerala, St. Theresa's College, Ernakulam, 1984.

Hallegua, Isaac Ben Elias, 'Letter of 1895 to Rev. J.H. Lord, Bombay', Sassoon ms. 935.

Hallegua, I.S., 'The Paradesi Synagogue of Cochin and Its Dying Community of Jews', Cochin, photocopied ms. for private circulation by author, 1988.

Hallegua, S.H., 'Simchat Torah in Cochin', *Kol Bina*, vol. 6, no. 1, September 1986, p. 6.

Hastings, James E., ed., *Encyclopedia of Religion and Ethics*, New York: Charles Scribner's Sons, 1958.

Hertzberg, Arthur, ed. and intro., *The Zionist Idea: A Historical Analysis and Reader*, New York: Atheneum, 1977.

Hillel, Rabbi De Beth, *Travels of Rabbi De Beth Hillel*, Madras: privately published, 1832.

Isenberg, Shirley Berry, *India's Bene Israel: A Comprehensive Inquiry and Sourcebook*, Bombay: Popular Prakashan; Berkeley: Judah L. Magnes Museum, 1988.

———, 'Indian Nationalism and India's Jews', *Indo-British Review* 15, 1 (1988), pp. 91-110.

Johnson, Barbara C., 'Shingli or Jewish Cranganore in the Traditions of the Cochin Jews of India, with an Appendix on the Cochin Jewish Chronicles', M.A. thesis, Northampton: Smith College, 1975.

———, '"Our Community" in Two Worlds: The Cochin Paradesi Jews in India and Israel', Ph.D. thesis, Amherst: University of Massachusetts, 1985.

———, 'The Emperor's Welcome: Reconsiderations of an Origin Theme in Cochin Jewish Folklore', in *The Jews of India*, ed. Thomas A. Timberg, New Delhi: Vikas, 1986, pp. 161-76.

———, 'For Any Good Occasion We Call Them: Community Parties and Cultural Continuity among the Cochin Paradesi Jews of Israel', in *Studies of Indian Jewish Identity*, ed. Nathan Katz, New Delhi: Manohar, 1995, pp. 53-82.

Kaelber, Walter O., 'Asceticism', in *The Encyclopedia of Religion*, ed. Mircea Eliade, New York: Macmillan, 1987, vol. I, pp. 441-5.

Kasher, Rabbi Memachem M., *Hagadah Shelemah, The Complete Passover Hagadah*, Jerusalem: Torah Shelema Institute, 1967.

Katz, Nathan, *Tampa Bay's Asian-Origin Religious Communities*, with assistance from Meher M. Noshirwani, Tampa: National Conference of Christians and Jews, A Religious History of Tampa Bay Reports Series, no. 1, 1991.

———, 'The Judaisms of Kaifeng and Cochin: Parallel and Divergent Styles of Religious Acculturation', *Numen: International Review for the History of Religions*, vol. 42 (1995), pp. 118-40.

Katz, Nathan and Ellen S. Goldberg, 'The Last Jews in India and Burma', *Jerusalem Letter* (Jerusalem Center for Public Affairs) 101 (15 April 1988), pp. 1-8.

———, 'Asceticism and Caste in the Passover Observances of the Cochin Jews',

Journal of the American Academy of Religion, LVII, 1 (Spring 1989), pp. 52-83.

———, 'The Ritual Enactments of the Cochin Jews: The Powers of Purity and Nobility', *Journal of Ritual Studies* 4, 2 (Summer 1990), pp. 189-225.

Koder, Cecil, 'Palestine Is Our Only Destination', Cochin, poem ms., n.d.

Koder, S.S. et al., eds., *Commemoration Volume*: *Cochin Synagogue Quatercentenary Celebrations,* Cochin: The Kerala History Association and the Cochin Synagogue Quatercentenary Celebration Committee, 1971.

Koder, S.S., 'A Hebrew Letter of 1768', *Journal of the Rama Varma Archaeological Society* 15 (1949), pp. 1-6.

———, 'The Jews of Malabar', *India and Israel* (1951), pp. 31-5.

———, 'Kerala and Her Jews', a paper read before the Kerala History Convention, 18 May 1965, Cochin, privately published, 1965.

———, 'Kerala and Her Jews', in *Jews in India '64 with Who Is Who*, ed. E. Elias and E. Isaac, Ernakulam: Indo-Israel Publications, 1965, pp. 21-34.

———, 'History of the Jews of Kerala', *The St. Thomas Christian Encyclopedia of India* 2 (1973), pp. 183-5.

———, *History of the Jews of Kerala,* Cochin: privately published, 1974.

———, 'Saga of the Jews of Cochin', in *Jews in India,* ed. Thomas A. Timberg, New Delhi: Vikas, 1986, pp. 121-42.

Kohut, George Alexander, 'Correspondence between the Jews of Malabar and New York a Century Ago', in *Semitic Studies in Memory of Rev. Dr. Alexander Kohut,* ed. George Alexander Kohut, Berlin: S. Calvary & Co., 1897, pp. 420-34.

Kushner, Gilbert, *Immigrants from India in Israel*: *Planned Change in an Administered Community,* Tucson: University of Arizona Press, 1973.

Lesley, Arthur M., 'Shingly in Cochin Jewish Memory and in Eyewitness Accounts', *Journal of Indo-Judaic Studies,* vol. 3, 2000, pp. 7-19.

Lord, Rev. J. Henry, *The Jews in India and the Far East,* rpt, Westport: Greenwood Press, 1976; Kolhapur: Mission Press,. 1907.

Machazor Shingli, Amsterdam: Proops, 1769. ('Shingli Beth'.)

Machazor L'Yomim Nora'im, Amsterdam: Proops, n.d.

Maimonides, *Rambam Mishneh Torah Hilchot Chametz U'Matzah,* tr. Rabbi Eliyahu Touger, New York and Jerusalem: Moznaim Publishing Co., 1988.

Mandelbaum, David G., 'The Jewish Way of Life in Cochin', *Jewish Social Studies,* vol. 1, no. 4, October 1939, pp. 423-60.

———, *Society in India,* 2 vols., Berkeley: University of California Press, 1970.

———, 'Social Stratification among the Jews of Cochin in India and in Israel', *The Jewish Journal of Sociology,* vol. 17, no. 2 (1975), pp. 165-210.

———, 'A Case History of Judaism: The Jews of Cochin in India and in Israel', in *Jewish Tradition in the Diaspora*: *Studies in Memory of Walter J. Fischel,* ed. Maswari Caspi, Berkeley: Judah L. Magnes Museum, 1981, pp. 211-30.

———, 'Social Stratification among the Jews of Cochin in India and in Israel', in *Jews in India*, ed. Thomas A. Timberg, New Delhi: Vikas, 1986, pp. 61-120.

Marriott, McKim, 'Interactional and Attributional Theories of Caste Ranking', *Man in India*, vol. 39, no. 2 (1959), pp. 92-107.

———, 'The Feast of Love', in *Krishna: Myths, Rites, and Attitudes*, ed. Milton Singer, Honolulu: East-West Centre Press, 1966, pp. 200-12.

Marx, Alexander, 'Contributions a l'Histoire des Juifs de Cochin', *Revue des Etudes Juives*, vol. 89 (1930), pp. 293-304.

Mendelssohn, Sidney, *The Jews of Asia, Especially in the Sixteenth and Seventeenth Centuries*, London: Kegan Paul, Trench, Trubner, 1920.

Menon, C. Achyuta, *The Cochin State Manual*, Ernakulam: Cochin Government Press, 1911.

Menon, Ramesh, 'The Namboodiris: Traumatic Decline', *India Today* (15 July 1991), pp. 90-2.

Moens, The Rt. Worshipful Adriaan, *Memorandum on the Administration of the Coast of Malabar, Dated 18th April 1781 A.D.*, tr. Rev. P. Groot and A. Galletti, notes by A. Galletti, rpt, New Delhi: Usha Publications, 1984.

Narayanan, M.G.S., *Cultural Symbiosis in Kerala*, Trivandrum: Kerala Historical Society, 1972.

Neusner, Jacob, *The Idea of Purity in Ancient Judaism*, Leiden: E.J. Brill, 1973.

Nevatim Moshav Synagogue, *Shirim L'Moadim Shabbatot, Hatunah U'Brit Milah*, Israel: Moshav Nevatim, 1963 (in Hebrew).

Parasarathy, Anand, 'Marriage of the Decade', *Frontline* (9-22 January 1988), pp. 77-9.

Peters, Joan, *From Time Immemorial: The Origins of the Arab-Jewish Conflict over Palestine*, New York: Harper & Row, 1984.

Pirkei Avos: Ethics of the Fathers, a new translation with a concise commentary anthologized from the classical rabbinic sources, commentary by Rabbi Meir Zlotowitz, ed. Rabbi Nosson Scherman, Brooklyn: Mesorah Publications, Artscroll Mesorah Series, 1989 (1984).

Pollak, Michael, *Mandarins, Jews, and Missionaries: The Jewish Experience in the Chinese Empire*, Philadelphia: Jewish Publication Society, 1980.

Pool, David de Sola, ed. & tr., *Seder HaTefilot: Book of Prayers According to the Custom of the Spanish and Portuguese Jews*, 2nd edn, New York: Union of Sephardic Congregations, 1986 (1941).

Rabinowitz, Louis, *Far East Mission*, Johannesburg: Eagle Press, 1952.

———, 'A Jewish Wedding in South India', *Jewish Affairs* (July 1952), pp. 41-4.

Rader, Rosemary, 'Fasting', in *The Encyclopedia of Religion*, ed. Mircea Eliade, New York: Macmillan, 1987, vol. 5, pp. 286-90.

Rahabi, Ezekiel, 'Letter of 1768', published in Hebrew by Naphtali Herz Wesseley, *Ha-Meassef*, Koeningsberg (1790), vol. VI, pp. 129-60; in abridged

English translation by S.S. Koder in *Journal of the Rama Varma Archaeological Society*, vol. XV (1949), pp. 1-6; manuscript translation by I.S. Hallegua, Cochin, 1987.

Rahabi, Naphtali Elijah, see Roby, N.E.

Redfield, Robert, 'Relations of Anthropology to the Social Sciences and to the Humanities', in *Anthropology Today: An Encyclopedic Inventory*, ed. A.L. Kroeber, Chicago and London: University of Chicago Press, 1953, pp. 728-38.

Reinman, Shlomo, *Masa'oth Shlomo b'Eretz Hodu, Burman, v'Sinim*, Vienna: Schur, 1884 (in Hebrew).

———, 'Masa'oth Shlomo b'Kogin', in *Mikotsin l'Eretz Yisrael*, ed. S. Weil, Jerusalem: Kumu Brinah, 1984, pp. 31-9 (in Hebrew).

Reissner, H.G., 'Indian-Jewish Statistics, 1837-1941', *Jewish Social Studies*, vol. 12 (1951), pp. 349-65.

Reynolds, Holly Baker, 'The Auspicious Married Woman', in *The Powers of Tamil Women*, ed. Susan S. Wadley, Syracuse: Maxwell School of Citizenship and Public Affairs, Foreign and Comparative Studies/South Asia Series, no. 6, 1980, pp. 35-60.

Riemer, Jack, ed., *Jewish Reflections on Death*, New York: Schocken, 1972.

Roby, N.E. (Naphtali Elijah Rahabi), 'The White Jews of Cochin', *The Jewish Chronicle* (6 September 1901), p. 17.

———, *Divrei Y'mei HaYehudim b'Cogin* (Sassoon no. 268), Cochin ms., 1911.

———, ed., *Sefer Hupat Hataniyam*, Cochin ms., Bombay: Judah Ashenazy, 1917-18.

———, *Toldot Beit Rahabi be Cogin*, Cochin ms., Berkeley: Judah Magnes Museum, 1939.

———, ed., *Sefer Tefilah l'Moshe*, Cochin ms., n.d.

Roland, Joan G., *Jews in British India: Identity in a Colonial Era*, Hanover and London: University Press of New England, published for Brandeis University Press, 1989.

Rosenfeld, Rabbi Abraham, tr. and ann., *Seder HaYom l'Tisha B'Av*, New York: The Judaica Press, 1989.

Ross, Israel J., 'Cross-Cultural Dynamics in Musical Traditions: The Music of the Jews of Cochin', *Musica Judaica*, vol. 2, no.1 (1977-8), pp. 51-72.

Roth, Cecil, ed., *Encyclopedia Judaica*, Jerusalem: Keter Publishing House, 1971.

Salem, Avraham Baruch, *Eternal Light or Jewtown Synagogue*, Ernakulam: S.D. Printing Works, 1929.

Saphir, Yaacov, *Eben Saphir*, Lick: L. Silbermann, 1866 (in Hebrew).

———, 'HaYehudim b'Kogin', in *Mikotsin l'Eretz Yisroel*, ed. S. Weil, Jerusalem: Kumu Brinah, 1984, pp. 21-30 (in Hebrew).

Sarphati, Mosheh, *Piqas* (*Record Book*) *of the Paradesi Synagogue*, Cochin manuscript in Library of Ben-Zvi Institute, Jerusalem (n.d).

Sartre, Jean-Paul, *Anti-Semite and Jew*, New York: Schocken Books, 1965 (1948).

Sassoon, David S.D., *Ohel Dawid: Descriptive Catalogue of the Hebrew and Samaritan Manuscripts in the Sassoon Library, London*, 2 vols., London: Humphrey Milford, 1932.

Schermerhorn, R.A., 'Jews: A Disappearing Minority', in *Ethnic Plurality in India,* Tucson: University of Arizona Press, 1978, Chapter 10, pp. 238-61.

Schneerson, Rabbi Menachem M., *Haggadah for Pesach, with an Anthology of Reasons and Customs*, tr. Jacob Immanuel Schochet, Brooklyn: Qehot, 1985.

Segal, J.B., 'White and Black Jews at Cochin: The Story of a Controversy', *Journal of the Royal Asiatic Society*, vol. 2 (1983), pp. 228ff.

Simon, A.I., 'The Songs of the Jews of Cochin and their Historical Significance', *Bulletin of the Rama Varma Research Institute*, vol. 13 (1947).

Smith, Jonathan Z., *Imagining Religion from Babylon to Jonestown*, Chicago and London: University of Chicago Press, 1982.

———, *To Take Place: Toward Theory in Ritual*, Chicago and London: University of Chicago Press, 1987.

Soloveitchik, Rabbi Joseph B., 'The Halakhah of the First Day', in *Jewish Reflections on Death*, ed. Jack Riemer, New York: Schocken, 1974, pp. 76-83.

Spector, Johanna, 'Jewish Songs from Cochin, India, with Special Reference to Cantillation and Shingly Tunes', *Proceedings of the Fifth World Conference of Jewish Studies* (1969), pp. 245-65.

———, 'The Music of the Jews of Cochin with Special Reference to Shingli Tunes', in *Commemoration Volume*, ed. Koder, 1971, pp. 177-85.

———, 'Shingli Tunes of the Cochin Jews', *Asian Music*, vol. 3, no. 2 (1972), pp. 23-8.

Strizower, Schifra, *Exotic Jewish Communities*, New York: Thomas Yoseloff, 1962.

Subrahmanyam, Sanjay, *The Political Economy of Commerce: Southern India, 1500-1650*, Cambridge: Cambridge University Press, 1990.

Suffrin, A.E., 'Asceticism (Jewish)', in *The Encyclopedia of Religion and Ethics*, ed. James Hastings, New York: Charles Scribner's Sons, 1958.

Swiderski, Richard Michael, *Blood Weddings: The Knanaya Christians of Kerala*, Madras: New Era Publications, 1988.

Thomas, Lowell, 'The City of Black and White Jews', in *India: Land of the Black Pagoda*, New York and London: The Century Company, 1930, pp. 28-39.

Thurston, Edgar, assisted by K. Rangachari, *Castes and Tribes of Southern India*, Madras: Government Press, 1909, vol. II, pp. 460-92.

Timberg, Thomas A., ed., *Jews in India*, New Delhi: Vikas; and New York: Advent, 1986.

Tripathi, Gaya Charan, 'Navakalevara: The Unique Ceremony of the "Birth" and the Death of the "Lord of the World" ', in *The Cult of Jagannath and the Regional Tradition of Orissa*, ed. A. Eschmann, H. Kulke and G.C. Tripathi, New Delhi: Manohar, 1978, pp. 223-64.

Turner, Victor W., *The Ritual Process: Structure and Anti-Structure*, Ithaca: Cornell University Press, 1977.

Wadley, Susan S., ed., *The Powers of Tamil Women*, Syracuse: Syracuse University Maxwell School of Citizenship and Public Affairs, Foreign and Comparative Studies/South Asia Series, no. 6, 1980.

Walerstein, Marcia, 'The Cochini Jewish Wedding of the Malabar Community in India and Israel: Change in Custom, Symbol and Meaning', in *Jews in India*, ed. Thomas A. Timberg, New Delhi: Vikas, 1986, pp. 248-70.

Weil, Shalva, ed., *From Cochin to the Land of Israel*, Jerusalem: Kumu Berina, 1984 (in Hebrew).

———, 'Symmetry between Christians and Jews in India: The Cnanite Christians and the Cochin Jews of Kerala', in *Jews in India*, ed. Thomas A. Timberg, New Delhi: Vikas, 1986, pp. 177-204.

Whitehead, Right Reverend Henry, *The Village Gods of South India*, Calcutta: Association Press (YMCA), 1921.

Whitney, William Dwight, *The Roots, Verb-Forms and Primary Derivatives of the Sanskrit Language*, New Haven: American Oriental Society, American Oriental Series, vol. 30, 1945 (1885).

Yehudi, Adv. Prem Doss S., *Israel as Seen by an Indian*, Trivandrum: The Author, 1983.

Zalman, Rabbi Schneur, arr., *Shulchan 'Arukh Orech Chayyim*, 4 vols., Brooklyn: Qehot, 1985 (in Hebrew).

All Biblical quotations are taken from *The Jerusalem Bible*, Jerusalem: Koren Publishers, 1977.

Index

'Adeni, Eliahu 69
Aron, P.T. 39
Arti Samhita 136
Ashkenazi, Miriam 150-1,163
Ashkenazy, Isaac 38, 47, 59, 74, 151, 165
Ashkenazy, Judah 87-8
Asceticism 14, 51-70
Avo 121-3

Babylonia 32, 70
bar mitzvah/minyan 77, 89-91, 127, 128, 165
Bayly, Susan 21-2, 43
Beck, Brenda E.F. 99,103
Bene Israel 13, 41, 100, 107
Bhagavati-Bharakali 20, 43
Brahmins 19-20, 21, 51-2, 64, 92
brit milah 77, 82, 87-9, 94, 128, 129, 156, 165
Buchanan, Rev. Claudius 113

Caspi, Mishael Maswari 78
caste, caste system 13, 15, 22, 45, 51-70, 98-131, 134-6, 146
Castro, R. Jacob de 105
Chanukkah 23, 45-7, 50, 51
Cheraman Perumal 64, 82
Chill, Abraham 88
Chinese Jews 21, 134-5
Cohen, Jackie 34, 46, 151
Cohen, Jacob 17, 33, 34, 38, 58, 66, 68, 75, 82, 88, 152, 160, 166
Cohen, Sarah 17, 29, 30, 40, 55, 56, 59, 60, 73, 90, 110
Cohen, Sassoon 34
Cohen, Shalom 34, 73, 151
Cohen, Yaakob Daniel 40, 112
Cowen, Ida 78
Cranganore 12, 19, 38, 40, 64, 77, 98, 102, 103, 108, 109, 110-11, 112, 113, 114, 119
cumankali 81-2, 84, 90

Dharmashastra 13, 19, 62
Diwali 56
Doss, Prem Doss Yehudi 46-7, 166-7
Dumont, Louis 45, 61, 64, 136

Egnor, Margaret 82
Eliade, Mircea 54
Eliahu Hanabi (Elijah) 53-4, 88
Elias, Abigail 40
Ernakulam 30, 35, 37, 40, 46, 66, 73, 113, 128, 140, 142, 144, 155

family purity 21, 64
Funerals 77, 92-4, 165

Gandhi, Mohandas K. 98, 101, 123-4, 129
Gaon, Saadia 28
Gestalt psychology 14-15
Greenbaum, Aaron 70
Guru, Narayanan 124

Halakha 14, 20, 21, 22, 42, 43, 55, 57, 78, 98-9, 101, 130, 145, 163
Hall, T.C. 54
Hallegua, Brian 152
Hallegua, David 152, 164
Hallegua, Fiona 152, 164
Hallegua, I.C. 66, 91
Hallegua, I.S. 30, 34, 36, 151
Hallegua, Keith 91, 149, 152
Hallegua, Queenie 29, 57, 68, 74, 151
Hallegua, Samuel 39, 51, 66, 68, 74, 88
Hallegua, Sassoon 37
Hallegua, Seema 152
Hallegua, Shlomo 121
Hallegua, Ya'el 152, 164, 166
Hallegua, Yosef 30, 58, 68, 74, 75
Herzl, Theodor 142
hiddur mitzvot 43, 51
Hillel, R. David DeBeth 108, 109, 111, 112, 113, 118, 119
Holi 40, 50

Hoshana Rabba 35

Indian-Jewish identity 12, 19, 22

Jerusalem 13, 19, 47, 77, 111, 113, 123
Johnson, Barbara C. 45, 56, 89

Kaelber, Walter 54, 55
kapparot 33
Kashrut 21, 46, 57, 58, 61, 65, 163
Khona, D.B. 60, 66-7, 166
Kipling, Rudyard 11
Koder, Cecil 40, 139
Koder, Elias 39, 65, 157
Koder, Gladys 29, 51, 59
Koder, Gloria 147, 157
Koder, Julian 153-4, 161
Koder, Lily 12, 44, 149, 151
Koder, Naphtali 146, 161-2, 164- 5
Koder, Sammy and Simi 161, 163
Koder, Sattu 29, 30, 33, 38, 41-2, 51, 59, 68, 70, 134, 161
Kol Nidre 33
Krishna 10, 43, 50
Kurdistan 32
Kushner, Gilbert 143, 150, 162

Lag B'Omer 23, 67-8
Lesley, Arthur M. 40
Lord, Rev. J. Henry 112, 119

malqut 33
Mandelbaum, David 30, 33, 39, 40, 62, 90, 106-7, 111, 112, 113, 124-5, 152, 156
Manu 19, 62-3, 116
Manusmriti 62
marriage 78-87, 125-6, 165
Marriott, McKim 50, 53
Moens, Gov. Adriaan 106, 117-18
Moshav Nevatim 155, 162
Mota, Nehemia 46, 51, 68

Nambudiri 13, 28, 44, 51-2, 61, 63-5, 110, 116
Nayar 13, 20, 42, 44, 45, 61, 62, 78, 79, 116
Nestorian Christians 16

Paiva, Moses Pereyra de 108, 109, 110, 114
Parvati 43
Passover, Pesach 13, 14, 21, 23, 27, 28, 31, 38, 42, 47, 50, 51, 70, 77, 78, 86, 98, 121, 147, 151, 162, 163
pattankaran 77, 91-2
Perumpadappu family 43
Pollack, F.W. 143
Puri 43
Purim 23, 50-1, 55, 56, 59

Rabban, Joseph 19, 29, 77, 79, 82, 85, 102, 109, 110
Rabinowitz, Louis 78, 81, 83, 120, 144
Rader, Rosemary 54
Rahabi, Ezekiel 29, 111
Redfield, Robert 17
Reinman, Shlomo 74,78
Reynolds, Holly Baker 81, 82, 90
Rig Veda 62
Roby, Naphtali (N.E.) 36, 142
Rosh Hashanah 23, 28, 29-32, 77, 147, 149; Cakes 28, 59
Ross, Israel 32

Salem, A.B. 98, 99-101, 123-5, 129, 147-8, 153
Salem, Baby (née Koder) 125-6, 128, 153
Salem, Balfour 125-6, 128, 146, 153, 161, 165
Salem, Cynthia 128
Salem, Gamliel 39, 47, 58, 67, 87, 88, 126, 127, 153
Salem, Kenneth 39, 75, 128, 152
Salem, Leslie and Glennis 128, 153, 164
Salem, Raymond 17, 37, 39, 44, 47, 74, 88, 92, 99-101, 125, 127, 130, 141, 151
Salem, Reema (née Roby) 47, 59, 87, 126-7, 153
Sapir, Yaakov 39, 78
Sartre, Jean-Paul 11
Sassoon, David 123

satyagraha 101, 124, 129
Segal, J.B. 114
Shabbat 23, 27, 73-6, 77, 79, 85, 124-5, 126, 140, 143, 147, 148, 162-3
Shavu'oth 27, 67, 69-70, 77, 147
Shilappadikaram 81
Shingly tunes 31, 32, 35, 38, 83, 91
Shiva 43, 81
Shmini Chag Atzeret 23, 29, 30, 36-42, 77
Simchat Cohen 34
Simchat Torah 13, 14, 21, 23, 29, 30, 36-42, 50, 52, 78, 90, 98, 124, 129
Simon, A.I. 78, 110
Simon, Esther 'Pearlie' 165, 166
Simon, Leonore 152
S'lichot 28, 31, 33
Smith, Jonathan Z. 52, 65
Song of Songs 86
Spector, Joanna 32
Sukkot 23, 29, 35, 36, 147

Thomas, Lowell 35
Tibetan Buddhists 16
Tisha B'Av 23, 27, 66, 69-70, 77
Tolerance 15, 98, 134-6
Turner, Victor 52, 59, 60

Vishu 59

Walerstein, Marsha 78, 82, 86

Yemen 30, 32, 38, 56, 74, 79, 100, 110, 115, 145
Yom Kippur 21, 23, 27, 28, 29, 32-4, 36, 42, 60, 70, 125, 126, 147

Zimra, R. David ibn 103-5, 106, 107
Zionism, Zionist 15-16, 139, 140, 142-8, 160, 164, 167
Zohar 68-9, 87
Zoroastrians (Parsis) 16, 59